Getting to Maybe

Getting to Maybe

How to Excel on Law School Exams

Richard Michael Fischl

and

Jeremy Paul

Carolina Academic Press

Durham, North Carolina

ISBN 0-89089-760-3
LCCN 99-60901

CAROLINA ACADEMIC PRESS
700 Kent Street
Durham, North Carolina 27701
Telephone (919) 489-7486
Fax (919) 493-5668
E-mail: cap@cap-press.com
www.cap-press.com

Printed in the United States of America.

For Pam and Laurie

Contents

Preface   xiii

Acknowledgments   xix

Chapter 1 You're Not in Kansas Anymore   3
A Place Where "Knowing the Material" Is
Not Enough   3
Some Lessons You May Need To Unlearn   6
Lesson #1 — Undergraduate Exams and the
"Information Dump"   6
Lesson #2 — Sorting Through the Law School
Rumor Mill   8
Lesson #3 — The Dark Side of the Socratic Method:
The Rulebook vs. The Loose Cannon   11

Part I Issues in Living Color

Chapter 2 Issues as "Forks in the Road"   21

Chapter 3 Forks in the Law: Rule vs. Counter-Rule Issues   27
A. Patterns to Watch For   28
1. Traditional Rule vs. Modern Rule   28
2. Different Strokes for Different Folks   30
3. Common Law vs. Statute   31
B. How Professors Test Rule vs. Counter-Rule
Issues (and Why Students Frequently Miss Them)   32

Chapter 4 Forks in the Law: Competing
Interpretations of Statutes   37
A. Patterns of Ambiguity   39
1. Plain Meaning vs. Purposes Issues   39

2. Where Do Purposes Come From?   40
    a. Legislative intent   40
    b. Policy analysis   42
3. Purposes as a Source of Statutory Ambiguity   43
    a. Competing purposes   43
    b. The pattern of conflict: Broad vs. narrow
       purposes   46
4. Language as a Source of Statutory Ambiguity:
   Competing Meanings   48
B. Fact Situations To Watch For   52

**Chapter 5 Forks in the Law: Competing
Interpretations of Caselaw**   55

A. Desperately Seeking Similarity: When To
   Follow Precedent   56
B. Searching for Distinctions that Make a Difference   57
C. Patterns of Ambiguity To Watch For   59
D. Dealing with Multiple Cases   64

Chapter 6 Forks in the Facts   67

A. How Law Creates Forks in the Facts:
   Why Categories Matter   68
1. Rule vs. Exception   70
2. Statutory Boundaries   71
3. Sequential Categories   71
4. Crossing the Line   72
5. Categories as Elements of Legal Rules:
   Running the Gantlet   73
6. Open-Ended or "Evaluative" Categories   74
B. Why Categories Don't Settle Things: Sources
   of Factual Conflict and Ambiguity   75
1. Facts on Both Sides of the Category   75
2. Differing Standpoints   76
3. Differing Time-Frames   77
4. Differing Ways To Make Sense of the Facts   79
    a. Take things one at a time or view them
       as a totality   79

b. Lenses of generality 80
c. Linguistic ambiguity 82

Chapter 7   Taking It to the Next Level: "Twin Forks" 87

A. Linked Forks: One Good Fork Deserves Another 90
B. Reciprocal Forks: Back-and-Forth between Law
   and Facts 92
C. Concurrent Forks: Straddling a Statutory Boundary 94
D. Proliferating Forks: Competing Domains 96
E. Hidden Forks: Dodging the Statute 100
F. Background vs. Foreground: Variations on the
   Twin Forks Theme 102

Part II Strategies for Issue-Spotting, Analysis,
   and Argument: Heart, Brains, and Courage

Chapter 8   Taking Exams Seriously: A World Full
of Wicked "Whiches" 109

Chapter 9   How To Spot Issues, and What To Do
Once You Spot Them 117

A. Issue-Spotting 119
   1. What the Course Will Tell You If You Listen 119
      a. Classnotes and outlines 119
      b. Themes and "issues" 122
      c. Old exams and study groups 124
   2. What the Exam Will Tell You If You Let It 125
      a. Map the parties' claims and conflicts 125
      b. Don't stop with the first issue you see 127
      c. If the answer seems too easy, it probably is 128
      d. If you finish early, "check your work" 130
B. What To Do with Issues Once You Spot Them 131
   1. You Already Know More than You Think
      You Do 131
   2. From Issue-Spotting to Issue Analysis 133
   3. The Recipe for Argument Construction:
      Just Add Reasons 135
      a. Keep in mind who the real judge is 136

b. Once again, you already know more
   than you think you do   137
   (i) Patterns of argument for forks in
      the facts   137
   (ii) Patterns of argument for competing
       interpretations of statutes and cases   141
c. The crucial role of policy arguments   142
4. Where To Focus Your Fire   143
   a. Focus your fire on points in conflict   143
   b. Focus your fire on points that make a
      difference   144
   c. Focus your fire on issues emphasized by
      the professor   145
   d. Write till the facts run out   146
C. What *Not* To Do With Issues: Herein of "IRAC"   147

**Chapter 10 Czars of the Universe (Otherwise
known as "Policy Wizards")**   151
A. To Know and Not To Know—That Is the Answer   153
B. Touching All Parts of the Policy Kingdom   156
1. "Shaping" Society   156
2. Administering Policy   157
3. Doing the Right Thing   159
   a. The unfairness of change (consistency
      over time)   160
   b. Treat like cases alike   161
      (i) Consistency over space   161
      (ii) Consistency across social categories   162
      (iii) The distribution of wealth (consistency
         across economic class)   163
4. What Kind of Czar Are You?   165
5. Government Non-Interference and the Prime
   Directive: Even Czars Have Limits   166
C. Heads and Tails You Win   168
1. Getting Past the Obvious   169
2. One Good Argument Deserves Another   171
3. When in Doubt, Just Say No   173

4. Learning To Mix and Match 174
5. Accentuate the Multiple 177
D. Find the Fun and *Snap* the Test's a Game 180
   1. Trade-Off vs. Paradox 181
   2. The Pattern of Paradox 184
     a. The short run and the long run 185
     b. Intent vs. effects 186
     c. Law on the books vs. law in action 188
     d. Categories are many-splendored things 188
   3. Paradox Is an Attitude 190
   4. When in Doubt, Write It Down 192

Part III Test-Taking Tips — Your Very Own Ruby Slippers

Introduction 197

Chapter 11 Preparing for the Exam 199
Tip #1. Exam Preparation Takes All Semester 199
Tip #2. Focus Your Exam Study on Your Classnotes 202
Tip #3. Prepare Your Own Outline of the Course 203
Tip #4. Review the Professor's Old Exams 207
Tip #5. Consider What Questions *You* Would Ask 210

Chapter 12 Writing Exam Answers 215
Tip #6. Carefully Read the Exam Instructions and Follow Them to the Letter 215
Tip #7. Read Each Question Carefully, and Answer the Question Asked 219
Tip #8. Organize and Outline Before Writing Your Answer 223
Tip #9. Provide the Reader with a Brief Roadmap 226
Tip #10. Explain Your Reasoning 228
Tip #11. Draw Conclusions When They Are Called For 232
Tip #12. Argue Both Sides 234
Tip #13. Stick to the Facts and Circumstances Presented 239

Tip #14. Remember Who Your "Judge" Is   242
Tip #15. Watch Time/Credit Allocations   244

Chapter 13 Mistakes to Avoid   249
Tip #16. Don't Regurgitate Legal Rules and
Principles   249
Tip #17. Don't Repeat the Facts   252
Tip #18. Avoid Conclusory Answers   255
Tip #19. Avoid Disquisitions on Topics Outside
the Course   257
Tip #20. Don't Leave Your Common Sense at
the Door   259
Tip #21. Avoid Writing Jurisprudence Lectures   262
Tip #22. Don't B.S.   264

Chapter 14 Frequently Asked Questions   267
FAQ #1. Do You Need to Cite Cases by Name?   267
FAQ #2. Should You Type Your Exams?   269
FAQ #3. Does the IRAC Method Help?   271
FAQ #4. What If You Realize You've Made a
Mistake in Your Answer?   274
FAQ #5. What If You Think the *Professor* Has
Made a Mistake?   276
FAQ #6. What If You Don't Know What a
Word Means?   278
FAQ #7. Does the Professor Want "Black-Letter"
Answers?   280
FAQ #8. Should You Use Commercial Study Aids?   282

**Chapter 15 Putting Maybe to Work: Sample
Questions and Answers**   287
A. Torts   289
B. Property   295
C. Constitutional Law   305
D. Contracts   314

Sources   323

About the Authors   327

Preface

This book is aimed at every law student who has ever wondered how to progress beyond her teachers' repeated warnings that "learning the rules is not enough" to a sound idea of exactly what it takes to perform well on law school exams. This is no small question. Law students are expected to demonstrate top performance in a setting where everyone agrees that "knowing the answer" is the wrong way to think about excellence. For most entering law students, however, the obvious alternative to "knowing the answer" is "*not* knowing the answer." And clearly "I don't know" isn't what your professors are looking for either. So what lies between getting it right and not getting it at all? What kind of intellectual work is required to cope with exams on which some questions yield yes-or-no answers, but where the real trick is *Getting to Maybe*?

Both of us wondered about such questions a great deal as we traveled through Harvard Law School many years ago, and neither of us found much guidance beyond the occasional paraphrase of Justice Stewart's famous remark about obscenity, "I know it when I see it." So when we began teaching together at the University of Miami in 1983, we decided soon thereafter that we would devote the same level of analytical rigor to the exam process that our colleagues expected us to deploy in our more traditional research. We have been working on this book, off and on and mostly clandestinely, ever since.

We have believed all along that the law school exam is a topic worthy of academic interest. Law professors give the kind of exams they do precisely because they believe that students who perform well have demonstrated the skills identified with good lawyering. So we decided that if we could succeed in providing an accurate description of those skills, we would have helped legal educators everywhere to define more precisely the content of a first-rate legal education.

But we also knew from the start that mere academic concerns would not be enough to spark interest in our work among many in our intended audience. So we have devoted particular care to sharpening observations about exams that we believe will be directly useful to student readers seeking to improve their own performance. We don't believe that any book on exams can substitute for hard work and learning the law. But we are confident that the conscientious student who works through our book will be rewarded at the end of every semester. This is, after all, a "how-to" book.

What proved most gratifying to us as we progressed with our project was that we discovered no clash between our desire to challenge teachers and students to think seriously about what goes into exams and our goal of helping students write better answers. Indeed, it's the combination of these goals that we hope will earn *Getting to Maybe* a place among the classic books aimed at beginning law students. This is not a book about legal reasoning generally, because its focus is solely on exams. But neither is it a book of simple exam-taking tips—although you'll find many within—because law school exams involve complicated legal reasoning, a fact astonishingly ignored in the many current books that purport to tell students how to write top-flight answers.

What we have done instead is to tackle the exam process by breaking it down into discrete analytical components. Many people describe law school exam questions as hiding legal issues within complicated fact patterns. We compare it with Martin Handford and his wonderful drawings that hide Waldo in a maze of design and color. By watching other people, and practicing on one's own, virtually anyone can get pretty good at locating Waldo. Imagine, however, if you could sit down with Mr. Handford and have him describe for you how he hides Waldo in the first place. That's our task in Part I of the book—"Issues in Living Color"—in which we seek to explain why "issues" (rather than merely chaos and confusion) lurk within those long hypotheticals. We identify aspects of the legal system that create patterned ambiguity where newcomers arrive expecting to find a rulebook instead. Such ambiguity is at the core of law school exams, and virtually every practicing lawyer to whom we have spoken has applauded the idea of figuring out what makes something an "issue." Issue recognition, they tell us, is crucial to subsequent success at the bar.

To put Part I to work for our readers, however, we needed to go well beyond merely describing what an issue *looks like*. We want students to develop study habits that actually fit the skill of spotting issues expected on the typical exam. Like virtually every other guide to exam-taking, this one recommends that our readers study hard, outline their courses, practice on old exams, and discuss the material with classmates. But in Part II, we go beyond the conventional advice to explain how to connect these familiar study techniques to the kinds of performance your professors expect. We hope in the process to vindicate professorial warnings about the dangers of hornbooks and commercial outlines, warnings that too many students ignore at their peril.

Our colleagues often remind us that spotting an issue is only half the battle and that many students fall down when the task turns to analysis. We agree. We doubt, however, that analytical difficulty is a product of students' moral or intellectual failings. Rather, we attribute many perceived student inadequacies to a breakdown in communication between students who expect to be judged on whether their answers are "correct" and professors who want discussion of both sides of difficult questions. So in Parts II and III we seek to remedy the communication gap.

The long, complicated exam question throws many students for one loop and then another. First, because each question contains multiple sources of ambiguity, students must write about how different parts of the law fit together in situations where the student is unsure whether each component of the law applies or not. There is nothing unfair about this. Clients arrive with difficult problems, just as medical patients sometimes end up in an emergency room with more than one complaint. It's hard enough to diagnose a single problem—is that pain in the patient's abdomen an ulcer, appendicitis, or what? But if the patient has multiple complaints, each with many possible diagnoses, then things get really complicated.

Legal problems are often similarly complex, and exam questions always are. So throughout the book we explore techniques for putting together the many components of a question in ways that will help the student organize and streamline the analysis. Just as the emergency room doctor must learn to focus on which patient complaints are relevant to proper diagnosis, the successful law student must keep her eyes on how each ambiguity in the question will or will not affect the ultimate outcome of a potential legal dispute.

The second way that student expectations are disrupted is a by-product of the first. Questions that pose multiple, interrelated issues will prove extremely frustrating to the student eager to proceed to a result. Once you get a feel for law school, you realize that you should celebrate every ambiguity you see within an exam question because you have that much more to discuss. But in the beginning, as you hurry through to reach conclusions, the temptation is to be annoyed, if not overwhelmed, by all the uncertainty. We show you how you can turn that uncertainty to your advantage by pausing long enough on each of the many ambiguities to provide the kind of discussion your professor wants.

In the end, of course, the proof of our method is in the pudding. So we close the book with sample exam questions from each of the basic law school courses we have taught — Constitutional Law, Contracts, Property, and Torts. We provide sample answers that illustrate the substantive techniques the book describes and some stylistic advice about how to write answers as well. There is no one way to write a good exam answer, and, as we say throughout the book, if you must choose between our advice and the specific instructions of the professor giving the exam, toss our book out the window every time. Our educated guess, however, is that much of what you read here will fit very well with what most of your professors expect on the exams you have taken or will be taking soon.

So relax, enjoy our book for what it is, and remember that the doubts you may feel today will be the issues you'll be confidently dissecting tomorrow. Not knowing the "right answer" is very different from having "no answer." And sometimes "maybe" may be the best answer of all.

Richard Michael Fischl
Coral Gables, Florida

Jeremy Paul
Hartford, Connecticut

March 1999

Acknowledgments

A number of friends read this manuscript at various stages, and we are grateful to them for their helpful suggestions. So thanks to Tom Baker, Ellen Dannin, Marc Fajer, Pat Gudridge, Jennifer Jaff, Duncan Kennedy, Julie Lipkin, Fran Olsen, Eve Paul, Tamara Piety, Katie Sowle, Catharine Wells, and Steve Winter.

We owe an equally large debt to the many scholars whose work has taught us and inspired us to identify and embrace ambiguity as it appears on law school exams and elsewhere. The nature of this "how-to" book counsels against adherence to the familiar academic style of prolific citation, yet the absence of references to specific sources may make it appear as though we invented the ideas in this book from whole cloth. Nothing could be further from the truth. Indeed, we see this book as a third-generation contribution to a style of legal education begun in the era of Karl Llewellyn and revived in the era of Duncan Kennedy. We have been particularly influenced by the work of those two scholars, which we cite formally in our list of sources at the end. We should also add that it was Duncan who first persuaded us that great teaching and great scholarship are not dichotomous categories.

We have also been influenced by and borrowed liberally from a host of talented scholars too numerous to mention. A few people, however, have done work making our task so much easier that we wanted to offer special acknowledgment. They are Terry Anderson, Jack Balkin, Jamie Boyle, Steven Burton, Jerry Frug, Peter Gabel, Morty Horwitz, Jennifer Jaff, Mark Kelman, Karl Klare, Edward Levi, Laura Little, Soia Mentschikoff, Fran Olsen, Pierre Schlag, Joe Singer, Deborah Stone, Irwin Stotzky,

William Twining, Pat Williams, and Steve Winter. Formal citations to their work can also be found in the back, and we urge those of you intrigued by what you find here to consult them for a deeper look than a book about exams can plausibly offer.

Finally, we would like to extend special thanks to the late Claude Sowle, Dennis Lynch, and the University of Miami School of Law for bringing the two of us together in a rare and extraordinary setting a decade and a half ago, and to the law schools at both Miami and the University of Connecticut for generously supporting our work on this project.

We couldn't have done this without you.

Getting to Maybe

Chapter 1

You're Not in Kansas Anymore

A Place Where "Knowing the Material" Is Not Enough

Every law student craves the answers to a few big questions. Can I handle the pressure? Will I make the Law Review? What kind of job can I get when I graduate? Does law school leave room for romance?

We suspect, however, that one question burns deepest in the hearts of all but the few students at the top of every class: "How come Student X did better on (say) the Torts exam than I did, even though I studied twice as hard and knew the material much better than she did?"

The point of this book is to provide you with an answer to that question from a law professor's perspective — a perspective we think you'll find useful, since it is invariably a professor who decides whether to give you or Student X the higher grade! But we want to begin the book by considering answers our *students* sometimes give to this "burning question," since we think those answers reveal some common misunderstandings about law exams:

a) Student X had a copy of a Torts outline put together by the guy who "booked" last year's class and who is now the professor's research assistant.

    b)   Student X ignored everything the professor said and read Glannon (or Emmanuel's) the night before the exam.

    c)   Student X is just smarter than the rest of us.

We hear these answers — or slight variations on them — all the time from students disappointed with their law school grades. And as usual, our students are on to something, for there's a grain of truth in each answer: It can help your examination performance to work with a good outline for the course; it might also help to step back from your own materials (your classnotes and casebriefs and outlines) to get a fresh overview from a high-quality commercial study aid; and of course it never hurts to be really smart.

But these answers also share a common yet misleading assumption about law exams — namely, that the key to excelling lies in what you "know" coming into the exam. On this view, if you could only get your hands on the definitive outline or the right hornbook — and if only you were smart enough to keep it "all" in your head for the three- to four-hour ordeal — you'd be on your way to Law Review and legal stardom in nothing flat.

In point of fact, you *do* need to "know the material" — the seemingly endless collection of cases, rules, policies, and theories examined in each of your courses — in order to excel in law school. But the rub is that knowing the material is only a starting point, for the typical law exam doesn't simply test your ability to recall — or even to understand really well — the many things you learned from the course in question. Rather, the typical exam tests your ability to *use* the material you've learned and to *apply* it to problems you've never seen before.

To get a sense of what we mean, forget about law for a moment. Assume instead that you are taking a graduate course in engineering and that you have spent the semester studying the properties of various building materials and a host of theories of design. You have dedicated virtually every waking moment to this course. You have read and re-read every assignment and taken copious notes; you have come to each class session meticulously well-prepared; you have taken down almost every word the instructor has uttered; you have saved and annotated every handout; and—during the two weeks just before the final exam—you have organized and reorganized and outlined and committed everything to memory with such success that, in the highly unlikely event that someone besides a classmate were to ask you to explain the differing properties of (say) plastic vs. glass, you could quickly rattle off everything that could possibly be said on the subject.

You enter the room for the final examination, and the proctor presents you with a large box containing a seemingly random assortment of materials of the sort studied in the course. On the blackboard, the proctor writes the following instructions: "Using the materials in the box before you, design and construct a widget according to the principles we studied in the course." (Unlike law students, engineering students know exactly what widgets look like!) Confronted with this daunting task, you would no doubt find the mass of information you have mastered in preparation for the exam helpful—indeed, crucial. But you would obviously be making a serious mistake if you left the contents of the box untouched and proceeded instead to compose an essay on the fundamentals of materials and design and to submit it for the grade. The point of the exercise is not, after all, to regurgitate what you know, but to use what you know on what you happen to find inside the box.

Perhaps the most important lesson we can teach you about law exams is that each question you will encounter is a lot like the engineering student's box: It's what you do with what you find inside the question that counts the most. In all likelihood, what distinguished Student X's performance from everybody else's on that Torts exam was less what she "knew" coming into the exam—let alone which outline she had or which hornbook she studied—than *what she did with the questions she encountered on the exam itself.* And the intellectual skills that enabled her to handle the questions so well can be learned and developed by virtually any student who is smart enough to get into law school and diligent enough to put in the time.

But truth be told, we legal educators generally don't do a very good job of teaching exam skills, at least not directly. We focus instead on the intricacies of legal reasoning and argument—and on the policies and theories that organize and complicate each area of the law—and we seldom explore in any depth the connection between those lessons and the challenge of law exam-taking. So even the most enterprising student has little choice but to draw upon sources that turn out to be less than fully reliable, for it's almost impossible to master law school exam-taking by relying on undergraduate habits, tips from fellow students, or even the Socratic dialogue in the classroom. In this book we'll tell you why those experiences may send the wrong messages, and we'll provide you with someplace else to turn.

Some Lessons You May Need To Unlearn

Lesson # 1—Undergraduate Exams and the "Information Dump"

Consider, first, the exam-taking habits pushed on you in undergraduate school and even before that. College-level testing often involves a demonstration of student knowledge. Who was William the Conqueror and what country did he invade and when? How many hydrogen atoms make up a water molecule? Such questions conform to a vision of memorize-and-regurgitate learning, and, to many students, law school initially appears to be the ideal spot for raising this kind of testing to new heights. How many days do I have to file that appeal? How many witnesses must there be for the will to be valid? Given the gargantuan number of laws "on the books," law professors could easily give closed-book exams filled to the brim with nothing but questions calling for esoteric knowledge of memorized legal intricacies. *But we don't.*

It's true that failing to grasp the basic points of your substantive courses will prove fatal to your exam performance. In Constitutional Law, for example, you need to know that *Marbury v. Madison* established our tradition in which the federal courts have the power to invalidate acts of Congress in the name of the Constitution. Going beyond the basics, however, to attempt to memorize verbatim every little rule and sub-rule you encountered during a course is unlikely to be particularly helpful, because law school exams are about much more than just accumulated knowledge. Indeed, testing principally for such knowledge would be foolish. As an attorney, you can almost always "look it up" if you need to; in fact, on most occasions, it would be irresponsible *not* to look it up, even if you were absolutely positive you remembered "it." Besides, to invoke once again our engineering exam analogy, a client seeking a lawyer's advice doesn't need someone who can recite legal rules from memory; rather, she needs someone who will use all that knowledge to help her solve her "box" of problems.

Exam-taking skills developed before law school, however, cause many students to persist in treating our questions *as if* they called for a memorized answer. To see what we mean, let's work through a concrete example.

Assume that you are attempting to answer an exam question on that favorite topic from first-year Contracts, the battle of the forms. Say the first thing you notice about the question is that the transaction at issue involves the sale of a customer list from an established firm to a start-up. (*Uh-oh*, you think. *Is that a sale of goods? It's a sale, sure enough, but isn't a customer list too intangible to be a "good" within the meaning of the U.C.C.?*) Then you see that the selling firm's offer requires payment upon delivery of the list, but the buyer's response promises to make payment "within thirty days." (*Oh, no*, you think. *Now I've got to figure out whether the Code or the common law applies. If this is a sale of goods, then there may be a contract under § 2-207 in spite of the differing terms. But if it's not a Code transaction, then the differing terms will kill the deal under the common law rule that a valid acceptance must form a "mirror image" of the offer.*) The hypothetical draws to a close, with the selling firm tendering the customer list and demanding immediate payment; the buying firm insisting on its own thirty-day term; and the seller seeking your legal advice regarding its rights in the dispute. (*Yikes*, you think. *If the case is governed by the common law, maybe the seller accepted the buyer's terms by performance—that is, by tendering the list after the buyer "fired the last shot" in the exchange of documents. On the other hand, if U.C.C. § 2-207 governs, then everything may turn on whether the difference between the conflicting terms is "material." A thirty-day difference in a payment schedule doesn't seem like that big a deal, but if the seller sold the list because of cashflow needs, maybe it is. But wait! Isn't § 2-207 supposed to deal with cases involving parties who do business by exchanging pre-printed forms replete with self-serving boilerplate? Does it make any difference that the parties here don't seem to be using any forms at all?)*

As we will shortly explain, the point of an exam question like this one is to get the student to identify each of the ambiguities noted in the parentheticals and to analyze the difference the resolution of those ambiguities might make to the rights and obligations of the respective parties. But in the face of exam pressure, many students respond by ignoring the ambiguities—indeed, by ignoring the facts stated in the question altogether—and treating the problem as an invitation to begin writing everything they know about the battle of the forms.

We refer to an answer of this kind as an "information dump." The student interprets the question actually asked—involving multiple issues, complex facts, and competing equities—as an opportunity to do what he used to do (and no doubt did very well) in college: Write an essay designed to persuade the grader that he "really understands" the battle of the forms. But what he has done instead is persuaded the grader that he couldn't—or, perhaps, that he just didn't want to—grapple with the vexing problems presented in the question he was asked. And, like the engineering student who writes an essay rather than building a widget out of the box of materials, chances are he won't be very happy with the grade he gets as a result.

Lesson # 2 — Sorting Through the Law School Rumor Mill

To be sure, students begin to hear that "law exams are different" from almost the moment they set foot on their law school campus. As with most "rumor mills," however, there's a good bit of misleading advice lurking within the conventional wisdom imparted by second- and third-year students.

Imagine a rookie basketball player whose teammate's advice on covering a superstar is "force him left." The rookie enters the game and invites the star to drive left. The star promptly does so, putting the ball in the basket with a beautiful left-handed shot. During the next time-out, the rookie presses his teammate, "I thought you told me to force him left!" Without batting an eyelash, the teammate responds, "You should see what happens when he goes right!"

Law students who trade the "information dump" for the "helpful hints" from their classmates and from upper-level students may have a similarly unsettling experience. "You told me to spot the issues," a student was recently overheard complaining to a colleague, shortly after the first-semester grades were released. "And the professor admitted that I saw most of them. But I only got a C+ on the exam!" The predictable response: "You should see what you'd get if you *didn't* spot the issues!"

Like "knowing the material," the ability to "spot the issues" is crucial to a successful exam performance; but like knowing the material, issue-spotting is nowhere near enough. Recall, for a moment, our hypothetical battle-of-the-forms question. An answer that read something like the following would almost surely get a passing grade at virtually any law school:

> The first thing we have to decide is whether the sale of a customer list is a sale of "goods" under the U.C.C. If it is, then the next issue is whether the buyer's "thirty-day" term is a "material alteration" of seller's offer. But if it's not a sale of goods, then the issue is whether the seller accepted the buyer's terms by performance.

The student has indeed "spotted the issues" and would no doubt get credit for that. But like the student who "dumps" information rather than *using* it, the student who merely "spots" the issues—without going on to explain why they are issues, what difference they make, and the arguments for resolving them one way or another—will at best end up somewhere in the undistinguished middle of the class. (In Part II of the book, we will explore in great length what you *should* do with issues once you spot them.)

There are two other exam-taking strategies frequently pro-
moted by well-meaning fellow students that may be equally misleading to a beginner. First, there is the suggestion that all you
need to do on the final is to show the professor that you've
"grasped the fundamentals of the course." This approach does
have one thing going for it: You can organize and draft your answers well in advance of the exam, and you won't have to waste
any time during the exam period itself reading—let alone thinking about—the professor's questions! The downside, of course,
is that this is simply a variation on the "information dump" we
talked about earlier, except this kind of undifferentiated "dump"
is likely to get you an even lower grade. Thus, the student who
responds to our hypothetical question by "writing everything she
knows" about the battle of the forms might get at least some
credit for signaling to the professor that she recognizes the basic
legal problem that the question addresses; by contrast, the student who responds by attempting to demonstrate that she's
grasped the "fundamentals" of *the entire Contracts course* is
likely to lead the grader to the conclusion that she didn't have
the faintest idea what the question was about.

The other strategy you are likely to hear about from your
classmates is the so-called "IRAC" method. The idea here is that
exam-taking can be reduced to four simple steps: (I) spot the
issue; (II) cite the rule that resolves the issue; (III) apply the rule
to the facts presented; and (IV) offer a conclusion that answers
the question. We will discuss the dangers of IRAC at greater
length later in the book, but for now suffice it to say that attempting to reduce law exam-taking to four simple steps is a lot
like attempting to reduce guitar playing to four simple chords:
It's not a bad way to start, but until you get well beyond it, no
one is going to mistake you for B.B. King. Indeed, you could
write a book about the many important exam-taking skills that
simply cannot be captured in IRAC or in any other one-size-fits-
all formula. (We have, and you're reading it!)

Lesson # 3 — The Dark Side of the Socratic Method: The Rulebook vs. The Loose Cannon

Perhaps the cruelest aspect of the law school exam process is visited upon those of you who look for lessons in the place you legitimately should expect to find them — inside the law school classroom. Many students enter law school expecting to memorize a massive quantity of legal rules for regurgitation-on-command — much in the manner that the interns and residents on the popular television series *ER* are asked to rattle off the names of a million-and-one body parts, symptoms, and diseases while making rounds with their senior colleagues. We have no idea whether *ER* accurately captures the rigors of medical training, but the law student who anticipates a memorize-and-regurgitate model of education is in for some big surprises at most American law schools.

One surprise is that most of the "rules" you are expected to master are buried in the text of judicial opinions. In spite of the fact that you're paying thousands of dollars a year to have a faculty of experts teach you the law, it turns out that your professors expect *you* to figure out the rules — often referred to as "case holdings" — on your own. What's worse, you never seem to get them right. Does the holding of *Romer v. Evans*, 517 U.S. 620 (1996), apply to all laws that discriminate against homosexuals or only to those that prevent them from securing the same protection others are afforded by civil rights statutes? Does the holding of *Hawkins v. McGee*, 84 N.H. 114, 146 A. 641 (1929), govern damages for every breach of contract; or for broken promises in the context of medical treatment gone awry; or just for "hairy hands"?

Nor can you find the solace of certainty in the statutory supplement. It may seem that at least *these* are rules you don't have to figure out on your own; after all, they are written down in black and white. But before you've even had time to breathe a sigh of relief, you discover that it is just as difficult to determine the meaning of a statute — or a provision from the Constitution or a section from the Restatement of Torts — as it is to figure out the holding of a case. When you offer an interpretation based on the "plain meaning" of the rule ("no vehicles permitted in the park" means *all* "vehicles," period), the professor is bound to respond with a series of perplexing questions. Is the "meaning" really so "plain"? Are tricycles among the "vehicles" to which the rule refers? What did the drafters *intend*? Were they even *thinking* about tricycles? What policies were the drafters trying to further? Do tricycles produce the noise, pollution, and risks to pedestrians we associate with automobile traffic?

Worse still, if you came to law school expecting simply to memorize and regurgitate rules, the biggest surprise may be that "determining the meaning of the rule" is just the starting point in legal analysis. A lot of time is also spent "applying the rule to the facts," a task that turns out to be every bit as daunting as determining the meaning of the rule itself. Was the uncle's promise to give his nephew a large sum of money if the latter refrained from smoking an offer proposing a bargain? Or was it merely a conditional promise to make a gift? If the host invites you, but not your boyfriend, to a party, and your boyfriend shows up anyway—injuring himself on his way in through an unlocked back door—is he considered a licensee or a trespasser?

A significant part of what law professors teach *and test* is designed to help you learn to cope with these kinds of questions. But many students find classroom discussion maddening because it's a rare professor who will stop to highlight the difference between good and bad efforts at rule identification or application.

What happens next is at the root of more exam disappointment than almost anything else we can describe. Students grow increasingly frustrated by the lack of hard-and-fast "answers" emerging from the so-called Socratic classroom, and, as a result, many are drawn toward one or the other of two highly simplified approaches to legal analysis and exam-taking. We'll refer to those approaches here as *the rulebook account* and *the judge as loose cannon*.

Simply put, the rulebook account is shorthand for the belief that once you know the rule, "the rule decides the case." On this view, "legal reasoning" is one part memorization and one part logic: The job of the judge, or the lawyer who appears before her, or the student on the exam, is simply to apply the governing rule to the facts at hand and to announce the result. ("To form a contract, the terms of the acceptance must be the 'mirror image' of those in the offer. In this case, the seller's offer called for immediate payment, and the buyer's would-be acceptance stipulated payment in 30 days. Therefore, there is no contract. Next case, please!")

With the possible exception of law enforcement personnel and others who've had frequent contact with the legal system, most non-lawyers—and thus most beginning law students—seem to think that the law works in this way, at least when it's working properly. As a consequence, the experience of the first semester of law school can come as quite a shock, since it typically consists of the study of case after case in which the rules, the facts, and the connection between the two can be argued in more than one way. (Recall, for example, all of the ambiguities and complexities in our battle-of-the-forms hypothetical—ambiguities and complexities that the simple syllogism at the end of the last paragraph completely glossed over.)

Students respond to this "gestalt shift" in different ways. One approach is to cling to the rulebook account. We suspect this is an instinctive reaction because "the rules" offer a lifeboat of seeming certainty in the raging sea of ambiguity explored in the law school classroom. (You know you're not swimming, but at least you won't drown.) Some students may even begin to think of the professor as a heretic and the Socratic inquiry as a form of religious persecution. Paradoxically, this stance often involves a firmer resolve and a strengthened belief in the importance of the rules. "Okay," they think. "Maybe some smarty-pants, overeducated preppy law professor can score picky debating points on helpless neophyte law students. But rules just *have to* decide cases, since the only other alternative is that judges are free to do whatever they want and to run utterly amok."

Yet another group of students comes to agree with this last point—*i.e.*, that the only alternative to "rules deciding cases" is "judges doing whatever they want"—but from that premise they are pulled toward a more cynical conclusion. Having studied case after case in which "the rules" could easily lead to more than one result, these students embrace the approach we refer to as the judge as loose cannon—that judges decide cases on the basis of values, or politics, or policy, or "what they had for breakfast," or some combination of such factors having nothing whatsoever to do with legal rules.

In point of fact, as our students line up on each side of this divide, they are in their own way re-enacting a long-standing debate in American law—a debate the roots of which go back at least as far as the beginning of this century. Fortunately for you (and for us as well!), we don't have to rehearse or resolve the debate between formalism and legal realism here. Instead, what we want to do is to show you how the extremely oversimplified versions of these positions that beginners frequently espouse—that is, "naive" formalism (the rulebook account) and "vulgar" realism (the judge as loose cannon)—can undermine your capacity to make persuasive legal arguments and, with it, your ability to excel on law school exams.

In a nutshell, the students who embrace the rulebook account tend to write exams that substitute rule-regurgitation for reasoning and analysis. On the upside, they frequently come to the exam having mastered, or even memorized, every little rule, subrule, and exception that was covered in the course—and, "just in case," some that the professor never even got to! But the trouble begins when they read the first question and encounter the sort of ambiguity that is typically present on a law exam. Perhaps it is a case in which more than one rule might govern (*e.g.*, a riparian property rights case that would come out different ways under the respective doctrines of reasonable use and prior appropriation). Or perhaps it is a case in which a single rule clearly governs, but the rule might be interpreted in one of two ways (*e.g.*, a proximate cause problem that might be decided one way by Cardozo and another way by Andrews). Or perhaps it is a case in which the rule and its meaning seem fairly clear, but the facts might be interpreted in more than one way (*e.g.*, a transaction— like the uncle's promise to give his nephew $5000 if the latter gives up smoking—that might fairly be characterized either as an offer proposing a bargain or as a conditional promise to make a gift).

Confronted with ambiguities like these, our rulebook devotee is stymied because there is no "rule" telling him how to resolve them. There is no small irony here: Since law professors almost invariably try to test what they teach, the chances are that the student's instructor spent substantial class time working through these very problems — or problems quite like them — attempting to demonstrate through lecture and/or Socratic discussion that there was more than one way of looking at each of them. Yet our student may well have stopped taking notes at the time because he was waiting patiently through all the argument and counterargument for a punch line — waiting, that is, for a rule to come to the rescue with some definitive resolution.

As a result, when he encounters such a problem on the final, he may well experience a sense that he is the victim of a malicious bait and switch: After spending the semester teaching the class rule after rule after rule, how could the professor have decided to test the very questions for which the rules don't provide clear winners and losers? Unsure of how to deal with problems that the law doesn't seem to solve, the rulebook devotee may retreat to his natural habitat and draft answers designed to demonstrate his mastery of the rules, all the while avoiding the ambiguities that would arise in attempting to apply them to the facts presented in the question. Yet the point of the typical law exam is precisely to see whether students can identify, analyze, and argue thoughtfully about such ambiguities, and so an answer that has simply wished them all away is unlikely to distinguish itself.

By contrast, a student who embraces the judge-as-loose-cannon approach tends to write exam answers that discuss everything *but* the rules. Once she picks up on what she sees as the principal lesson of the Socratic method — that rules don't decide cases because there is always another way of looking at things — she stops taking notes every time a legal rule is discussed. "What's the point in focusing on *that*," she thinks, "since the decision is always based on something else?" That "something else" may vary from professor to professor and even from case to case: Sometimes it seems to be "policy" (*e.g.*, the security of transactions in Contracts or loss-spreading in Torts); sometimes it's the "equities" presented by the facts (*e.g.*, the vulnerability of the impoverished tenant at the hands of the wealthy absentee landlord); sometimes it is the judge's "values" (when the professor agrees with her) or her "politics" (when he doesn't). Since in the view of such a student these extra-legal considerations are what really drive judicial decisions, she sees no need to spend precious study time mastering the intricacies of the seemingly pointless array of rules.

Come the final exam, she may well be in for a complete disaster. For one thing, since most exam questions test the student's ability to use legal rules to make arguments, it is now our unsuspecting student who has become the "loose cannon," entering the battle virtually unarmed. A central task of lawyering is to translate the facts, policies, equities, and values that support her client's case into the language of the law (*e.g.*, "the landlord breached the warranty of habitability and therefore the tenant should be able to withhold her rent"), and you simply can't do this unless and until you develop a facility with the rules that form the basic rhetoric of legal argument. For another thing, when it comes to a task that separates the best answers from the merely mediocre—*i.e.*, dealing with the ambiguities that complicate the legal analysis of the question—the loose-cannon student may not even be able to identify those ambiguities, since she has not taken the rules seriously enough to see how they might lead in several directions. (She is unlikely, for example, to figure out that the uncle's promise could be interpreted as proposing either a bargain or a conditional gift unless she understands the legal requirement of consideration.)

Of course, many students find themselves drawn simultaneously in both directions. Some conclude that "cross-dressing" may be the safest course and offer randomly alternating approaches—consciously or unconsciously—in the hope that *something* they say will please the grader. Others try to embrace both approaches at the same time. Like the atheist who hedges his bets by sending the children to church, the rulebook proponent may conclude an extended regurgitation of rules with an abrupt loose-cannon appeal: "Of course, it depends on your politics," he writes. "I champion the weak against the strong—just like the professor!—so I think the court should rule in favor of the family farmer and against the coal company. But a more conservative judge might come out the other way."

Ironically, in the end the two approaches leave the student in much the same sorry fix. The rulebook devotee may see the ambiguities on the exam, but he ignores them because he thinks the law requires an answer and he doesn't have one; the loose cannon cannot even spot the ambiguities, for she has ignored the rules because they only lead to . . . *ambiguities.* But like Dorothy in the Wizard of Oz, they've each had the ruby slippers all along, for if they had learned to embrace the ambiguities they have been so busy ignoring and denying, they'd be on their way to Law Review.

* * * * *

We said at the beginning of the chapter that the most important lesson we could teach you about law exams is that it's what you do with what you find inside the question that counts the most. The second most important lesson should be apparent from the foregoing discussion: What you will find inside the typical law exam question is ambiguity, and we think that learning to live with it—indeed, learning to search it out and exploit it— is the key to doing well on law school exams.

In the rest of the book, we will attempt to translate these basic lessons into a blueprint for concrete action as you pursue your legal studies and prepare for and take exams. Part I of the book ("Issues in Living Color") will help you learn the specific ways in which law professors use ambiguity to create "issues" on law exams. We have designed Part II ("Strategies for Issue-Spotting, Analysis, and Argument") to help you learn how to recognize those issues and how to deal with them as you draft your exam answers. In Part III ("Test-Taking Tips"), we offer more generalized advice on exam-preparation and exam writing, and we also address some "frequently asked questions" from our students. Finally, the book ends with a series of sample exam questions and answers from Constitutional Law, Contracts, Property, and Torts; the idea here is to provide you with an opportunity to see our advice put into in action.

Our aim is to *clarify*—not simplify—the examination process, and accordingly this book will require sustained effort on your part. We are confident, however, that there will be a big payoff in terms of improved academic performance. As for the romance part, you're on your own!

Part I

Issues in Living Color

Chapter 2

Issues as "Forks in the Road"

No doubt you've encountered the word "issue" with great frequency since you started law school, and you've probably figured out by now that it means different things in different contexts. When writing opinions, judges use the word as shorthand for "a question we must answer in order to decide this case." Attorneys drafting briefs, by contrast, often use the word as a tool of advocacy. (To recall an old joke, when the law is against him, a lawyer will try to make an "issue" out of the facts; when the facts are against him, he'll attempt to make an "issue" out of the law.) And law students struggling with casebriefs for their first-year courses surely suspect that "issue" is just another name for that unfathomable formula their professors consult to divine whatever it is that the case under discussion is really about.

So it should come as no surprise to you that the word has yet another meaning in the context of a law school examination. The typical exam question will tell a story that presents some sort of hypothetical dispute. The story may be as brief as a sentence or two, or it may go on for two to three pages. The question then asks you to identify (or "spot") the issues that would have to be resolved if the dispute became a lawsuit. In this context, we believe it is useful to think of issues as "forks in the road" of your analysis of the dispute. Like a "fork" you encounter in a real road, an issue presents you with a choice between two (and sometimes more) paths leading in different directions. But unlike a fork in a real road, exam forks are more like the divide in the Yellow-Brick Road, where the Scarecrow tells Dorothy she can go "both ways." Not only do exam forks permit you to travel in different directions at the same time; that is precisely what you *should* do, for the more paths your analysis explores, the better your answer will be.

Let's begin with a variation on the famous "Brooklyn Bridge" hypothetical—where an offer to make a unilateral contract is revoked when the offeree is "halfway across the Brooklyn Bridge" (or "halfway up the flagpole")—that virtually every law student encounters in her first-year Contracts course:

> Paul Patron offers Arlene Artiste $10,000 to paint a portrait of the Patron family. Artiste explains that her other commitments make it impossible for her to promise a completed work by a particular date, and Patron responds, "I don't *want* your commitment. I just want the portrait." After Artiste spends numerous hours doing preliminary sketches—but before she has put brush to canvas and begun the actual portrait—Patron advises her that he has changed his mind and is revoking the offer. What legal rights does Artiste have against Patron?

What "forks in the road" are presented by this hypothetical?

For one thing, you may recall that the traditional common law rule permits the offeror in the unilateral contract setting to revoke at any time before the offeree completes performance. If that rule is applied to the facts presented here, then Patron is perfectly free to back out of the deal, and Artiste has no right to stop him. But you may also recall that under the "modern" rule designed for this predicament—reflected in § 45 of the Second Restatement of Contracts—a binding option contract is created once the offeree "begins the invited performance." And if *that* rule is applied, then Patron is prohibited from revoking as soon as Artiste starts the commissioned work.

In sum, then, there is a "fork in the road" with respect to the law to apply to the facts stated in the hypothetical. If you take the "road" of the traditional rule, your analysis will lead to the conclusion that Patron is free to revoke his offer at any time before Artiste actually finishes the painting. But if you take the "road" of the rule under § 45, your analysis will lead to the conclusion that Patron's offer is irrevocable as soon as Artiste begins her performance. To put the matter in more conventional terms, we would say that there is an "issue" presented by the question because there are two different legal rules that might apply to the facts at stake, and each of those rules will lead to a different result. We call this a "rule vs. counter-rule" issue — but if that's too fancy, just think of it as a "fork in the law" — and we'll have lots more to say about issues of this sort in the next chapter.

But our map of the "forks in the road" in the Artiste/Patron example is not yet complete. To continue with our analysis, it is pretty clear where the "road" of the traditional rule will lead: Since Artiste has yet to complete the portrait, Patron is perfectly free to revoke his offer. But the "road" of Restatement § 45 leads to terrain that is more uncertain than our discussion has thus far acknowledged. True enough, under that provision Patron loses the right to revoke once Artiste "begins the invited performance." But is it clear on the facts before us that Artiste has met that requirement? On the one hand, it can certainly be argued that Artiste began the performance when she did the preliminary sketchwork: To an artist, such sketches are as much a part of portraiture as the brushstrokes on the final canvas, and thus from that standpoint Artiste "began the invited performance" at the moment she started work on her first sketch. But on the other hand, Patron asked for a family portrait — not a series of sketches — in exchange for his promise of $10,000. Accordingly, you could argue that from *his* perspective "the invited performance" would be limited to the actual painting of the commissioned portrait, and that the preliminary sketches were "mere preparations" for that performance.

In sum, then, we have encountered a second "fork in the road" in the problem, and this one relates to the way we interpret the facts. If you take the "road" that interprets the performance sought from the standpoint of Artiste's own understanding of her task, your analysis may lead to the conclusion that the preliminary sketchwork was indeed the "beginning of performance," creating an option contract that in turn prevents Patron from revoking his offer. But if you take the "road" that interprets the performance from the perspective of Patron's focus on the end-product he sought to purchase, your analysis may lead to the conclusion that Artiste had not yet begun the invited performance and that Partron is accordingly free to revoke. To put the matter once again in more conventional terms, we would say that there is a second issue in this hypothetical—quite apart from the rule vs. counter-rule issue we discussed earlier—because there are at least two plausible ways to interpret the facts presented, and each of those interpretations may lead to a different outcome. Not surprisingly, we call this issue a "fork in the facts."

* * * * *

We have good news and bad news—and then some more good news. The first bit of good news is that 99% of the issues you will encounter on law school exams will fall into one or the other of the two categories we've just identified: They will involve either a "fork in the law" or a "fork in the facts." (Indeed, as we will explain in Chapter 7, a pretty fair number will involve both kinds of fork at the same time.) Thus, to coin a phrase, if you've seen two issues, you've pretty much seen 'em all.

But now for the bad news. This insight will get you absolutely nowhere on a law exam unless you already know precisely which forks in the law and precisely which forks in the facts to look for. Thus, you couldn't spot the "forks in the road" of the Artiste/Patron example unless you already knew (a) that the common law permitted the offeror in the unilateral contract setting to revoke at any time before the offeree completed performance; (b) that the Second Restatement, by contrast, protects the offeree once she begins performance; and (c) that, even under the Restatement approach, the protection the offeree enjoys during performance may not extend to activities that are "mere preparations." And you wouldn't have had a clue about (a), (b), or (c) unless you had taken—and studied pretty carefully during—your Contracts course. In sum, you can't even *begin* a search for "forks in the road" on a law exam until you've grasped the material taught in the course itself. If you were hoping for a shortcut—a way to avoid all the work it takes to engage that material seriously and make it your own—you'll have to pursue that quest elsewhere.

But now for a little more good news. Each of the two kinds of issues we've identified—forks in the law and forks in the facts—appear on law exams in recurring *patterns*. And learning to recognize those patterns can help you to (1) organize a course in preparation for an exam; (2) identify the issues that you encounter on the final; and (3) develop strategies for analyzing the issues you identify. We address each of these points at some length in Part II ("Strategies for Issue-Spotting, Analysis, and Argument"); but we'll devote the remaining chapters here in Part I to exploring these recurring patterns and helping you learn to recognize them on your own.

* * * * *

Before we turn to that task, however, we have several important caveats about our "forks in the road" approach. First, we don't pretend for a moment that what we offer in this book is an exhaustive list of the issues that you will encounter on your law exams. Every area of law we've ever encountered has issues unique to it, and sophisticated lawyers who practice in even the most familiar areas — personal injury law, for example — are coming up with new ones all the time. What we've done here is to identify the issues you are most likely to encounter in the subjects most students study in law school. But for a life in the law, this is only a starting point.

Second, for exam-taking purposes, the most important issues of all are the ones that the professor stresses in your class. Most professors try to test what they teach, and so we cannot emphasize enough that the lessons you learn from this book — or for that matter from any commercial study guide — are no substitute for a mastery of your course material.

Third, resist the temptation — however understandable it may be — to treat the patterns of issues we identify as "answers" you can memorize and regurgitate on law exams. The point is not to memorize them; it is rather to learn how to use them in particular contexts. We'll have a lot more to say about this in Parts II and III of the book, but for now, just keep the following advice in mind: "*Utilize, don't memorize!*"

Finally, keep your eyes on the prize. The point is *not* the proper classification of the issues you encounter on your exams. In the end it really doesn't matter whether it's a "fork in the law" or a "fork in the facts"; indeed, if you use the "forks" terminology on an exam, your professor is likely to think you have lost it completely and lapsed into baby talk. We are firmly of the view that it's easier to identify issues if you learn to recognize the patterns in which they appear, and we think that the "forks" approach is an extremely effective way to do that. But what matters most is that you learn to recognize and deal with issues on your own, and the "right" way to do that is whatever way works best for you.

Chapter 3

Forks in the Law: Rule vs. Counter-Rule Issues

Although your professors don't talk about them in these terms, they've been teaching you about "forks in the law" since your first day of law school. Indeed, two kinds of "forks in the law" are so common in legal argument that you can expect to encounter them on virtually every law exam you ever take.

One kind of fork presents a choice between rule and counter-rule. This is neatly illustrated by our Artiste/Patron hypothetical, where the dispute in question would be resolved one way by the common law rule (which would permit Patron to revoke his offer at any time before Artiste actually completes the portrait) and another way by § 45 of the Second Restatement (which protects Artiste against revocation once she begins her performance).

A second kind of "fork in the law" presents a choice between competing interpretations of a single rule. For the classic illustration of a fork like this, consider once again the treatment of tricyles under a rule that prohibits "vehicles" in the park. There, the question might be resolved one way by an interpretation that focused on the language of the rule ("tricycles are 'vehicles' and therefore forbidden") and another way under an interpretation that focused on the rule's apparent purpose ("tricycles just don't pose the kinds of dangers in public parks that automobiles do").

In this chapter, we are going to focus on issues that present the first kind of fork: We'll call them "rule vs. counter-rule" issues. We'll start by offering a "map" of the patterns in which issues of this sort appear, and then we'll explore some of the reasons that students don't recognize them as "issues" when they encounter them on an exam.

A. Patterns to Watch For

For many lawyers, the dream client would be the one who walks into your office and presents you with a problem that can be resolved in her favor simply by citing a legal rule. "The court must rule for my client," you imagine yourself solemnly declaring, "because Rule X says so" — after which you close the case-file and collect your fee on the way out the courthouse door for a golf date.

If you've been in law school long enough to be reading this book, chances are you've already figured out that it doesn't work that way very often in the real world. One reason for this — and a reason that often comes as a surprise to students who find the prospect of learning just *one* rule for every situation challenging enough — is that it is frequently the case that the lawyer for the other side can respond to the rule you cite with a different rule, and under that rule his client rather than yours will prevail.

It's bad enough that your dreams of an easy win and a golf date are shattered; what's far worse, at least from the perspective of most law students, is that this means that there are twice as many rules to learn! Yet the bad news comes with a silver lining, for the way most law professors test this multiplicity of rules is pretty straightforward: They will give you a hypothetical that would be resolved in one way by Rule X and in another way by Rule Y, and chances are that the difference between the rule and the counter-rule will have been analyzed in some depth in the course of class discussion. Indeed, in American law these rule vs. counter-rule relationships appear in patterns, and here are some of the patterns you are most likely to encounter on your exams.

1. Traditional Rule vs. Modern Rule

In most of the subjects you'll study, a major theme is that law changes over time. As a result, you'll find yourself studying topic after topic in which you'll learn first about the "traditional" rule and then about the "modern" rule governing this or that particular problem. An excellent illustration is our Artiste/Patron hypothetical, where the traditional rule—a product of the common law—would permit Patron to revoke his offer at any time before Artiste completes the portrait, and the modern rule, established by the Second Restatement, would prohibit revocation once she begins the requested work.

No doubt you can readily think of additional examples of such traditional vs. modern rule relationships. Consider the following hypothetical, which raises a rule vs. counter-rule issue familiar to anyone who has taken Torts:

> The moment the light changes, Penny Pedestrian steps into the crosswalk without looking both ways. Meanwhile, Danny Driver, who just left his favorite tavern after downing three gin-and-tonics in the course of an hour, is driving his car at a speed well in excess of the posted limit and weaving wildly through traffic. As Pedestrian sets foot into the street, Driver races into the intersection from behind her and makes a sharp turn directly into her path, striking her and causing her serious bodily injury. What rights does Pedestrian have against Driver?

Do you see the issue? Everything turns on whether we apply the doctrine of contributory negligence (the traditional rule) or the doctrine of comparative negligence (the modern rule).

Thus, Driver's conduct (drinking and driving and speeding and weaving and making sharp turns) is clearly negligent—reckless, even—but Pedestrian's failure to look both ways before stepping into the intersection is probably negligence on her part as well. Under the doctrine of contributory negligence, Pedestrian's own lack of due care is a complete bar to her cause of action against Driver. By contrast, under the doctrine of comparative negligence, Pedestrian would be permitted to recover that portion of her damages attributable to Driver's negligence rather than her own; thus, if on these facts we consider Driver (say) 90% at fault and Pedestrian 10% at fault, Pedestrian can recover 90% of the damages from injuries resulting from the accident. Thus, once again we encounter an issue that is a consequence of rule and counter-rule leading to contrasting results.

2. Different Strokes for Different Folks

A second pattern to watch for occurs when different jurisdictions adopt different rules because of political, philosophical, or regional differences between the jurisdictions in question. If enough states have adopted a particular approach, your casebook and/or your professor is likely to describe it as the "majority rule" and to refer to the less popular approach as either the "minority rule" or even the "X rule," where X = the name of some state that takes the nonconforming approach. (When we were in law school, for example, there seemed to be a special "Massachusetts rule" for just about every topic.) In other contexts, however, you will learn that no rule has commanded a "majority." But regardless of the particulars, the point is that when the law on a topic is split in this way, you should watch out for a rule vs. counter-rule issue on your exam.

Consider the following problem, which is drawn from the riparian rights section of the typical Property course:

> For over a decade, Yasgur has diverted water from the stream running through his land to run a generator providing electricity for his family farm. Beau purchases the land just upstream of Yasgur and diverts a small portion of the stream to water his flock of sheep. Because of the diminution in flow, the stream no longer has the force to power Yasgur's generator. What rights does Yasgur have against Beau?

As in the other cases we've looked at so far, the issue presented here once again involves rule and counter-rule. But this time, the conflict is not between traditional and modern rules, but rather between contemporary rules embraced by different jurisdictions.

Thus, under the riparian rights doctrine favored by many Western states — the rule of prior appropriation — Yasgur may well have a claim against Beau for the diminution in flow, since Yasgur's rights to his usage of the stream predated Beau's by many years. But under the rule of reasonable use, which is applied in many Eastern jurisdictions, Beau is entitled to her fair share of the stream no matter how much longer Yasgur has owned the adjacent lot. As long as Beau's use is a reasonable one—as watering sheep from a stream running through farm country would seem to be—the fact that it deprives Yasgur of the flow to which he'd grown accustomed is irrelevant.

Other familiar instances of such "different strokes" issues abound. Consider, for example, a variation on the Driver/Pedestrian hypothetical we examined a few moments ago. Assume that Pedestrian's husband Harry looked on helplessly and in utter horror as Pedestrian was struck by Driver's recklessly driven car, but that Harry managed to avoid contact with the errant vehicle himself. While Driver's conduct was clearly the cause of severe "emotional distress" on the part of Harry, Harry's rights against Driver may turn on another "different strokes" issue: Some states require a physical impact before permitting a plaintiff to pursue a claim for emotional distress (in which case Harry would lose for want of such impact), while other states permit plaintiffs to pursue a claim without such impact (in which case Harry may well be able to succeed in his claim).

3. Common Law vs. Statute

Let's end this section with one more variation on rule vs. counter-rule issues. In each of the hypotheticals discussed thus far, the issue arises in the context of a conflict between two rules that each has its basis in the common law. But—in your coursework as well as on your exams—you will also encounter issues that arise because of a difference between a common law rule and a statutory rule. Indeed, as state legislatures enact more and more statutes regulating matters historically governed by the common law, you are likely to confront this kind of issue on your exams with increasing frequency. Consider, then, the following illustration:

> Billy Buyer mails Sally Seller a purchase order for 1000 of Seller's widgets, offering to pay her advertised price of $2 per widget on delivery and requesting immediate shipment. Seller replies by sending Buyer an acknowledgment of order, promising to ship 1000 widgets immediately and agreeing to the price and payment terms. Seller's acknowledgment also states that "Seller expressly disclaims any warranties with re-

spect to any items shipped pursuant to this acknowledgment." After Buyer receives Seller's acknowledgment—but before Seller ships the goods—Buyer telephones Seller and states that he is backing out of the deal. What rights, if any, does Seller have against Buyer?

Do you recognize the issue from your Contracts course?

On the one hand, under the common law "mirror-image rule," the terms of a would-be acceptance must mirror the terms of the offer in every respect. Although Seller's acknowledgment accurately recapitulates the description of goods, quantity, price, delivery, and payment terms stated in Buyer's purchase order, it "breaks the mirror" by adding a term—*i.e.*, the disclaimer of warranties. As a result, the acknowledgment is not an acceptance of the offer, and there is no contract that would preclude Buyer from backing out. On the other hand, under the pertinent statutory provision—U.C.C. § 2-207—an otherwise valid acceptance forms a binding contract in spite of the fact that it purports to add terms not found in the offer. And if the statutory rule were applied in this case, the Seller's acknowledgment would operate as an acceptance of Buyer's offer, thus binding Buyer to the contract and preventing him from backing out.

B. How Professors Test Rule vs. Counter-Rule Issues (and Why Students Frequently Miss Them)

As the foregoing examples suggest, rule vs. counter-rule issues are pretty straightforward: As long as you're familiar with the particular rule vs. counter-rule relationship in question, you aren't likely to miss it when it appears on an exam. Yet law professors find that students—even students who have studied hard and prepared well—miss these issues with surprising frequency. Our view is that the principal reason for student error is not that students fail to see the rule vs. counter-rule situation, but that they don't understand that when they've seen one what they've seen is an "issue."

In our experience, many students ignore the rule vs. counter-rule situations they encounter because they figure that, at the end of the day, only one rule will govern the case at hand and their job is (a) to figure out which rule it is and (b) to apply that rule to the facts presented. Their thinking goes something like this: "Hey, I know this one: There's some old rule that lets the offeror revoke even if you're halfway up the flagpole, and there's a Restatement section that fixes all that. So who cares about the old way? The professor asked us to discuss the rights of the parties, and that must mean under the law that would apply today. Now where's my copy of the Restatement . . . ?"

Truth be told, these students may be on to something. Sometimes the professor has in fact constructed the question in such a way that the student will be "right" if he applies (say) the Restatement and "wrong" if he applies the common law rule. But here's an important test-taking tip: If the professor went to the trouble of teaching you about the difference between the Restatement and common law rules governing the revocation of offers — and if she also went to the trouble of designing a problem that would come out one way under one rule and another way under the other — chances are pretty good that she expects you to recognize this difference and is ready to award issue-spotting points to the students who do. And while it's true that no self-respecting lawyer would pay much attention to the "old" rule in a setting in which the Restatement alternative obviously governed, it's equally true that no self-respecting law student should pass up the chance to earn additional exam points so easily!

But if you are attempting to answer a question in which the choice between rule and counter-rule seems to be that straightforward, you ought to take this as a signal that you may be missing something in your analysis of the problem. Since lawyers can only fantasize about the dream client whose case can be resolved by the straightforward application of a single legal rule, law professors rarely give exam questions that are this simple either. Indeed, at least nine times out of ten, the professor will try to construct a hypothetical in which the choice between rule and counter-rule is not nearly so clear-cut. Fortunately, such hypotheticals tend to appear in patterns too, and, fortunately for those of you with the good judgment to be reading this book, we're going to help you learn to spot them.

Watch for the unidentified or imaginary jurisdiction. One common way that professors test rule vs. counter-rule issues is to set the facts of an exam question in an unidentified or even imaginary jurisdiction (*e.g.*, "Pleasantville" or "Remulak" or "the State of Ames"). When you encounter a rule vs. counter-rule issue in this setting, you can be sure that the professor is expecting you to analyze the facts at hand under both the rule and the counter-rule, since the choice between the competing rules is obviously up for grabs.

Watch for the jurisdiction whose law wasn't explored in the course. Sometimes you'll encounter an exam question set in a jurisdiction whose law you *do* know; when that happens, your job is to apply that law and then move on to other issues. If, for example, your Torts course examined Florida's approach to comparative negligence in painstaking detail, and on the final you encounter a question involving an accident that (a) occurred in Florida between Florida residents and (b) is the result of plaintiff's negligence as well as defendant's, you'd be making a serious mistake if you saw this question as an opportunity to provide a lengthy rule vs. counter-rule analysis of the difference between comparative and contributory negligence. The professor has taught you Florida comparative negligence and has designed a question specifically asking you to apply that law. It is therefore virtually certain that she wants you to focus like a laser beam on that task. And while you might earn some issue-spotting points for offering a sentence or two contrasting the Florida law analysis with the analysis under competing approaches the professor has emphasized (*e.g.*, contributory negligence), an extended discussion of an approach that obviously doesn't apply to the facts at hand will almost surely be penalized; indeed, if your discussion suggests that you are hedging your bets because you don't know which rule applies in Florida, you may well be on your way to a grade you won't be very happy with.

But many law school courses—and especially the classic common law courses like Contracts, Torts, and Property—examine "majority" vs. "minority" approaches and "traditional" vs.

"modern" rules and rarely focus in on the current law of a particular jurisdiction. If you encounter a rule vs. counter-rule issue on an exam in a course taught like this, it's a safe bet that the professor isn't testing to see whether you can guess which rule will apply, even if she has set the facts of the problem in some specifically identified jurisdiction (*e.g.*, Idaho). She is far more likely to be testing you on what she taught you and trying to see whether you recognize that more than one rule might apply to the facts at hand.

Watch for traditional vs. modern rule issues where the modern rule has not been judicially adopted. When students learn about traditional rules and modern common law rules in a particular area of the law, many conclude that they need to know the modern rule and that the rest is "history." ("I didn't come to law school to learn how to practice in 19th Century England," cracked one of our students in this connection.) But this attitude can lead to serious mistakes, for the so-called "modern" rule is frequently only a trend that many jurisdictions have not yet adopted and, for all we know, might never embrace. Indeed, sometimes the modern rule isn't even a bona fide trend, but is merely the approach taken by a handful of cases that have captured the fancy of the members of the American Law Institute and inspired a black-letter formulation in the latest Restatement of Law. And as we frequently remind our students, the Restatement is a beautiful thing, but (a) it isn't a statute and (b) it isn't "law" unless and until a court (or some other authoritative body) says it is.

In the end, then, our advice here is the same as in the previous point: If an exam question places you in Jurisdiction X and your professor has stressed that Jurisdiction X has adopted the modern rule on the relevant topic, then that's clearly the rule you should emphasize in your answer. But if you encounter a traditional vs. modern rule issue in virtually any other setting, you would be making a serious mistake to ignore the traditional rule and simply assume that the modern rule has been adopted.

Chapter 4

Forks in the Law: Competing Interpretations of Statutes

As you saw in the previous chapter, in order to test a rule vs. counter-rule issue on a law exam, the professor may invent a factual scenario in which the choice between two competing rules represents a "fork in the law": each rule takes your analysis of the problem down a different path. Law professors examine a second kind of "fork in the law" — we call them "competing interpretations" issues — in much the same manner. Once again, we design hypotheticals that can be analyzed in more than one way, but here the choice confronting the student will involve different readings of the *same* rule. The rule in question may come from any one of a number of sources, but we're going to focus here on the two you are most likely to encounter on your law exams: statutes and cases. We'll cover statutes in this chapter and caselaw in the next.

* * * * *

We've already described the classic example of a competing interpretations issue: Does a rule that reads "No vehicles permitted in the park" apply to tricycles? The answer to that question depends on the meaning of the rule, and the meaning of the rule is not nearly so clear as it might seem to someone who's never been a victim of the Socratic method. One way to read the rule is to give the word "vehicle" its common or "dictionary" definition. If we do that, the only question is whether tricycles fall within that definition and, since they probably do, we are ready to conclude that they are barred from the park. But another way to read the rule is to focus on the reasons for the prohibition. And if we read the rule that way—and conclude that the point of the rule is to reduce pollution, noise, and the risks of serious injury to pedestrians in the park—we may well decide that it wasn't designed to apply to tricycles.

The first time you encounter a problem like this in law school, it is tempting to conclude that the problem is just sloppy drafting. "What's the big deal?" someone might pipe up in class. "Why didn't the drafters just say '*motorized* vehicles,' since that is obviously what they meant? Wouldn't that fix the problem and spare the rest of us all this tedious discussion?" "Fair enough," responds the professor. And then she poses a question that creates a ripple of nervous laughter through the classroom: "But would your rule apply to motorized *wheelchairs?*"

As the first month or two of law school is bound to convince you, the problem of statutory ambiguity seems to lie right there in the words; and adding more words, or different words, won't make it go away. This is more than a little scary. After all, it's hard to imagine a rule that's shorter and simpler than "No vehicles allowed in the park." When we turn to the far more complex provisions of the U.C.C., the model penal code, and other statutes you study in law school, the possibilities simply boggle the mind!

Indeed, many law schools dedicate entire courses to the problem of interpreting statutory materials, and many fine books and articles have been written on the subject. So we can't reduce the subject to five or even fifty easy lessons. But what we *can* do is help you learn to recognize a statutory ambiguity—what we call a competing-interpretations issue—when you encounter it on a law exam. As in the previous section, the way we'll do that is by describing the most common patterns of ambiguity and then the kinds of problems law professors design to test them.

A. Patterns of Ambiguity

1. Plain Meaning vs. Purposes Issues

By far the most common pattern of competing interpretations is illustrated by our "No vehicles permitted in the park" hypothetical. One way of reading that rule is to focus on the *language* (tricycle = a "vehicle"); another way is to focus on the rule's *purposes* (tricycles just don't pose the same threats to the park and its users as cars do). Disputes that turn on this conflict—an interpretation of a rule that is based on the so-called "plain meaning" of the words used vs. an interpretation based on the "purposes" that the rule was designed to accomplish—endlessly arise in legal practice, and it should therefore come as no surprise that professors test them with great frequency on law exams.

Consider a second example:

> Horace Wholesaler receives an order from Reba Retailer for 50 high-end audio components at a total price of $20,000. Wholesaler sends Retailer an acknowledgment of order by e-mail, promising immediate shipment of the ordered goods. Prior to shipment, Wholesaler reneges on the deal. Retailer sues, but Wholesaler asserts that the U.C.C.'s Statute of Frauds bars the claim. What result?

Do you see the plain meaning vs. purposes issue? On the one hand, an e-mail message that appears only as an electronically generated image on a computer screen may not constitute a "writing"—let alone a "signed" writing—under the plain meaning of the terms of U.C.C. § 2-201(1) (requiring "a writing signed by the party against whom enforcement is sought"). On the other hand, if the Statute of Frauds was enacted to avoid "he said/she said" testimonial disputes by requiring a verifiable record of certain kinds of transactions, that purpose would seem to be served every bit as well by a saved message readily retrievable from a hard drive as it is by hardcopy gathering dust in a file drawer.

2. Where Do Purposes Come From?

For most students, it's easy to see the plain meaning of a rule: You know what words like "vehicle" and "writing" mean and, when you hit a rough one, you can always look it up. But purposes are a different matter, and unfortunately you won't find *those* defined in any dictionary or encyclopedia. So where do purposes come from? We'll discuss the two most common sources in the law-exam setting: legislative intent and policy analysis.

a. Legislative intent

The most obvious place to start in a search for a statute's purpose is the horse's mouth: What clues do we have about what the "authors" of a particular rule—Congress; the state legislature; the city council—were attempting to accomplish? We can find those clues in a number of places:

- *Legislative history.* The mass of material lawyers refer to as "legislative history"—official reports of legislative committees that drafted the bill; statements made by legislators during floor debates; and even testimony given to the legislative body by outsiders—may shed light on what it was the drafters were attempting to achieve by enacting the statute in question. For example, recall once again our "No vehicles permitted in park" hypothetical. If the discussion in the various committee reports focused exclusively on automobile and truck traffic—citing studies of pollution and noise levels; accident statistics; damage due to weight loads; and the like—you'd have a sound basis for arguing that the purpose of the rule had nothing to do with tricycles.
- *Other provisions of the statute.* Another place to look for purposes is other provisions of the statute in question. To continue our "vehicle" hypo, the presence of a provision that makes revocation of the operator's license the key sanction for violations of the rule would suggest that the drafters were worried about grown-ups in cars, trucks, and motorcycles—not children on tricycles—when they enacted the rule.

- *Official comments.* Uniform statutes like the U.C.C. are frequently accompanied by an "official comment" specifically designed to explain the purpose of the various provisions. (Although the Restatement is not a statute, the "reporter's note" serves a similar purpose in interpreting its provisions.) To recall once again our e-mail under the Statute of Frauds hypo, the Official Comment to § 2-201 reveals that the purpose of the "signed writing" requirement is "to afford a basis for believing that the offered oral evidence rests on a real transaction"—a purpose that may be satisfied as well by a saved e-mail message as a hardcopy document.
- *Real-world catalysts.* What was the legislature reacting to when it enacted the statute in question? Frequently there is some dramatic event that prompted the legislature into action, and this too may shed light on the purpose of a statute. If, for example, the "No vehicles permitted in the park" rule had been enacted in the wake of a tragic accident in which a sport utility vehicle had struck and fatally injured a group of joggers running together in the park, this would offer further evidence that the risks the rule was designed to eliminate were of the sort associated with automotive—rather than tricycle—traffic.

* * * * *

We can easily imagine your reaction to all of this: "Are you guys *sure* there isn't just some dictionary I can use to find a statute's purpose? Am I really supposed to know the details of the legislative history and all that other stuff for every statute and every provision we read in class?"

As usual, we've got good news and bad news. The good news is that 99% of the time, if a law professor is going to test you on the purpose of a statute, then she will teach you about it—and do so quite explicitly—during the course. The bad news is that many students will dismiss the discussion of such material as "beside the point," since they think they came to law school just to "learn the rules." Thus, when class discussion turns to a close reading of a Senate report—or a careful analysis of the umpteenth Official Comment—they put their pens and pencils down and wait for what they view as the only thing that matters: "So . . . what's the rule?"

This is a terrible strategy for preparing for law practice and an even worse one for exam preparation. In practice, recognizing the difference between the purpose of a rule and its plain meaning is something you'll need to do all the time, but you won't do it very well if you don't learn to pay close attention to the ways that lawyers decode statutory purpose. Yet you'll be even worse off on an exam, for you're likely to miss altogether the issue the professor is trying to test: If you don't know the purpose of the rule, how will you be able to tell when that purpose differs from the rule's plain meaning?

b. Policy analysis

Lawyers can't always count on having direct evidence of legislative intent; for many statutes, the legislative history will be too sketchy to be of much use, and the other sources we've suggested may be unavailable or inconclusive as well. So what do we do then?

The short answer is that we engage in "policy analysis," and perhaps the best way to do that is to imagine that you are a legislator who is trying to decide whether to support or oppose a bill containing the rule in question. What policy or policies is the rule designed to further? Why do you suppose your colleagues want to see it enacted into law? What problem or problems (social, commercial, legal, etc.) are they worried about and why do they think this rule will fix them? Whether you decide to support it or not, what is it that the rule is supposed to accomplish?

Your professors have pressed you to engage in this kind of thinking from the first day of law school, and while it is befuddling at first ("How would *I* know what the rule was designed to accomplish?" more than one student has no doubt silently mused. "*I* didn't write it!"), it is a skill that gets easier with practice. Indeed, by the end of the first semester, most students have begun to ask policy questions on their own.

Of course, if you attend class regularly and take good notes, you won't have to make guesses about the policies behind the rules you encounter on an exam. As we said in connection with our discussion of legislative intent, chances are that the professor will have thoroughly explored the policies behind any statute she thinks is worthy of testing on the final.

At the same time, most professors would be delighted to encounter a policy analysis that goes beyond a mere parroting of points made in class. And from time to time, most of us also test you on rules and statutes you've never seen before. So developing a facility with policy analysis—in addition to good note-taking—is an important test-taking skill. A major theme of this book is that issues and arguments appear in patterns in the law—and that studying those patterns is the best way to learn to deal with those issues and arguments—so it shouldn't surprise you that there are patterns to what we're calling policy analysis as well. Indeed, we've devoted an entire chapter to this topic—Chapter 10 ("Czars of the Universe")—and we encourage you to work your way through that material very carefully as you try to develop this skill.

But we bet you're already better at policy analysis than you think you are; read on, and see if you don't agree.

3. Purposes as a Source of Statutory Ambiguity

a. Competing purposes

Imagine a statute that protects "whistleblowers"—employees who "disclose to law enforcement personnel any violation of the law by the employer"—against discharge or other discipline in retaliation for their "whistleblowing." Imagine that the statute also states a prerequisite for such protection: The employee is required to "notify the employer before disclosing the violation to law enforcement personnel." Now let's try your hand at policy analysis. Which of the following policies is the pre-disclosure notification requirement designed to further?

    (a) To ensure that employees fulfill their obligation of loyalty to the employer before taking matters "outside the family";

  (b) To ensure that an employer is aware of a violation of the law and has an opportunity to correct it before facing an investigation by law enforcement personnel;

  (c) To encourage and facilitate voluntary employer compliance with the law in order to avoid the costs—to the taxpayers as well as to the employer—associated with government agency enforcement proceedings;

  (d) All of the above.

If you picked (a), (b), or (c), congratulations! All three are policies that might indeed be furthered by the requirement of pre-disclosure notification, so you can relax a little bit about your ability to do policy analysis. (We told you that you were up to it!)

If you picked (d), you have also figured out the next point we want to make: Most rules have more than one purpose. What this means is that there is yet another source of ambiguity in statutory interpretation. In addition to the plain meaning vs. purposes issues, there are also issues that pit one statutory purpose against another. Consider, for example, how our whistleblower statute would apply to the following situation:

> Emma Employee is killed in an on-the-job accident at Silver Spoon Pharmaceuticals, Inc., and the state occupational safety and health agency has begun an investigation of the incident. Without a word to her employer, Wanda Whistleblower contacts agency officials and volunteers information about a safety violation—subsequently remedied by the employer—that directly contributed to Employee's death. Silver Spoon retaliates by discharging Whistleblower, who sues for relief under the statute. What result?

The analysis under a plain-meaning interpretation of the statute is pretty clear: Whistleblower didn't "notify the employer before disclosing the wrongdoing to law enforcement personnel." So she's out of luck.

But what about an interpretation that focuses instead on the statute's purposes? The short answer is that it depends on *which* purposes we're talking about. If we start with (a)—requiring employees to fulfill a duty of loyalty by notifying the employer before "taking it outside the family"—the result may well be the same as it would be under a plain-meaning interpretation of the rule: Whistleblower loses because she didn't notify the employer first.

But if we focus instead on (b), we might conclude that pre-disclosure notification was not necessary in this case. After all, the employer was already aware of the violation and has already corrected it, so those reasons for pre-disclosure notification are moot. Similarly, at the time of the disclosure, the employer was already facing an investigation by law enforcement personnel, so policy (c) — avoiding unnecessary agency proceedings — is beside the point as well.

(Note, by the way, that we've identified two "forks in the road" in this problem. We started with a plain meaning vs. purposes fork, but our analysis of purposes led us to a second fork, when we discovered there were competing purposes. We call this a "twin fork," and we'll have more to say about twin forks in Chapter 7).

* * * * *

Policy analysis is not the only source of competing purposes. An examination of legislative intent — through legislative history and the like — will also frequently reveal competing purposes. One obvious reason for this is that there may be as many different purposes as there are legislators; another is that any given legislator may be moved by multiple purposes. These differing and multiple purposes will frequently surface during the course of legislative deliberations.

Consider once again the problem of applying our "No vehicles permitted in the park" rule to tricycles. It may be clear from the committee reports and the floor debates that the legislators were concerned about many things, and most of them — pollution, noise levels, wear and tear on the park roads — may have nothing to do with tricycle traffic. That part of the record suggests that permitting tricycles in the park is perfectly consistent with the statute's purposes.

But assume that the legislative history is also rife with concerns about the park's role in enhancing the quality of life for elderly people who live in the surrounding apartments. Perhaps a representative of an advocacy group promoting the interests of the elderly was a key witness before the committee that drafted the bill; perhaps one of the catalysts for the statute's enactment was an incident in which a teenager on a bicycle struck an elderly couple. You get the picture. To the extent that "protecting the elderly users of the park" is viewed as one of the statutory purposes, the case for applying the prohibition to tricycles will be much stronger.

In the end, our point is that you should avoid the trap that befalls many law students. Having discovered that the purpose of a rule may provide a way of interpreting it that is different from a mere application of plain meaning—and having decided that this is a pretty neat trick—they stop thinking and rely on the first purpose they see in the legislative history or through policy analysis. Our advice: Don't forget to push on those purposes, for there is frequently more than one!

b. The pattern of conflict: Broad vs. narrow purposes

There is a pattern to many competing purposes issues that is easy to recognize once you see how it works. When lawyers argue about the interpretation of a statute, one side will frequently speak in terms of the "broad" purposes behind the statute and the other side will describe its purposes as relatively "narrow." Indeed, even when those terms are not explicitly invoked, you'll often find that broad vs. narrow purposes is what the lawyers on opposite sides of a case—or judges in the majority and those in dissent—are really arguing about. Broad vs. narrow purposes issues come in at least two versions.

Spin vs. counter-spin. One way to think about broad vs. narrow purposes is to put yourself in the position of the most enthusiastic supporters of a statute (on the one hand) and then of its most outspoken critics (on the other). Imagine the "spin control" that each group might attempt at a press conference on the day the statute is enacted. Typically, the supporters will declare victory in the most sweeping terms, whereas the critics will put the best possible face on defeat by acknowledging only a minor setback.

If, for example, the statute in question is a federal environmental protection act, the supporters might portray its enactment as a great victory that "marks a dramatic shift in our Nation's environmental priorities" that will "forever change the way America does business." By contrast, opponents may begrudgingly acknowledge defeat by countering that the statute is "obviously not intended to affect the sound practices of the vast majority of American businesses" and insisting that "it is aimed only at the excesses of a small number of recalcitrant polluters."

When a case comes along challenging the EPA's authority under the statute to establish strict emissions standards for industry, the lawyers on each side are likely to cast the broad vs. narrow purposes of the statute in similar spin vs. counter-spin terms. Thus, lawyers defending the strict standards will declare that the statute's purpose was to "mark a dramatic shift" in environmental policy that was obviously intended to force many firms to "change the way they do business." But lawyers challenging the standards will find them to have "gone beyond the salutary goal of targeting recalcitrant polluters" and to have intruded on the "sound environmental practices of countless law-abiding firms whom Congress never intended to reach."

Floodlight vs. laser beam. In a second version of the broad vs. narrow purposes debate, a broad purpose is invoked to diffuse or weaken the effect of a statute, whereas a narrow purpose is invoked to sharpen its focus and effect. To return again to "No vehicles permitted in the park," if the purpose of the prohibition is stated in the most broad and general terms — "to protect the park and the public" — the threat posed by tricycles may seem *de minimis* when compared with the pollution, noise, and physical dangers associated with other kinds of traffic. But if the purpose is stated narrowly — "to protect the elderly, the infirm, infants and their stroller-pushing nannies, and other frequent users of the park" — the threat from tots-on-trikes may well loom larger.

* * * * *

Competing purposes issues frequently fall into this pattern, with one side offering a broad and the other a narrow account of the purposes of the statute in question. Learn to recognize the pattern, and you'll "know it when you see it" on an exam.

4. Language as a Source of Statutory Ambiguity: Competing Meanings

A moment ago, we urged you not to stop your search for issues with the first purpose or policy that comes to mind. The same advice applies when you are focusing on the plain meaning of a rule, for—quite apart from the rule's purposes—the "meaning" of the language used frequently isn't very "plain" at all. We've assumed all along, for example, that a tricycle fits the dictionary definition of "vehicle," but the Oxford English Dictionary offers *six* definitions of the term, only one of which is relevant here.* Moreover, lawyers arguing about the meaning of terms used in a statute are frequently working out of multiple "dictionaries," looking to such sources as history and commercial context as well as to common usage to determine the meaning of statutory terms.

To train you for this kind of work, law professors frequently draft exam questions that involve competing interpretations of the words used in rules and statutes. What follows are some of the "dictionaries"—besides Black's and the old-fashioned one— that you must learn to consult.

The dictionary of statutory context. We frequently can look elsewhere in the statute to shed light on the meaning of disputed terms. In the easiest case, the legislature has actually provided its *own* dictionary and included a section in which various terms used in the statute are defined. In other cases, a bit of detective work may be necessary. Consider once again our vehicle hypothetical. Perhaps there is a section of the statute that prescribes different penalties for different vehicles violating the rule, and perhaps the specific vehicles listed are "motorcycles"; "cars";

---

* "A means of conveyance, usu. with wheels, for transporting people, goods, etc.; a car, cart, truck, carriage, sledge etc. . . .; [a]ny means of carriage or transport . . . ." The other definitions refer to things that may end up in the park from time to time—*e.g.*, "[a] song, play, film, etc. that is intended or serves to display the leading actor or performer to the best advantage"—but were almost surely not what our imaginary city council had in mind when it adopted the rule.

"light trucks and vans"; and then larger "trucks" with increasing numbers of wheels. This suggests that when the word "vehicle" is used elsewhere in the statute, it should be given that narrower meaning, rather than its broader "plain meaning."

The dictionary of history. It's 2020 and "hardcopy" has been completely eliminated from most forms of human communication—partly due to the proliferation of electronic communications media and partly due to the fact that we have finally run out of trees. The members of the committee charged with revising Article II of the U.C.C. have long since died and been replaced by a new generation, and hopes have dimmed somewhat for a quick resolution of a battle that's now been going on for half a century. As a consequence, the U.C.C.'s Statute of Frauds (§ 2-201) reads exactly as it did in 1970, quaintly requiring "a writing signed by the party against whom enforcement is sought."

In that setting, the meaning of "writing" that is so "plain" today may well have changed with the social and business practices to which it once referred—and as you've no doubt already figured out, those developments will alter our analysis of the e-mail hypothetical. Thus, a lawyer arguing that an e-mail message is a "writing" may well simply be stating the obvious, and the party responding that § 2-201 is not satisfied by e-mail will have to cite "the dictionary of history": At the time of its enactment, "writing" meant printing, or typing, or handwriting on paper or a similar medium producing "documents," and the prospect of communication via e-mail wasn't even contemplated by most folks.

Precisely because today's "plain" meaning frequently becomes tomorrow's "historical" meaning, issues pitting historical meanings against other interpretations—based on current meanings or on statutory purpose—are extremely common in law practice and on law exams. (Indeed, you are even more likely to encounter issues pitting historical meanings against other interpretations in the context of Constitutional Law than in the context of statutes.)

The dictionary of commercial context. Imagine a municipal ordinance requiring restaurants to install and maintain two flush toilets "for every 40 seats." Does that rule apply to sofas and chairs in a restaurant's lobby or waiting area? Stools at the bar? A bench at the "take-out" counter? Rocking chairs out front?

These are all "seats" under a plain-meaning interpretation of the rule, but to someone doing business in the restaurant industry, "40 seats" (as in a "40-seat facility") may have a more specialized meaning and refer to "seats available for meal service." For a large restaurant, the difference between the two interpretations could be worth thousands of dollars in plumbing. (The difference could also be worth a lot to a patron whose child has waited until the last moment to announce the need for a bathroom!)

Disputes that raise this issue—*i.e.*, a conflict between a plain-meaning interpretation and an interpretation that draws meaning from the "commercial context"—arise with great frequency in the context of statutes designed to regulate a particular trade, industry, or profession. When dealing with such a statute on a law exam, then, watch for terms that may have a specialized meaning in the commercial context in question.

The dictionary of the common law. We've saved the hardest for last, so fasten your seat belts. Statutes frequently use terms (like "tenant" or "independent contractor") that had a well-developed meaning at common law. With equal frequency, statutes are enacted for the purpose of *changing* the common law. What happens when the same statute does both of these things at once: *i.e.*, modifies the common law, but uses common law terms in the process? A concrete example may help you see the potential statutory ambiguity:

> An upscale tobacco merchant sends a signed letter to a group of selected customers announcing bargain prices on a list of rare cigars and expressly guaranteeing those prices for a two-week period. Three days later, one of the selected customers attempts to purchase two cigars from the list, but the merchant refuses to honor the price guarantee. What legal rights does the customer have against the merchant?

You may recall that, at common law, the merchant's promise would have been unenforceable for want of consideration, under the famous rule of *Dickinson v. Dodds*, 2 Ch.D. 463 (C.A.

1876). You may also recall that the "firm offer" provision of the U.C.C. — § 2-205 — was specifically designed to reverse that rule. In pertinent part, that section provides:

> An offer by a merchant to buy or sell goods in a signed writing which by its terms gives assurance that it will be held open is not revocable, for lack of consideration, during the time stated . . . .

Is our merchant's letter a "firm offer" under this rule? It's clear that we have a "signed writing" from a "merchant" that "gives assurance" — indeed, in the language of our letter, *guarantees* — "that it will be held open" for two weeks, and our customer turned up at the shop well within that time period. But what's not clear is whether the letter is also an "offer," and the answer depends on what we mean by that term.

On the one hand, if "offer" keeps its common law meaning, the merchant's letter may fail under the common law rule that treats price lists, advertisements, catalogs, and the like as mere invitations to deal and not offers. But on the other hand, the purpose of § 2-205 is to hold merchants to commitments they make and deprive them of technical objections that are the common law's equivalent of "but-Simon-didn't-*say*-I'd-sell-cigars-at-those-prices!" On that view, we should dispense with the common law technicality and interpret the word "offer" more broadly, to protect the customer's reasonable commercial expectations — based on the merchant's own signed and written assurances — that the merchant would sell the listed cigars at the "guaranteed" prices during the stipulated time period.

As the foregoing suggests, issues that present a conflict of this sort — between the common law meaning of a term and a meaning based on statutory purpose — can be subtle and more than a little complex. But in a world where statutes are ever more frequently enacted to "displace" the common law, you should expect to encounter issues of this sort often, in legal practice as well as on your exams.

B. Fact Situations To Watch For

Most law professors try to test what they teach, so the best way to enable yourself to recognize competing-interpretations issues is to pay careful attention to the statutory ambiguities your professor emphasizes. If she stressed one or more of the issues we've discussed—the tension between the plain meaning of some statutory provision and its purpose, say, or between the different policies underlying a particular statute—chances are that those issues will show up somewhere on the final. Beyond that, our experience suggests that there are several factual situations that law professors routinely use to test competing interpretations of statutes, so it's a good idea to become familiar with them.

- *Variation on a hypothetical examined closely in class.* One fact pattern to watch for is the scenario that presents a slight variation on a hypothetical that was closely analyzed in class. If the professor devoted substantial time and attention to analyzing the "No vehicles permitted in the park" rule and its application to tricycles, watch for skateboards, wheelchairs (motorized and otherwise), and golf carts on the final!

- *New application of an old statute.* Watch for the scenario in which a statute that's been around for awhile is invoked in a factual setting that was unimaginable at the time of enactment—like the Statute of Frauds applied to a transaction memorialized via e-mail or voice-mail. Precisely because they present situations that the drafters of the statute didn't envision, new-situation/old-statute hypos are a great vehicle for testing the tension between plain-meaning or historical-meaning interpretations (on the one hand) and statutory-purpose meanings (on the other).

- *New or imaginary statute.* Professors who want to test their students' ability to engage in statutory interpretation (rather than just the capacity to regurgitate arguments from class discussion) may design a question asking you to apply a statute you've never seen before—a recently enacted statute, perhaps, or even one that the professor has invented out of whole cloth. When you encounter a problem like this, *don't freak out*. Indeed, you should count your blessings, for this is one setting in which the professor won't expect you to know anything about legislative history! On the other hand, this is an excellent way to test policy analysis—where you have to come up with statutory purposes on your own—so keep an eye out for issues that involve policies pitted against one another and/or against the plain language of the statute.

- *A statute making a cameo appearance in a common law claim.* Finally, watch for the setting in which a statute is invoked in the context of a common law claim or defense—for example, a tenant who withholds rent on the basis of the landlord's violation of the housing code, or a defendant in a negligence suit who offers compliance with a regulatory statute as proof of reasonable care. Professors frequently invent statutes for use in settings like these, and in our experience students miss competing-interpretations issues because they focus like a laser beam on the common law and pay too little attention to the statute. (For example, consider a hypothetical in which an owner is taking her cat on a commercial flight, and the cat escapes from its cage and bites another passenger; the passenger sues for negligence, and the owner defends on the ground that the cage complied with pertinent FAA regulations. The "B" exam will identify and analyze the tort law issue—does statutory compliance establish reasonable care?—but the "A" exam will take it to the next level by focusing on competing purposes of the statute as well: Are the FAA regulations designed to protect passengers from the prospect of feline attack? If so, compliance with those regulations may be relevant to the issue of the owner's reasonable care. But if the regulations are merely intended to protect cats from unnecessary discomfort during turbulence and to ensure that cages fit unobtrusively in the space beneath a seat, then their relevance to the duty of care with respect to fellow passengers is substantially diminished.)

Chapter 5

Forks in the Law: Competing Interpretations of Caselaw

A now-famous law school classmate once aptly described the experience of reading your first judicial opinion as a lot like "stirring cement with your eyelashes." And for most students, it only gets worse when you go to class, where the professor can ask you virtually *anything* about the case, and for every question there seem to be a dozen different and equally plausible answers.

Believe it or not, the law exam may be just the compass you need to help you negotiate this challenging terrain. For when it comes to testing your understanding of the cases you've studied, an exam problem typically asks only one question and expects only one answer. The question is "should you 'follow' the case?" and the answer (you guessed it!) is "maybe." (Actually, that's two answers, but more on that in a moment.)

The typical exam question involves a scenario that is a variation—it may be a slight variation or it may be a dramatic one—on the facts of a case you've studied in class. (The parties may be arguing over the "capture" of oil deposits rather than wild animals, for example, or about the regulation of the Internet rather than broadcast television.) The scenario thus presents you with another instance of what we've been calling a "fork in the law." If you "follow" the earlier decision (the "precedent"), you'll reach one result. But if you don't follow the precedent—if instead you "distinguish" it—your analysis may come out the other way. (*E.g.*, the oil deposits case may lead to one result if we "follow" the rule of *Pierson v. Post* and to another if we "distinguish" that case.)

Just as the "forks in the law" we studied in the last chapter depend on how you interpret a statute, the choice between following and distinguishing a precedent depends on how you interpret the earlier case. And in the same way that statutory ambiguities appear in patterns you can study and learn to recognize—plain meaning vs. purposes; competing purposes; etc.—there are recurring patterns of ambiguity in caselaw as well. After a few more words about following and distinguishing cases, we'll devote the rest of the chapter to exploring those patterns.

A. Desperately Seeking Similarity: When To Follow Precedent

Let's say your Constitutional Law teacher asks you to evaluate an imaginary statute that outlaws human cloning. The challenge may be brought by an infertile person who seeks to clone himself. (Not as far-fetched a scenario as it was when we used this problem a short while ago on an exam!) You have read every case for the course six times, and you're sure you have never read anything about cloning. So your first reaction is: This isn't fair. I studied so hard, and she asks me about something we never learned.

As usual, however, you know more than you think. Odds are very good that you have read *Planned Parenthood v. Casey*, 505 U.S. 833 (1992), the Supreme Court case reaffirming a woman's constitutional right to choose, prior to the viability of the fetus, whether to carry a pregnancy to term. Suppose that instead of viewing the case in the narrow terms of abortion rights, you were to describe *Casey* more broadly as guaranteeing a right to control one's own "reproduction." (This kind of broadening is a common lawyer's tactic and pervades public commentary about court cases.) Now you have an argument that your course included a case about cloning, even though you didn't see it that way at first.

You can challenge the anti-cloning statute on the ground that *Casey* protects "reproductive freedom" and your client is being denied the freedom to "reproduce" himself. This challenge will generate a debate over the *meaning* of *Casey*, just as our discussion of statutes involved a whole set of debates over the meaning of statutory provisions.

There are two things to notice about this debate. First, it is easy to see how a vigorous and interesting controversy about *Casey* could occur before a court even got to the question of cloning. So, to use our terminology, there is a "fork in the law" about what *Casey* protects ("abortion rights" vs. "reproductive freedom") that, in theory, could be answered without regard to whether cloning then fits under the category of "reproductive freedom." Once categorization becomes the issue, the government might contend, for example, that "reproductive freedom" should include *in vitro* fertilization but not cloning, since the former involves two sets of DNA and thus resembles natural conception whereas the latter does not. (The categorization issue — as you might have gathered — involves a "fork in the facts," a topic to which we will return in the next chapter.)

Second, the debate over the meaning of *Casey* is emblematic of perhaps the most common pattern of ambiguity in caselaw: What varies in the different ways of looking at *Casey* is the "level of generality" at which the holding is stated. The low level of generality makes the case sound as though it's only about "abortion." The higher level of generality looks to "reproductive freedom." We'll have more to say about this pattern and several others to watch for in a moment.

B. Searching for Distinctions that Make a Difference

Some exam questions force students to struggle to find the analogy between a case they have read and the fact pattern the exam presents. Many students, for example, may simply miss the similarity between "abortion" (the case they know) and "cloning" (the exam issue). But students who spot the similarity right away face an equally grave danger. For it is just as much a mistake to zero in on similarities and forget to explore the *differences*. And where the similarities are hard to see (comparing cloning to abortion), the differences should stick out like a sore thumb. Indeed, one more clue to "finding Waldo" is to remember that your professors are trying to build variations on cases you already know. So there will almost always be similarities *and* differences. If you can spot one easily, look for the other. Most of the time, it will be hiding there somewhere.

When it's the differences you are focused on, remember that mere identification is good, but what will really move you to the head of the class is explaining why those differences should matter—why they are significant enough to justify a result different from the one reached in the precedent. Consider, for example, the following problem, taken from a real exam.

A visiting scholar is renting a house for a year and hoping to renew the lease in May. The house's owner, however, has the house on the market in December. The owner tells the scholar he can renew only if the house isn't sold by May. The scholar's time in the house has alerted him to certain defects (basement flooding after big rains, loud parties every Thursday night in the house across the street, sparking from the electrical outlets). He decides, however, to tell neither his landlord nor prospective buyers about these defects, because he hopes that last-minute discovery will spoil a deal and give him a chance to renew. What happens instead is that the defects aren't discovered until after the closing, when new owners move in. The new owners are furious and bring suit not only against the sellers (who knew nothing of the defects) but also against the scholar who was present and silent when the house inspections took place. The question asks for an evaluation of the scholar's liability.

Most Property students are familiar with cases establishing that sellers have an obligation to disclose certain defects to buyers prior to a sale. Yet our question involves the disclosure obligations of a tenant, not a seller. Students who notice this distinction will clearly be on the road to a good answer. But there is further to go. It's never enough merely to notice that some fact or facts within your exam question make it different from the case or cases you have read. You have to explain why the legal system should take special note of the different facts. Professors will be very unhappy with answers that conclude the tenant is liable because "there is a duty to disclose." Here you miss the different facts altogether. But professors will also be unhappy with answers that say merely "the scholar is not liable because he is not a seller." The scholar presumably also has a different last name from the party found liable in the case you studied. Yet you know intuitively no one cares about that. So, why does it matter so much that we are talking about a tenant and not a seller? Answer that and you are on the road to an "A."

C. Patterns of Ambiguity To Watch For

The case says so. The easiest way to be sure that you need to pause and discuss a fact in your exam that differs from the facts in the case you've read is that the case will tell you. For example, in the case related to our visiting scholar example, the judges might say in clear language, "We hold that the seller of a home is liable for failing to disclose hidden defects." Your professors will delight in writing exam questions that feature someone *like* a seller (a tenant with a financial interest in the sale), but who is not a seller, to force you to discuss whether the case should apply or be extended to cover the new situation.

Rule vs. rationale. We're sure you've noticed that our fact pattern about the visiting scholar strains a bit to construct a financial interest on the scholar's part in hiding the defects from the buyer. Such contortions are often found in exams for a simple reason. The professor is trying to contrast what may be a narrow formulation of the rule in the case, "seller liability," with what may be a broader rationale suggested by the case's logic. If the case that imposes liability on sellers does so on the ground that it's not fair for one party to gain financially from hiding information from another, then the rationale may suggest finding the visiting scholar liable even though the rule itself doesn't cover tenant liability. Indeed, concentrating on the rationale for a case holding is precisely the way to tell whether the facts in your exam question differ from the facts of cases you already know in ways that are relevant to your answer.

The visiting scholar example reflects perhaps the most familiar contrast between a rule (formulated narrowly to cover the facts of the case — "sellers") and a rationale (formulated broadly based on underlying principles — "prevent gain from silence"). Here the exam facts are not covered by the rule but are arguably covered by the rationale. But it's just as easy to write questions the other way around, where the facts are covered by the rule but *not* the rationale.

For example, caselaw in a jurisdiction may establish rules that landlords must provide heat to every room in an apartment or violate the warranty of habitability. The cases may also preclude tenants from waiving the warranty obligations. Suppose your exam question has a rich, well-educated tenant who rents a large, luxury apartment. The landlord informs the tenant that heat in two of the rooms is broken and is unlikely to be repaired. Tenant signs a lease acknowledging the problem and explaining that he will use those rooms for computer equipment that does not need heat. The tenant moves in and begins withholding rent on the ground that the landlord is in breach of warranty. Technically, the tenant can rely on the cases. The landlord, however, may argue that the reasons for the rules are to protect poor tenants from waiving their right to the basics and this tenant is taking advantage. Once again, a court will have to choose between rule and rationale, but — in contrast to our visiting scholar hypo — this time it is the rule that applies (tenants can't waive the warranty of habitability) and the rationale that does not (this tenant doesn't need that kind of protection).

Levels of generality: Narrow vs. broad holdings. Another way to describe the difference between the rule of a case and its rationale is to describe one of the two as a "narrow holding" and the other as a "broad holding." The technique here parallels the one we encountered in contrasting broad and narrow interpretations of statutes, and there is virtually no limit to how "narrow" or "broad" a good lawyer can go. We saw it again when we discussed the application of *Casey* to human cloning: a narrow holding would focus on abortion and have no apparent application to cloning, whereas a broader holding that emphasized reproductive freedom might come out the other way. Let's continue with our visiting scholar example and examine the various ways in which we might describe the holdings of the precedent case.

- An extremely narrow holding might limit liability to situations where the facts precisely parallel the precedent: sellers of residential property who don't disclose known defects. Since our visiting scholar is not a seller, he would be home free under this holding.

- A broader holding focuses somewhat less on the facts of the precedent case and more on its rationale: We impose disclosure liability on sellers not because they are "sellers" but because they have a financial interest in the transaction, and it's not fair to permit persons with such an interest to benefit from hiding material information from other parties. This broader holding might lead to liability for the visiting scholar because of his obvious interest in the transaction. On the other hand, since his interest is less "financial" than it is "personal"—he likes the place and wants to avoid the hassle of moving—perhaps even this broader holding would not apply to him.

- An extremely broad holding—that is, a holding that pays virtually no attention to the particular facts of the precedent case and focuses exclusively on underlying rationales or principles—might require disclosure of known defects in any situation where "good faith" demands it. Under this holding, liability for the tenant who keeps his own counsel in the hope that the defects will tube the deal between seller and buyer is a virtual no-brainer.

A useful analogy—one that can help you learn to argue your way back and forth between narrower and broader readings of a case—is to think about a parent dealing with an errant child. What lesson is the child supposed to learn when she is admonished for leaving a favorite toy on the living room floor? (1) The narrowest "holding" would focus on leaving that particular toy in the living room when dad is cranky; (2) a broader "holding" might mean "no toys allowed in the living room"; (3) a broader "holding" still would mean "pick up after yourself." When the child leaves an article of clothing on the bathroom floor, it is easy to imagine the parent citing the earlier admonishment for proposition #3 and the child responding, "But you said 'toys.'" (Obviously, law professors did not invent this argumentative technique!)

Finding the rationale in case language. We have assumed so far that you can easily discern the rationale for cases you have studied. This won't always be so. Sometimes the court will be cryptic, and you'll have to rely on class notes and discussions — or on policy analysis of the sort we described in the previous chapter — to decipher why the court ruled as it did. Sometimes, however, the court will be quite forthright about its rationale. The case of *Johnson v. Davis*, 480 So. 2d 625 (Fla. 1985), for example, which imposes seller liability for nondisclosure, explains: "One should not be able to stand behind the impervious shield of *caveat emptor* and take advantage of another's ignorance. . . . The law appears to be working toward the conclusion that full disclosure of all material facts must be made whenever elementary fair conduct demands it." Students analyzing the visiting scholar example and relying on *Johnson v. Davis* were obviously rewarded for taking the court's own statement of rationale as evidence that the rule should be extended to cover the scholar's situation. (They were rewarded even more if they also saw the other side and argued that "fair conduct" does not include imposing a burden on persons, like the scholar, who are not parties to the buyer/seller transaction.)

Multiple rationales. The final pattern here precisely parallels the case of "competing purposes" we discussed in the previous chapter. Cases can often be interpreted as based on several rationales, and these may point in different directions and even conflict with each other. The rule requiring disclosure by sellers could stem from the court's desire to ensure that the party in the best position to have information about defects should be required to disclose. On this theory of unearthing information, requiring disclosure by the tenant — as the party in possession — would appear to be a logical outgrowth of the rule. But if the disclosure rule is justified on the grounds of "encouraging trust

between contracting parties," then extending disclosure .
ments to the tenant appears unnecessary (although perhaps ι.
ant should owe a disclosure duty to landlord). And, if we place
the seller disclosure rule in the broader context of *caveat emptor*,
then we may affirmatively oppose the expansion of liability to
tenants. Here we might say that we want buyers to be vigilant
when inspecting property, and we permit lawsuits against sellers
only because we frown so heavily on fraud. Unlike a deceptively
silent seller, the silent tenant won't be taking the buyer's money.
In the tenant's case, then, buyer vigilance may resurface as the
courts' principal concern.

* * * * *

A word about technique: Applying vs. extending a case. We
have been talking so far as if there are only two things you can
do with a precedent: follow it or distinguish it. But following
precedent can be somewhat more complicated than this analysis
suggests. One way to follow precedent is simply to "apply" the
earlier case to the present facts; another way is to "extend" the
earlier case to reach this one. The difference is subtle but important; indeed, it is the sort of difference that can separate a "B"
exam from an "A."

Recall one last time our visiting scholar hypothetical, and assume you have just finished crafting an argument that *Johnson v.
Davis* (the case imposing liability for nondisclosure on sellers)
should be distinguished. One way to argue the other side—that
is, to argue that we should follow *Johnson*—is to insist that the
earlier case has already settled the matter at hand by holding
that *any* party with a financial interest in the conveyance has an
obligation to disclose known defects. Thus, your argument continues, the resolution of the visiting scholar case is simple and
straightforward: Since the visiting scholar had a financial interest
in the conveyance, and since he knew about the defects, *Johnson*
"applies" and the visiting scholar is accordingly liable for
nondisclosure. (Note, by the way, that we've relied on a "broad"
holding of *Johnson*—broad enough to impose liability beyond
sellers to include others with a financial interest in the property.)

But assume instead that *Johnson* contains language specifically limiting the reach of the holding to sellers. (*E.g.*, "Seller of-

fers a 'parade of horribles' that it asserts will follow if we impose liability for nondisclosure in this case, predicting a 'slippery slope' that will eventually lead to lawsuits against mortgage companies, tenants, and even the gardener and the young lad who cuts the lawn. But we need not decide today whether other parties with such varying degrees of financial interest in the transaction would be liable for nondisclosure.") In those circumstances, an argument that *Johnson* "applies" to the visiting scholar is obviously a dog that just won't hunt; he's a tenant, not a seller, and the court expressly declined to decide his case in *Johnson*. But an argument that the earlier case should nevertheless be followed here is by no means foreclosed, for you are still free to contend that the rationale that moved the *Johnson* court should persuade the court here to confront the issue that *Johnson* avoided and "extend" the earlier case to cover the visiting scholar.

Understanding the difference between applying and extending a precedent can thus help you to write exam answers that impress the grader in two ways. First, she'll be impressed by your careful reading of the precedent and by your recognition of the fact that you weren't free simply to "apply" the precedent to the new facts. Second, she'll be impressed that this obstacle didn't prevent you from developing an argument for following the precedent by "extending" it rather than merely "applying" it.

D. Dealing with Multiple Cases

Although we have now described many ways that exam questions can create doubt about case application, we have been purposely oversimplifying the matter. That's because so far we have unrealistically written as if there's only one case relevant to the problem you face on your exam. We suspect many of you noticed this in our discussion of human cloning. Sure, you mused, *Casey* could be read to suggest that "reproductive freedom" is the core of privacy protected by the Constitution. But what about the long-accepted practice of outlawing bigamy? (*See Reynolds v. United States*, 98 U.S. 145 (1879).) Doesn't this suggest that some types of reproductive activity may be limited? And what about *Bowers v. Hardwick*, 478 U.S. 186 (1986)? Doesn't that case, upholding Georgia's statute criminalizing sodomy, suggest that the Constitution protects only "traditional practices," and won't this make it harder to fit human cloning under a *Casey* rationale? It sure does.

The point here is that exam problems often ask you to evaluate scenarios for which a whole line of cases may be relevant. This is particularly true in Constitutional Law, though not because of anything intrinsic to that subject; there are famous lines of cases in other law school courses (*e.g.*, the indefiniteness cases in Contracts and the takings cases in Property), and when you research a particular problem in the real world you will almost invariably discover a complex grid of precedent. But given the recent trend toward teaching first-year common law subjects as reduced-credit single-semester offerings—with the result that professors in those courses feel greater pressure to emphasize breadth of coverage over depth of analysis—you are unfortunately less likely these days to encounter extended lines of cases outside the Constitutional Law context.

Certainly, if you were asked to answer a question about human cloning it might make sense to consider the many cases decided under the privacy rubric that begins in the birth control case. (*Griswold v. Connecticut*, 381 U.S. 479 (1965).) And when you consider a line of cases, each of them may provide a rule (*Roe's* trimester system) and articulate a rationale ("personal freedom"). So when evaluating a line of cases you may have conflicting rule formulations within a case or among cases, and you may have conflicting rationales within one case or among cases. The basic building blocks for writing your answers are the same as those described in the previous sections, so we need not multiply examples here. You just need to remember how many more possibilities for ambiguity are available to the professor for writing questions and to you for crafting dazzling answers.

Finally, on the subject of dealing with multiple cases, there will be some exam questions where you may not be deciding how to apply a line of cases to a new problem like cloning. Instead, the new problem may call upon you to decide which of two seemingly independent lines of cases applies. Consider, for example, *U.S. Term Limits v. Thornton*, 514 U.S. 779 (1995), where the Supreme Court had to decide how to classify a rule barring long-time officeholders from appearing on the ballot. Was it a "ballot access" measure under the line of cases granting broad leeway to government, or an additional "qualification" for public office under the line of cases limiting legislative authority? We'll describe the two lines of cases problem more fully in the "Competing Domains" section of Chapter 7.

Chapter 6

Forks in the Facts

If we were writing an introduction to legal reasoning, or, worse still, a book on legal theory, we would now devote a lengthy section to explaining the difference between what we are calling "forks in the law" and what we want to discuss next, "forks in the facts." As we have explained, our legal system has so many different sources of law (statutes vs. common law, multiple jurisdictions, conflicting precedents, etc.) that it's often very hard to tell from consulting available legal materials exactly what the law is. Moreover, even when you have only one statute or case to rely on, there are typically a number of plausible interpretations available. Once again, then, it's not clear what the law is. Exam questions that force you into discussions of different rules or interpretations are based on what we've been referring to as "forks in the law."

It will come as no surprise to you as a law student, however, that even when the plaintiff and defendant agree on the applicable law, and even on a particular interpretation of that law, plenty remains for the parties to argue about. A significant number—indeed, we would guess a majority—of actual legal disputes turn not on questions of what the law is, but on questions of how the law actually *applies* to a particular case. Both parties may agree, for example, that an anti-discrimination statute prohibits gender discrimination at places of public accommodation. But the owners of a private golf club may argue that their golf course is not a "public" place, while the woman who wants to play the course may vehemently disagree. We call such disputes about the application of law to particular situations "forks in the facts." In this chapter, we will describe some of the reasons why you will encounter so many situations in which applying the law takes some creativity, and we will once again map out patterns of forks that appear in law practice and, above all, on law school exams.

A. How Law Creates "Forks in the Facts": Why Categories Matter

You can't begin to see why law school exams generate so many hard problems until you grasp the importance of categories to legal disputes. We'll start then with a simple vignette to contrast the difference between ordinary and legal conversations. Imagine you and a group of friends were gathered together thinking about where to go to lunch. One friend, Tony, says he's dying for a plate of pasta and suggests you head to an Italian place. Another friend, Spanky, says he's in the mood for a diner. A third friend, Solomon, offers a concrete suggestion. "Why don't we go to Joe's Place?" he says. Joe's Place, it turns out, is just around the corner. It has booths with red vinyl benches, jukeboxes at each booth, and red-and-white-checkered tablecloths. It serves hamburgers, fries, malteds and sandwiches, but the house specialties are various pasta dishes with delicious homemade sauce. The right half of the menu is printed in Italian, and pictures of Frank Sinatra and Joe DiMaggio are on the walls.

If your friends are anything like ours, the suggestion of Joe's Place will change the focus of attention away from the type of place and onto the particular restaurant. Both Tony and Spanky are likely now to think about whether they would be happy eating at Joe's. Solomon's suggestion might not do the trick. Tony might say he doesn't like the pasta dishes there. Spanky might say the sandwiches aren't up to snuff. This will be a concrete dispute about the quality of Joe's Place. But it's unlikely Tony would say something like, "I love the pasta at Joe's Place, but I really wanted to go to an Italian restaurant, and it's not really Italian." If he did, everyone else would label him a stick in the mud. The same would be true if Spanky raved about Joe's yet resisted the selection because "it's not really a diner."

Unlike ordinary conversation, legal disputes—like our debate over the meaning of "vehicle"—will often pair plaintiff and defendant arguing about things like whether Joe's Place is really an "Italian restaurant" or really a "diner." That's because the legal rules will often divide the world into categories, with one legal rule applying to one category and a different rule applying to a second category. Homeowners, for example, may owe a different level of duty to invitees than they do to trespassers. Suppose, however, that I see a dangerous situation on your property and enter, uninvited, to try to stop it. Let's say I fear your child will fall in a pool. If I'm hurt on the way in because I step in dangerous chemicals you have carelessly left on the ground, I might sue you to recover for my injuries. Ordinary people might argue simply about whether I made the right call about saving your kid. (Was he really going to drown?) Common law courts, however, may respond to this situation by attempting to determine whether, because I entered uninvited, I was really a "trespasser." Or, because I had good reason to enter, whether my status was converted to that of an invitee. This kind of problem forms the core of countless legal disputes—and of even more exam questions.

Again, if this were a book on legal reasoning, we would provide a more detailed description of why the law tends to rely on categories. The simple explanation is that the very notion of the rule of law has a sequential component. People want the law to be established *before* the disputed conduct occurs. Lawmakers cannot imagine every situation that might occur and establish a rule for it in advance. But the law can group activities into broad categories and establish rules covering each. The categories help citizens see the rules as being in place prior to an actual dispute. Judges who appeal to the categories already in place appear to have less room for partial or biased conduct than those who are told simply to reach a fair result.

In this book, we aren't interested in whether this simple defense of law's categories is persuasive. Many of your professors will devote time to discussion about whether the law's reliance on categories really achieves objectives like predictability and reduced bias. But virtually every lawyer will agree that the law uses categories extensively. What we want to explain is how such categories contribute to the "forks in the facts" that form the core of so many law school exam questions. In this chapter we will illustrate a variety of ways in which laws are structured by category and then we'll explain why it's often difficult to look at a particular set of facts and determine which category they fall into.

1. Rule vs. Exception

There is perhaps no more common legal formulation than having a particular area of law governed by a basic rule but then permitting exceptions that apply to certain less common situations. The general rule under the commerce clause is that a state cannot alter the flow of commerce in ways that favor its own citizens over those of other states. But there is an exception for those situations in which the state is acting as a "market participant" and not a "market regulator." The general rule is that acceptance of an offer forms a valid contract at the time it is placed in the mail. But one exception makes acceptance of an offer under an "option contract" valid upon receipt and another permits the party making the offer to say in the offer that acceptance is valid only on receipt. ("I must hear from you by Friday.")

The general rule is that the prosecution can't use evidence the police have discovered during a warrantless search. But there may be an exception if the evidence was in the officer's "plain view" at the time it was seized. The general rule is that there is no duty to rescue, but there is an exception if the person refusing to give aid somehow created the peril or otherwise has a special relationship to the victim. The general rule is that a landowner may exclude strangers from her property. But if the landowner invites the general public in (let's say to gamble at a casino or shop at a mall), then the law may invoke an exception that requires the owner to admit people he doesn't want (let's say card-counters or leafleteers).

A standard exam technique is to generate a situation in which it remains unclear whether the general rule or the exception applies. If you consider the categories in our examples, it's easy to see how this can be done. It's often hard to say whether a particular offeror has opted out of the mailbox rule; whether a state is regulating or participating in a market; whether evidence really was in plain view; or whether the landowner's invitation to the public was sufficiently general to trigger the exception. Such problems make good exam questions.

2. Statutory Boundaries

Terms in statutes very often constitute categories that determine whether the statute applies. Article II of the Uniform Commercial Code, for example, applies to "the sale of goods." Let's say you hire me to cater a party, and a dispute arises. If the Code has desirable provisions from my point of view, I may argue that I have sold you food. Since food is a good, I'll contend the Code applies. You'll argue that you hired catering "services" and that the food was merely incidental. In that case, the Code won't apply. Similarly, suppose I sell you a customer list. That's clearly a sale; but is it a "good" under the meaning of the Code?

Or, to reconsider another example we used earlier, statutes may prohibit discrimination in "places of public accommodation." Yet it's often unclear whether a particular establishment fits the statutory definition. Is a country club a place of public accommodation? How about a community reading group that meets weekly at the home of one of the participants?

There are few more common exam techniques than requiring you to read statutory language carefully to determine whether the facts at hand fall within or outside of the categories established by the statute.

3. Sequential Categories

Many areas of law are organized based on a sequential chain of events. At some "magic moment" in the chain, events will have proceeded far enough that the law will shift the transaction from one category into another. In contract law, for example, buyer and seller may discuss the particulars that might form the basis of a contract between them. As long as the language is sufficiently conjectural, however, the law may characterize the conversation as "preliminary negotiations." Once one party puts a sufficiently concrete proposal to the other, however, the law may characterize that proposal as "an offer." If the other party accepts, a binding contract may be formed.

In criminal law, we see a similar structure. A deranged individual can sit in his attic all day long plotting how to kill his wife. He can write his plans in his personal journal and draw pictures about how the crime might take place. All these activities the law might characterize as mere preparations. Once, however, the potential murderer engages in an "overt act" toward completion of the crime, let's say putting poison into a bottle of champagne he knows his wife plans to drink next week, then the law may characterize his activities as "attempted murder."

Writing facts that leave you in doubt about which side of the sequence you are on is another classic exam technique.

4. Crossing the Line

The metaphor of proceeding step by step from one category into another is sufficiently powerful that even when the law divides conduct in ways that might not always be sequential we still often talk about crossing a line. It may be that what distinguishes a preliminary inquiry (any chance you might sell your watch) from an offer (I'd like to buy your watch) is the language chosen rather than some "magic moment" in a sequential chain. Sexual harassment cases force courts to distinguish between harmless office flirting and impermissibly unwelcome advances. It may be the first or the tenth meeting between the supervisor and employee that includes the improper behavior. So courts will be judging not the chain of events but the quality of the defendant's conduct to inquire whether any incident or the behavior as a whole went beyond "the point of no return." But, as the rhetoric suggests, although the court's inquiry is qualitative (what did the defendant do?), it will often be portrayed as sequential (did the defendant "go too far"?). In this context, too, you can expect to find exam questions that ask you to spot issues like "which side of the line" the defendant's conduct is on.

5. Categories as Elements of Legal Rules: Running the Gantlet

One of our favorite Torts teachers has a basic rap (although he'd never call it that) that he gives early in the semester to help relieve exam anxiety. Four words, he says, are all you need to make a good start on answering any Torts question. Those four words are "duty, breach, cause, and harm." This is good advice, if you think about how virtually any tort suit will require the plaintiff to prove each of these four elements. But it's an even better strategy if you think about how to generalize the point.

Many areas of the law require one party to prove several elements to make out a case. Criminal law, for example, often demands that the government prove all the "elements" of a crime. These might include "intent," "an overt act," and "causation of the forbidden result." Adverse possession often requires that the purported adverse possessor prove that she has had "actual possession of the disputed acreage and that the possession be adverse or hostile, open and notorious, continuous, exclusive, and for the time period required by statute in the jurisdiction."

Notice how the party with the burden of proof must satisfy each element to make out the case. So, it doesn't matter if the government can show intent and harm if the defendant engages in no overt act. (If I sit alone in my house wishing you'd die, and you drop dead of a heart attack, I've committed no crime.) We call this kind of legal structure "running the gantlet" to remind students that *each* element must be satisfied. (This contrasts with a multi-factor analysis, which is more like a recipe for a vegetable stew: The absence of a particular ingredient won't spoil the dish, since it's the overall mix that's crucial. Nuisance law, where courts weigh all the surrounding circumstances, is a good example of a multi-factor "stew.")

Now consider how wonderful "gantlet running" is for exam writers. Your professor may view it as a personal challenge to see if she can write a question where there is doubt about each of the several elements of a particular doctrine. And take our word for it, she can. So when you find convoluted exam scenarios that occur on deserted islands, this is a mere by-product of your professor taking a doctrine like adverse possession (an exam favorite) and testing her creativity. Can remote ocean locations really be possessed openly and notoriously? If boats come ashore every now and then, does this destroy exclusivity? If the marooned island dweller sticks to one side of the island, does she possess the whole thing? If the island dweller leaves on her boat for several weeks at a time, does this undermine her claim of continuous possession? As we'll explain further in Chapter 9, there's a tendency when you see an ambiguity in one part of the story (is possession actual?) to assume you have scoped out the whole question. But doctrines structured as a series of elements provide multiple opportunities for hard issues. Don't stop until you've "run the gantlet."

6. Open-Ended or "Evaluative" Categories

Classic issue-spotting exam questions get most of their mileage from what might be called borderline categories (preliminary negotiations vs. offer; flirting vs. harassment; residential vs. commercial lease). We would be remiss, however, if we failed to mention the many situations in which the law places an evaluative label or category on a party's behavior, and lawyers (and hence students) are expected to argue whether that evaluative label applies or not. Here, it's not so much whether one of two labels (offer vs. preliminary negotiations) is applicable (a or b?), but whether a single, more open-ended label governs *at all* (yes or no?). Contract law often imposes an obligation to perform in "good faith." So an exam scenario may expect you to characterize a party's action as in good faith or not. Tort law often imposes an obligation to act as a "reasonable" person. So an exam may expect you to argue about whether particular conduct was or was not reasonable. Nuisance law requires the plaintiff to show "substantial" harm. So, is the harm "substantial"? What you'll need to do on exam questions like this is to ask yourself which facts in the question support a claim that the action was in "good faith"; that the behavior was "reasonable"; that the harm was "substantial." And, equally important, what facts cut the other way?

B. Why Categories Don't Settle Things: Sources of Factual Conflict and Ambiguity

We imagine many of you reading the previous section have a nagging objection to the whole endeavor. Sure, you have learned in law school that the law divides things into categories and that determining which category governs is often crucial to outcomes. But what you want to know is why figuring out which category applies is such a mystery. Why aren't the law's categories sufficiently determinative to permit you to ignore all this "maybe" business and to focus your energies instead on learning rules and routinely applying them to the facts? In this section, we hope to explain that despite the legal system's best efforts, doubts about proper categorization will be with us as long as we have law. We will detail many sources of that ambiguity so that you'll know how to look for them buried inside the complex fact patterns that make up your exams.

1. Facts on Both Sides of the Category

Think back to our story about the Italian restaurant and the diner. Notice how we included facts that made Joe's place sound like a diner (booths, jukeboxes, malteds) and facts that made it sound Italian (wall photos, menu language, pasta dishes). This is an extraordinarily typical technique when drafting an exam question. The professor will take two well-established legal categories and write a story in which some facts point in one direction and some point in another. And, we might add, the professors here are taking their cues from real life. There's just no reason to expect that actual events will occur along the precise lines of legal categories. Your job, then, is to see how the exam facts reflect ambiguity and make the arguments for one characterization as well as the other.

In Property, you might get a landlord-tenant question involving an unrenovated loft used as a music studio, where the outcome depends on whether the lease is governed by residential or commercial rules. The teenage musicians might actually be living there with the landlord's knowledge and tacit consent. (He may have given them a key to the building for after-hours use denied to other tenants.) But the building may be otherwise commercial, and the space may have no kitchen facilities. The heat may be turned off at midnight. Yet there might be a shower in the loft space. The lease might have the words Commercial Lease written at the top in big letters. In sum, there are facts that support the "residential" lease characterization and facts that suggest a "commercial" transaction. So you need to be prepared to argue either way.

In Contracts, your exam might contain a lengthy letter from a seller to a buyer. The letter begins, "We would consider an agreement on the following terms." This sounds like preliminary negotiations because the seller offers merely to "consider" an agreement. Yet the same letter may close, "It is vital that you let us know immediately whether these terms are acceptable to you, so we can begin our own procurement efforts." This sounds more like an offer. Since there are facts on both sides of the preliminary negotiations vs. offer line, you'll find yourself using the language to argue each way. Indeed, as we move to the following sections, you'll see that linguistic ambiguities are often a source of "forks in the facts."

2. Differing Standpoints

It may be that the facts are entirely clear but they may look different from the standpoint of different actors. Suppose a supervisor is speaking with an employee who is active in union organizing and has recently gotten married. He says to her, "Congratulations, in your position it's a really good thing you got married." If the law prohibits "threats" made by employers, is this a "threat?" The supervisor may say he was merely trying to congratulate her on her good fortune. Yet the employee may see this as an implicit reference to her organizing activity: It's good she got married because she's going to need that income when she's out of a job.

Or think back to Patron's offer to pay Artiste $10,000 to paint a portrait, where the question was whether the preliminary sketchwork was "mere preparations" or the "beginning of performance." From Patron's perspective, the deal is for a portrait, and thus the fact that no paint has touched the final canvas may suggest performance has not begun. Yet Artiste's understanding of what a portrait entails may lead her to conclude that doing the sketches is very much part of the process, maybe even the hardest part. (Think about a paper you wrote for school where you had done all the research and an outline but hadn't actually begun writing. You would certainly say you had started the paper. Yet a professor demanding a 25-page paper might well give you zero credit if that were all you submitted.) So, even when the facts themselves are undisputed, the different perspectives of the parties may make it very unclear whether the facts fall in one legal category or another.

3. Differing Time-Frames

The same set of facts may often be characterized very differently depending on how far back in time you go to evaluate the situation. The most striking example of this phenomenon we've ever seen was on a television news show. The reporter opened by describing an automobile accident in which a white driver seemingly driving at a safe speed and obeying all traffic laws ran down and killed an African-American pedestrian who was crossing the street on her way to work. Black faces in local taverns were then shown denouncing the death as a product of blatant racism. White faces in different bars appeared next to accuse the first group of finding racism everywhere, even in a simple traffic accident. Since there was absolutely no reason to believe the driver had acted wrongly or possessed any ill will, it was hard to imagine how racism could have had anything to do with the death.

The story then switched, however, to how it was that the African-American pedestrian came to be in the middle of the street where she was killed. It turned out that she had taken the bus to work, and that she worked in a large suburban mall a good way down the road from the traffic accident. The bus did not stop in front of the mall, and the pedestrian crosswalk from the bus stop to the mall side of the street was, by all accounts, very dangerous. African-Americans in the community had been lobbying for months to add a bus stop right in front of the mall to reduce the traffic risk. Their efforts had failed, however, and, based on the television account, there was every reason to believe that powerful interests didn't want to make it too easy for African-Americans to travel from the inner city to the suburban mall. The short time-frame, focusing on the accident only, made racism appear an absurd charge. But the longer story created an entirely different impression.

Manipulating time-frames like this works for exam writers as well as television journalists. In torts cases, there is a well-known rule/exception structure whereby one party has no duty to aid another unless the potential rescuer somehow caused the victim's peril. Exam writers, then, will search for examples in which, at the moment of truth, the victim seems responsible for his own fate. So, a farmer might be strolling his grounds and hear a young child screaming from the bottom of a well into which the child has fallen. From a narrow time-frame, this appears a classic case in which the farmer is under no legal duty to attempt a rescue, whatever his moral obligations. But the exam writer may also include facts that reveal the well to be on the farmer's property. It may be noticeably marked with a "danger" sign and as carefully shielded from accidents as is reasonable, yet the farmer may have previously seen children too young to read or otherwise appreciate the danger playing nearby. This broader time-frame suggests that maybe the farmer does have a duty to aid. Of course, on an exam your professor will want you to present the case both ways.

Exam questions on self-defense in criminal law often make use of a similar structure. Where the murder victim has been terrorizing the defendant over a long period, the defendant may reasonably believe that the victim's latest conduct (*e.g.*, picking up a bottle) threatened her life. But if we focus on the fatal incident alone, self-defense might appear a more difficult claim. Note, by the way, that differing time-frames may help you to identify both a "fork in the facts" and a "fork in the law" in the same exam question. Thus, to continue our example, you may use time-frames to discuss the application of a particular legal test (*e.g.*, "reasonable belief of imminent threat") to the facts: A short time-frame suggests that defendant overreacted whereas the longer time-frame makes her self-defense claim seem far more reasonable. But you may also use the differing time-frames to discuss the proper interpretation of the test itself: If we give "imminent" a plain-meaning interpretation, defendant is in trouble; but if we look to the underlying purpose—to sort out real from fancied threats—the longer time-frame may support defendant's claim. We will have more to say about such "twin forks" in the next chapter.

4. Differing Ways To Make Sense of the Facts

a. Take things one at a time or view them as a totality

Imagine a Contracts exam question in which one issue is whether an offer has been made. The alleged offeror has made the following statements: "I'd really like to buy your watch." "If I were to buy that watch I'd probably pay around $300." And "I have your $300 right here." It's pretty clear that none of these three statements, taken on its own, would constitute an offer to buy the watch. On the other hand, if you take all three together, perhaps an offer has been made. This kind of ambiguity obviously makes for a good exam question.

One way to describe the ambiguity about whether the three statements count as an offer is as yet another kind of "fork in the facts." Here, the clash is between seeing each of the statements in isolation and looking instead to the "totality of the circumstances." You'll find the same clash in antitrust, where a set of allegedly anti-competitive practices might be viewed individually as just within bounds of the law but collectively over the line. So too labor law cases might involve a set of anti-union management practices where each one falls just within the legal limits yet the union argues that "taken together" they constitute an unfair labor practice.

From a student's perspective, there may be a puzzle about why such "forks in the facts" exist. This is one of those cases in which our rulebook devotee might expect to encounter well-established rules settling such questions as whether multiple statements could or could not be combined into an "offer." And, as it turns out, sometimes there are rules on issues like this. In contract law, for example, the so-called "modern view" adopts a "totality of the circumstances" test for many interpretive questions.

The presence of such a test will change the debate, but it won't make the one-at-a-time vs. taken-together dispute disappear. Thus, a good lawyer—and a successful law student—

would start an analysis of our watch hypothetical by acknowledging that the question presented is whether the statements constitute an offer in the "totality of the circumstances." But there is still a fork in the facts, for one side will focus on the individual staements and emphasize their failure to add up to an offer ("totality"= the sum of the statements), while the other side will argue that taken together the statements do indeed meet the legal test (the whole is greater than the sum of the parts).

And of course, in some areas of the law, the well-settled rule desired by the rulebook devotee will give way to a murky divide between competing interpretations. The recent impeachment battle, for example, highlighted such an ambiguity in our understanding of perjury. Must perjury refer to a specific (*i.e.*, "isolated") statement that is false and material, or can perjury be inferred from the totality of the witness's statements that as a whole are intended to mislead? The U.S. Senate was never required to resolve this ambiguity, but as a student taking exams you'll want to watch for both forks in the law and forks in the facts generated when the facts may be viewed in isolation or taken as a whole.

b. Lenses of generality

As we described in the chapters on "forks in the law," exam writers will often seize upon doubts over the meaning of rules by writing questions that hinge on stating a rule at varying levels of generality. An antitrust question about publication of a price list, for example, may be analyzed differently depending on whether the precedents are portrayed as broadly banning "anti-competitive practices," which might include publishing a price list, or as narrowly prohibiting "price-fixing," in which case mere publication may be permitted.

Sometimes, however, even when there is general agreement on the formulation of the rule, a similar ambiguity creeps down into what seems more like fact application. For example, many courts agree that one way in which tort plaintiffs can establish proximate cause is simply by showing that the defendant could foresee the plaintiff's harm. There is no need to show that the defendant could have predicted the precise set of facts giving rise to the harm. Yet virtually any exam question testing foreseeability will give you a chance to revisit this issue in determining whether the stated harm was foreseeable.

Let's say the question asks about a landlord who fails to provide hot water. The tenant boils water on the stove to pour into the tub to bathe her child. As she carries the pot full of water, she slips and spills the water on her child, causing severe burns. Were the child's injuries proximately caused by the landlord's breach of the warranty of habitability? You can argue for the tenant by stressing that the accident is the kind of event the landlord should have expected might happen when residential tenants are forced to get by without hot water. On the landlord's side, your first instinct might be to suggest that the precise chain of events leading to the injury (boiling, slipping, and spilling) was too unusual for the landlord to foresee. But then you recall that proximate-cause *rules* don't require that the landlord be able to foresee the precise chain of events. Don't give up! You can still make the causation argument for the landlord by remembering that there are many different levels of generality, not just two polar choices.

The landlord's position isn't merely that the precise chain of events was unpredictable, but that the type of accident that occurred was not a foreseeable outcome for failing to provide hot water. So you might argue for the landlord that matters would be different if there were a snake bite that couldn't be cleaned properly. No one would predict a snake, yet everyone knows hot water is needed to clean injuries. In contrast, burns like the one this tenant suffered may simply be too remote a possibility to hold the landlord accountable. Or at least you could so argue on the landlord's behalf.

To take a second example, a rule of law may distinguish between permissible "puffing" and unlawfully deceptive practices. A manufacturer can advertise a vitamin supplement as "good for you," even if many objective observers might disagree. But commercials that tout the supplement for cancer prevention better have evidence to back up the claim. Notice how "general" claims sound more like puffing whereas "specific" claims require greater levels of proof. Your exam writer may try to invent a fact pattern that falls between the two well-recognized examples. Suppose, for example, that the manufacturer advertises that the supplement is "guaranteed to make you feel ten years younger." In cases like this the legal categories—permissible puffing vs. unlawfully deceptive practices—are little more than placeholders for factual judgments. So you'll need to argue the statement in and out of each category. "Ten years younger" sounds pretty specific. But claims about "feelings" may be too vague to be more than mere puffery. Paying careful attention to how facts can be presented through different lenses of generality—and thus be argued into different categories (foreseeable or not, puffing or deception)—is another trick for answering the issue-spotter exam.

c. Linguistic ambiguity

Our last example of "forks in the facts" should be the most familiar, since our chapters on "forks in the law" devoted significant attention to the multiple sources of meaning for words appearing in cases and statutes. Words also make up the principal components of legal categories that rely on lay understandings, and, of particular relevance here, words are the key part of every contract. Any of your exams can choose to highlight the ambiguity in everyday language as a way of seeking argument about which category best fits the facts.

Your Contracts exams in particular will require you to read language with great care to determine the nature and meaning of the parties' agreement or lack of agreement. In theory, debates over contractual terms could be described as a hybrid between "forks in the law" and "forks in the facts." To illustrate the point, recall the famous case of *Raffles v. Wichelhaus*, where the parties used the same word ("Peerless") but meant different things (because they were each referring to a different ship named Peerless). On the one hand, you could analyze this problem—as we do here—as a "fork in the facts" arising from linguistic ambiguity: If we look at what the parties *said*, they have an agreement and hence a contract; but if we look at what they *meant*, the case comes out the other way. But you could also analyze the problem as a "fork in the law" arising from the same ambiguity: If contract law focuses on outward manifestations, then there's a contract because the parties' manifestations were the same; but if contract law focuses on subjective intentions, then there's no contract because they meant different things. In this book, we aren't writing about theory, so there's no point in worrying about whether this ambiguity is better described as a "fork in the law" or a "fork in the facts." Instead, just familiarize yourself with linguistic ambiguity as another source of issues you are likely to encounter on your exams.

Borderline cases. Some legal categories simply track ordinary experience in ways giving rise to interesting issues when actual experience proves other than ordinary. When we studied criminal law, courts had different rules governing searches and seizures depending on where the search was conducted. Police were afforded far greater latitude to search automobiles than homes. The distinction was built on claims about differing expectations of privacy in the two settings. So our professor asked us what the rules were for searching a Winnebago (a large motor vehicle that people may live in). This was a perfect exam question because it required knowledge of the two categories and discussion of the reasons for the divide that might help determine how to classify the borderline case. Similarly, property law often distinguishes between fixtures that stay with a house and chattels that the seller may take with him. The basement boiler is a fixture. The dining room table is a chattel. But what about the two-ton hot tub that sits in the pool house next to the built-in pool?

Words vs. actions. It's very common for there to be a difference between what people say and what they do. So why not write a question that emphasizes that difference? Let's say you have a probationary employee whose contract is very explicit that during her probationary period she may be fired at any time for any reason. The contract further states that her probationary period will end after six months, unless the employer approves her for upgrade to regular status at an earlier time. During the six-month period the boss says nothing about an upgrade. But after three months he buys her expensive new office furniture, orders her business cards, and has her name embossed on the door. In the fourth month, the boss gives her three new assignments that clearly will take until the end of the year to finish. And in the fifth month, he fires one of her colleagues and transfers all that work to her as well. When she receives an offer of secure employment from another firm, she declines, citing how safe she feels in her current post. If in the sixth month the boss comes to her and says she's fired because her work is no good, does she have any claim for breach of contract? The "words" used suggest one result, for the contract established a six-month probationary period, and the employer never actually said it was approving her for upgrade to regular employment status. But she will surely argue that her boss's actions tell a different story.

Written vs. oral statements. To continue the theme of job security, consider the all-too-common case of an employer whose formal written policy makes clear that all employees are subject to termination "at will." Yet in an exam question the company recruiter tells the employee that "no one has been fired here in 20 years," and that "a person like you can count on absolute job security, something you couldn't find anywhere else in the industry." When the exam question seeks a response to the employee's discharge, it's important to note the contrast between the written and oral statements and discuss which should take precedence and why.

Literalism vs. reasonable expectations. Your exam question tells the story of a mortgage company that takes the following actions. The borrowers apply for a loan on a home and supply the company with detailed financial information. A thorough credit check is done. Then the mortgage company sends an appraiser to the home who tells the borrowers that appraisal will be done in a couple of days. Three days later the company faxes the borrower a letter spelling out the details of the loan agreement. The first line of the letter says, "Congratulations, your loan has been approved." The mortgage company's representative also calls the borrower's insurance company to make sure the home is properly insured. Then the mortgage company's attorney phones the borrower and asks when a closing date might be set. A date is chosen and the borrower liquidates several mutual funds to have sufficient cash for the closing.

A week later, the mortgage company calls the borrower and says the deal is off. It turns out that the appraised value of the home was $50,000 less than the $250,000 expected, and a close reading of the three-page, single-spaced letter that the company had faxed reveals the following clause: "This agreement is conditioned on all necessary repairs being completed and a formal valuation of the house being completed at $250,000." The mortgage company thinks this removes any issue of its liability. Your job on an exam that poses these facts would be to highlight the obvious conflict between a "literal" term hidden in the maze of fine print and the "reasonable expectations" of the borrower based on the opening sentence of the letter together with the mortgage company's other conduct.

Multiple sources of meaning. Parties may use words in their contracts that have different meanings depending on what context you draw meaning from. A written contract for a dozen boxes of frozen hamburger rolls might mean "12 boxes" if you take the literal meaning or "13 boxes" if the commercial custom of a "baker's dozen" is to be applied. One party may reply to another's offer to sell goods by saying, "I accept your gracious offer, but I'd like to talk to you a little more about the terms." If we read this comment through a lay understanding of terms we may see mere continuing negotiations. But if we hold the speaker to the legal meaning, we may say that "acceptance" of an "offer" means that the parties have already concluded a contract.

Of course, the best exam questions may pose a long fact pattern in which several of these different ways of looking at facts are all combined into one story. Now that you have learned how to spot them one at a time, the next challenge is how to tackle multiple ambiguities simultaneously.

Chapter 7

Taking It to the Next Level: "Twin Forks"

Take a deep breath! You have now read through an extraordinary number of ways in which the law produces ambiguous situations that will provide ammunition for your professors to construct exams. So we have some more good news. Our experience has been that most law students actually become quite good at mastering the forms of ambiguity we have described. Some get there sooner than others, and so one thing you want to do is develop study techniques that speed your ability to spot exam issues. We'll talk more about that in Parts II and III.

Typical issue-spotting exams, however—like actual law practice—are yet more difficult than may be suggested by a description of any particular fork. That's because many exam questions will throw more than one ambiguity at you simultaneously. This is the phenomenon of "twin forks" to which we have referred in earlier chapters, and that we are now ready to tackle directly.

Return once again, then, to the classic example—famously analyzed by Lon Fuller and H.L.A. Hart—of a rule banning vehicles in the park. We have explained at least two different ways you might discuss the question whether the prohibition applies to a motorized wheelchair. (Let's give tricycles a rest for a moment!) First, you might talk about the right way to interpret the underlying rule. Should it be read through the lens of plain meaning or with its broader purpose in mind? From the perspective of this "fork in the law," the focus will be on reading the legal materials to find clues within them about the intentions of the statutory drafters. And you can almost imagine the particular example of the motorized wheelchair lurking in the background while the foreground debate concerns "what the law is."

Under either the plain-meaning or purpose-based alternative, however, you must still address the proper treatment of the wheelchair, the problem we've called a "fork in the facts." There is no ready-made answer to whether particular things are literally "vehicles" that can be invoked to solve the wheelchair case. Is a toy car a vehicle if its wheels spin? What if they don't? And if the rule is read according to purpose, let's say keeping the park quiet, is a motorized wheelchair too noisy? (And, of course, these issues don't even include the obvious point that the rule could be supported by other purposes, such as keeping the park safe.)

This kind of "issue within an issue" is what makes the vehicle example so engaging, and we think helps account for its lasting power as an educational tool. We're calling issues within issues "twin forks" to highlight that you must choose one side or the other and then, either side you choose, you must choose again.

Not all your professors will be as jurisprudentially inclined as Hart and Fuller were. But all of them will take advantage of twin forks as perhaps the core technique in drafting an exam question. If it's not explained to you (and certainly no one ever explained it to us), it can throw you for a loop. Once you understand it, however, it will look like a life raft rather than a dreaded source of confusion.

Take, then, a typical problem of the kind you'd expect to find on an exam. You know that your child was beaten up in the local public school and that the prospective buyer of your house has children he intends to send there. As a seller of the home, do you have an obligation to disclose the violent incident?

Suppose you were sure about the law. Let's say you knew that in the relevant jurisdiction home sellers are under a duty to disclose all information pertinent to the market value of their home. You might still be unsure about the correct answer to the exam question. So you might offer your professor a discussion about whether one violent incident is a sufficient basis for concluding that there's anything wrong with a school that is otherwise attractive to the buyer. Your child may be particularly prone to fighting, or there may just be one bully around who is about to graduate. As you show the ambiguity in the application of the market-value rule to these facts, you score points merrily along the way.

Now suppose instead that you didn't notice the possibility that one incident might not be indicative of a threat to the home's value. Instead, you simply assumed that this incident would be something you must disclose under a rule based on market value. But you are entirely unsure of what the law really is in the relevant jurisdiction. You remember the cases and don't really know whether they support a rule that requires disclosure of "anything" that affects market value or merely disclosure of "defects" in the house that affect market value. So you might offer your professor a discussion about the best way to read the cases. The facts in all the cases may involve defects in the house, but the expressed rationales appear to extend to all information about market value. You might raise "slippery slope" questions like whether you would be under an obligation to disclose information from a study you just read casting doubt on the future economy of the state. Again, you'd be merrily racking up points as you focused like a laser beam on this one particular ambiguity in the law.

Now let's suppose that *neither* issue escapes you. You have the sinking feeling as you read the question that you aren't sure quite what the law is (defects or market value), nor are you sure whether even if you knew the law you'd know how to resolve the case. (Could defects be extended to cover things about the local school? Will the market value of the house really hinge on one incident?) Remember that from the professor's perspective your ability to spot both sources of ambiguity makes you a good student. That's why our book is called *Getting to Maybe*.

But from your own internal perspective, especially if you haven't thought much about exams, you have every reason to feel confused. As you may see it, there are two things you are supposed to "know." "What's the law?" and "how does it apply?" Gasp! You're not sure about either one.

Once again, however, you know more than you think you do about this "twin fork." Much more! And here's what you know. You know that resolution of the issues you have identified will get you to a result in the case. So you know that if the rule is market value, and the violent incident is significant, then the seller must disclose. You know that if the rule is market value, but the incident isn't significant, then disclosure's not required. You know that if the rule is to disclose "defects," and "defects" is read narrowly, disclosure won't be necessary because the school is not the house. You also know that if "defects" is read as a surrogate for any information the seller may have special access to as a result of living in the house, then disclosure may be required. If you tell your professor all these things, and then you also give some reasons that courts might embrace each of the possible interpretations, your answer will be very well-received. (We promise!) We'll talk more in Part II about what reasons supporting differing interpretations might look like. For now, however, we want to show you enough examples of "twin forks" so that they will come to seem routine.

A. Linked Forks: One Good Fork Deserves Another

Recall our very first example of "forks in the road":

> Paul Patron offers Arlene Artiste $10,000 to paint a portrait of the Patron family. Artiste explains that her other commitments make it impossible for her to promise a completed work by a particular date, and Patron responds, "I don't *want* your commitment. I just want the portrait." After Artiste spends numerous hours doing preliminary sketches — but before she has put brush to canvas and begun the actual portrait — Patron advises her that he has changed his mind and is revoking the offer. What legal rights does Artiste have against Patron?

You will recall that we saw two different "forks" in this hypothetical. First we saw a fork in the law that matched the common law rule (an offer to make a unilateral contract may be revoked at any time before acceptance is complete) against § 45 of the Second Restatement of Contracts (an offeror may not revoke once offeree begins performance). Then we saw a fork in the facts: Did the preliminary sketches constitute a beginning of performance under § 45, or were they "mere preparations" before performance was actually begun?

In terms of scoring points on an exam, it's obviously twice as good to see two issues than to see only one. But the message of this chapter is that you are better off still if you can see *relationships* between issues. For one thing, seeing the relationship between different issues will sharpen your understanding of their significance and hence the analysis you provide in your answer. For another, relationships between issues appear in *patterns* on law exams, and studying these patterns will enhance your ability to recognize issues in the first place.

Consider, then, the relationship between the two issues we've identified in the Artiste/Patron illustration, for it is an extremely common one on law exams. The professor drafts a problem presenting a rule vs. counter-rule issue, but when you start to apply the rules to the facts presented in the problem, you encounter a second issue—frequently a "fork in the facts." We call this a "linked forks" pattern, because one of the "roads" you encounter at the first fork leads directly to a second fork.

Thus, in the Artiste/Patron case, either the common law rule or the rule from Restatement § 45 might apply. If we apply the common law rule to the facts, the analysis comes to an end, for the offeror is free to revoke. But if we apply § 45 to the facts, we encounter a second issue and the analysis must continue. If the sketchwork is the beginning of performance, then Artiste is protected against revocation; but if the sketchwork is "mere preparations," then Patron is free to revoke.

The links may not stop there. Assume we have a question presenting a slight variation on the facts we've examined thus far:

> Paul Patron offers Arlene Artiste $10,000 to paint a portrait of the Patron family. Artiste explains that her other commitments make it impossible for her to promise a completed work by a particular date, and Patron responds, "I don't *want* your commitment. I just want the portrait." After Artiste spends numerous hours doing preliminary sketches—but before she has put brush to canvas and begun the actual portrait—Patron advises her that he has changed his mind and is revoking the offer.

Artiste continues work on the project, in spite of Patron's purported revocation. She finishes the portrait, but citing Patron's attempt to back out of the deal, she refuses to sign it. Patron rejects delivery of the portrait, and Artiste sues for breach of contract. What result?

Let's analyze the variation step-by-step. Once again, we begin with the rule vs. counter-rule fork; once again there is a link between one of the rules (*i.e.*, § 45) and a second issue ("beginning of performance" vs. "mere preparations"). And once again, if the sketchwork is "mere preparations," then Patron is free to revoke and our analysis comes to an end.

But did you see that the facts we've added create a link to yet another issue? Thus, if the sketchwork does constitute the beginning of performance under § 45, then we confront yet another "fork in the facts." Under Restatement § 45, Patron's duty to pay for the portrait "is conditional on completion of the invited performance in accordance with the terms of the offer." Did Artiste meet this condition? If so, then Patron would seem to be liable for the promised $10,000. But if Artiste's refusal to sign the portrait violates "the terms of the offer," then Patron is still home free — at least until Artiste relents and signs!

The classic "issue spotter" question on law exams has multiple "links" like this, and in our experience students needlessly miss the second (and third and fourth . . .) links because they think they are through when they identify the *first* one. We discuss this common mistake at greater length in Part II of the book, but you can avoid that problem by learning to recognize this "linked forks" pattern and looking for it on your exams.

B. Reciprocal Forks: Back-and-Forth between Law and Facts

Recall another hypothetical from an earlier chapter:

Horace Wholesaler receives an order from Reba Retailer for 50 high-end audio components at a total price of $20,000.

Wholesaler sends Retailer an acknowledgment of order by e-mail, promising immediate shipment of the ordered goods. Prior to shipment, Wholesaler reneges on the deal. Retailer sues, but Wholesaler asserts that the U.C.C.'s Statute of Frauds bars the claim. What result?

The question, you may also recall, is whether the e-mail message constitutes a "signed writing" under § 2-201 of the U.C.C. One issue—a "fork in the law" involving competing interpretations—is whether we give the "signed writing" requirement of that provision a plain-meaning or a purpose-based interpretation. Under a plain-meaning interpretation, you can almost hear Clint Eastwood: "Read my lips: It says signed *writing*." By contrast, under a purpose-based interpretation, we might conclude that the goal of avoiding testimonial disputes about the existence and terms of a contractual commitment is served perfectly well by any verifiable record of the transaction in question, including a saved e-mail message.

But let's say we follow the plain-meaning path at the fork. Is the case over, or is there another issue? We may have a "fork in the facts" as well. On the one hand, an e-mail message that appears only as an electronically generated image on the screen of a computer monitor is an awful long way from ink on paper. On the other hand, e-mail is generated by the same means (*i.e.*, typing words on a keyboard) as most writing and can be reformatted and printed out on paper as easily as it can be saved to the hard drive. (Maybe we'll get to make Clint's day after all!)

Indeed, that debate might lead us right back to the meaning of the term "writing" in the statute. After all, it's already been applied to several successive generations of technology: handwriting, typing, word-processing, and laser-printing. Perhaps we've hit yet another question of competing interpretations: the dictionary meaning of "writing" vs. a commercial meaning that might focus on the way that people make and memorialize business deals in the late 1990's.

If you're still awake, here's the larger point. One way to describe what just happened is that it is another example of "linked forks." We start with a fork in the law (plain meaning vs. a purpose-based interpretation of "writing"). The path of plain meaning links to a "fork in the facts" (e-mail = writing vs. e-mail ≠ writing), but also to another "fork in the law" (dictionary meaning vs. commercial meaning of "writing").

But there is another, perhaps easier way to understand this example. When a legal problem forces us to apply "law" to "facts," there are at least two ways to do that. You can "hold the facts steady" and ask what the law is. (Here, do we give "signed writing" a plain-meaning or a purpose-based interpretation? And if we opt for the plain meaning, do we refer to the dictionary or to the commercial context?) Or you can "hold the law steady" and ask what the facts are. (Here, is e-mail "writing" or not?)

We're sure you are thinking that it's rather artificial to speak in terms of holding facts steady while moving law or doing it the other way around. You are right. On your exams, and in law practice, you'll find yourself instead moving back-and-forth between the law and the facts without giving the matter much conscious thought. That's why we call the analysis described here "reciprocal forks," because the best answer will move back-and-forth from one dimension of the problem to the other.

But it doesn't matter what you *call* it—whether you think of it as a "reciprocal fork"; or as simply another example of "linked forks"; or in some other way that makes more sense to you—as long as you learn to *recognize* the pattern in order to "know it when you see it" on an exam.

C. Concurrent Forks: Straddling a Statutory Boundary

Most of the statutes you study in law school—especially those you explore in your first-year courses—govern subjects that were previously governed by the common law. Indeed, for most of those subjects, the common law still governs any transaction that is "outside" the statute, and thus the "boundary" between what lies inside and what lies outside the statute is a matter of some importance. Consider the following hypothetical:

Betty Bookbinder enters a contract with Larry Lawyer to bind Lawyer's collection of appellate briefs in 37 matching volumes. Lawyer selects a cover from among Bookbinder's extensive selection of fine leathers and stipulates, among many other details, that his name should appear on each cover in gold 24-point Old English lettering. When Bookbinder delivers the bound volumes on the promised date, Lawyer notices that his name is in 22-point lettering instead of 24-point and refuses to accept the volumes. If Bookbinder sues for breach of contract, what result?

You may have recognized that the facts here are drafted to straddle the statutory boundary distinguishing a "sale of goods" governed by Article II of the U.C.C from a mere "service," which is outside the Code and hence governed by the common law. On the one hand, the transaction might be characterized as a sale of specially manufactured goods—Bookbinder is in effect selling Lawyer a substantial quantity of fine leather and providing custom work to ensure a fit between the product and Lawyer's needs—bringing it within Article II. But on the other hand, the dominant component of the transaction may be viewed as a service—Bookbinder is binding a collection of briefs that already belong to Lawyer—and the transaction would therefore be governed not by the statute but by the common law. In sum, the facts can be argued on either side of the statutory "boundary," making this a classic "fork in the facts."

But you may have noticed that the hypothetical also contains a second fork—a rule vs. counter-rule issue that we have called a "fork in the law." Thus, Lawyer's right to reject the volumes turns on whether we apply the U.C.C.'s perfect tender rule (§ 2-601) or the common law doctrine of substantial performance. If we apply the perfect tender rule, Lawyer has the right to reject the volumes because his name appeared in 22-point lettering rather than the 24-point lettering required by the contract. But if we apply the common law doctrine of substantial performance, we are likely to conclude that the slight defect does not constitute a material breach. On that view, Lawyer cannot reject the volumes and must satisfy himself with a counter-claim for any damages he's suffered as a result of the non-conformity.

We call these "concurrent forks," for the path you take at the "fork in the facts" determines the path you must choose at the "fork in the law." If we characterize the transaction as a sale of goods, then the U.C.C.'s perfect tender rule (§ 2-601) applies, and Bookbinder is out of luck. But if we characterize the transaction as a service, then Bookbinder may find refuge in the common law doctrine of substantial performance.

You will encounter "concurrent forks" in most areas of legal practice and in virtually every course you take in law school. Sometimes the statutory boundary will look like the boundary between two adjacent states. (On one side of the line, she's an "employee" protected against sexual harassment by Title VII of the Civil Rights Act; but on the other side of the line, she's an "independent contractor" whose only source of legal protection against such harassment is the common law.) Sometimes the statutory boundary will look more like the perimeter of an island. (If the country club is inside the line, then it's a "place of public accommodation" and its racially discriminatory membership policies are prohibited by the state human rights statute; but if it's outside the line, then the country club may be free to discriminate under the common law.)

The point, again, is to learn to recognize the larger pattern: Watch for the "fork in the facts" that straddles a "statutory boundary," for there's almost sure to be a "fork in the law" lurking nearby.

D. Proliferating Forks: Competing Domains

Believe it or not, most law professors strive to make the study of law easier rather than harder for their students, and one way we try to do that is by dividing up the subject areas we teach (Contracts, Torts, Property, etc.) into discrete topics (offer and acceptance; interpretation; remedies; etc.) and each of those topics into sub-topics (*e.g.*, money damages; specific relief) and even *sub*-sub-topics (*e.g.*, the rule of *Hadley v. Baxendale*; the duty to mitigate damages; etc.). The advantage to dividing up our subjects this way is that it permits students to focus in on one set of rules, cases, and/or principles at a time—an approach that is far less daunting than trying to grasp the "seamless web" of the law all at once and, in any event, a lot easier to outline as you prepare for the final!

The downside, however, is that real-world legal problems seldom fit neatly into a single section of even the most sophisticated outline. Instead, they blend and bleed from one section to another, frequently crossing even the most cherished boundaries of the course syllabus and the casebook's table of contents. As scary as that might seem to the beginning law student, the skilled lawyer welcomes the opportunity it provides to frame a case in a way that gives the greatest advantage to her client—and to resist her opponent's efforts to frame the case in some other way.

In an effort to assist you in developing this important skill—*i.e.*, of learning to analyze and argue your way back and forth across the boundaries we teach you—law professors frequently design fact patterns that straddle different doctrines, or different cases, or even different bodies of law. We refer to these as "competing domains," and the "statutory boundary" situation we just finished discussing (where a hypothetical is designed to straddle the boundary between what's governed by a statute and what's governed by the common law) is an important example of what we mean. Indeed, it is such an important example—and, more to the point of this book, it is so frequently tested on law exams—that we thought it deserved separate treatment in its own section.

But there is a much longer list of competing domains problems than any book could provide. And since some of them are a bit more complex than anything we've studied so far, we offer a few examples to give you a feel for what different competing domains may look like:

- In Contracts, you learn about the doctrine of "consideration" as well as the doctrine of "promissory estoppel." A classic competing domains question for that course presents a single fact pattern that straddles the two doctrines—*e.g.*, the nephew who gives up smoking in order to fulfill a condition on his uncle's promise to give him $5000 and whose forbearance could thus be characterized as either bargained-for consideration or merely detrimental reliance.

- In Property, you may study one case that gives a landowner the unrestricted right to pump percolating water from his property and a second case holding a landowner liable for the subsidence of neighboring land resulting from excavation. A competing domains question would present facts that straddle the two cases—*e.g.*, a landowner who pumps percolating water from his own land in such quantities and in such a manner as to cause subsidence on neighboring farms.
- In Employment Law, you may study the body of caselaw that protects public-sector employees against discharge in retaliation for exercising the right to free speech protected by the First Amendment. You may also study the common law "employment-at-will" doctrine that would permit private-sector employers to fire their employees for the same conduct. A competing domains question would present facts that straddle the two bodies of law—*e.g.*, the discharge of a teacher at a "charter school" for statements she makes regarding a school bond issue, where the charter school might be characterized as either a public employer (so that the discharge would violate the First Amendment) or a private employer (so that the discharge would be lawful under the at-will rule).

So why do we think problems like these involve "proliferating forks"? Let's take a slightly closer look at yet another competing domains problem. Assume, for example, that in your Torts course you studied a case imposing on property owners a duty of reasonable care regarding property conditions for the protection of their business invitees, and a second case holding that a landowner owes no such duty to a "social guest," since the latter is considered a mere licensee. A question on the final presents a fact pattern that straddles the two cases: Freda Friend comes to Homer Homeowner's house for a Tupperware party—so she's right on the line between a business invitee and a social guest—and during her visit she sustains an injury that results from Homeowner's lack of due care regarding the condition of the property.

Consider the issues that will arise when you analyze this problem. Obviously, we have a "fork in the facts": Friend might be characterized as either a business invitee or a social guest. But do you see that we also have "concurrent forks"? As in our "statutory boundary" case, the path you take at the "fork in the facts" determines the path you must choose at the "fork in the law." If we characterize the injured party as a business invitee, then Homeowner owed her a duty of care and its breach is actionable. But if we characterize the injured party as a social guest, then Homeowner owed her no such duty and the result is *damnum absque injuria*.

But we're not finished yet, for there are "reciprocal forks" buried in this hypothetical as well. As in our hypo dealing with e-mail under the Statute of Frauds, we can "hold the law steady" and take the facts back and forth between the business invitee and the social guest characterizations. But we can also "hold the facts steady" and see whether there is also more than one way to read the law. Perhaps you can offer a "broad" reading of the business invitee case so that it clearly covers the Tupperware party and thus enables Friend to recover; and perhaps you can likewise offer a "narrow" interpretation of the social guest case that will permit you to distinguish Friend's situation. On the other hand, perhaps you can narrow the former case and broaden the latter, and thus reach the opposite result.

In sum, the competing domains case presents two patterns that we've already explored—concurrent forks and reciprocal forks—but the rub is that it presents both patterns simultaneously. (Need to see it again? In the case of the discharged teacher, there are concurrent forks [if the charter school is a *public* employer, then the First Amendment prohibits retaliation for free speech, but if it's a *private* employer, then discharge is permissible under the at-will rule] and also reciprocal forks [you can try to broaden and narrow the cases that define "public" and "private" employers to cover or distinguish the charter school at issue here].) Apart from learning to recognize a fact pattern straddling competing domains, the key to success on questions like these is to sort carefully through the different "forks" in play—and to avoid getting tangled up in knots, a point we'll return to in Part II of the book.

E. Hidden Forks: Dodging the Statute

Imagine that you are taking your Property final and that you encounter an exam question in which a large corporation wants to purchase the land it is leasing from a farm family of modest means. Hoping for the return of better times (or a much better price), the family has thus far refused to sell. The roof of an abandoned farm building on the leased property is leaking badly and would cost the family about $30,000 to repair. Although the large corporation has no use for the building in question, it cites the leak and invokes the provisions of a landlord/tenant statute to excuse further payment of rent, hoping to force the family into selling the property at a bargain price.

A quick review persuades you that under a plain-meaning interpretation of the statute, the family can kiss its farm goodbye. But two considerations persuade you that there must be more to the exam question than this. For one thing, the professor spent a lot of time in class stressing the fact that the statute in question was the result of years of lobbying and protest activity on the part of community groups representing low-income tenants; surely their supporters in the legislature would never have dreamed that their handiwork could be used in this way. For another thing, you have 45 minutes to deal with this question and a look at your watch reveals that you've got 39 of them left. So there simply must be a way to approach the problem beyond the straightforward conclusion that the farm family loses because the statute *says* so.

Fortunately, you've read *Getting to Maybe*, and so you know what to look for. If a plain-meaning interpretation of the statute works against the family, perhaps they can invoke the history and purposes the professor emphasized to argue the case the other way. Recalling the things you can do with the word "vehicle," you begin to wonder whether the corporate lessee is the kind of "tenant" the statute was designed to protect, or whether the provision excusing rent payments in the face of serious defects was intended to apply to unoccupied buildings.

But now that you think about it, you recall reading a case for class that held that a corporate lessee—specifically, a law firm providing legal services to the poor—was a "tenant" within the meaning of the statute. And you recall a second case—involving an abandoned structure that posed hazards to the tenants' children—that extended a landlord's obligations to vacant buildings on the rental property. That wily law professor has drafted the question in a way that seems to "paint you into a corner"; whatever will you do?

As they say in the movies, what you need to do is "get the hell outta Dodge," and in this case Dodge is the statute. In fact, what you need to do is what we call "dodging the statute," and it is really just a variation on the sort of purpose-based arguments we've already used to deal with particular words or phrases or provisions that appear in a statute. The difference here is that you use the purpose-based argument to claim that the statute doesn't apply to the case before you *at all*, because the concerns that prompted the legislature to enact the statute are not even remotely present on the facts. We're not saying this argument is always or even usually a winner; what we are saying is that it is a perfectly respectable argument that a skilled lawyer representing the farm family is likely to make in the circumstances. (The first lawyer who argued that § 2-207 of the U.C.C.—which by its terms covers all non-conforming acceptances—doesn't apply unless the parties are entering a transaction via pre-printed forms went out on precisely this limb, yet there's now a growing body of caselaw accepting that argument.)

So why do we deal with this problem in a chapter called "twin forks"? We've already discussed the competing-interpretations fork: a plain-meaning application (the corporate tenant is permitted to invoke the statute to withhold payment of rent) vs. "dodging the statute" (the statute doesn't apply because it wasn't intended to cover a case like this). But if we dodge the statute, what law governs? Like the "statutory boundary" situation we discussed earlier, if we take the case "out" of the statute, we typically find ourselves back in the familiar environs of the common law.

Sometimes, getting back to the common law will lead directly to a result. In our example, if the lease is silent on the issue, you might conclude that the common law would treat the mutual obligations of landlord and tenant as "independent covenants." This would mean that the corporate tenant would be obligated to continue paying the rent in spite of the farm family's failure to ensure that all the buildings on the leased property were safe and in good repair.

It's quite possible, however, that the common law rule protecting tenants would go well beyond the terms of the statute and relieve the corporation of its rent obligation until the farm was placed in "reasonable" or "habitable" condition. So dodging the statute—a tactic that is easy to miss, since we normally think of statutes as unavoidable—may be a good strategy but not the end of the story.

Once again it's worth focusing on the larger pattern. The choice you make at the competing interpretations fork (do we follow the plain meaning and apply the statute, or do we invoke its purposes to avoid it?) determines the choice with respect to a different fork in the law (if the statute applies, its rules govern the transaction; if it doesn't, the case is governed by the common law). Note finally another aspect of the argument around the statute. Taking the holdings of the cases individually made things seem impossible when you considered the separate holdings that commercial tenants are protected and that unoccupied buildings are covered. Yet viewing each of these holdings as the furthest a court might go from the statute's core purpose —*i.e.*, protecting vulnerable tenants—made it possible to argue that combining them to cover your facts would contravene statutory intent. (See our discussion of multiple cases back in Chapter 5.)

F. Background v. Foreground: Variations on the Twin Forks Theme

Our experience is that the majority of exam questions include twin or multiple forks in which each branch you choose has a direct bearing on the ultimate outcome of a dispute. So, if you pick one version of the law the case will come out one way, and if you pick the alternative legal rule or interpretation you'll get the opposite result. Ditto for the facts.

As we move into our discussion of exam preparation and answer construction, however, we must stress an important point regarding the many ambiguities that we have identified. Not every choice you face on an exam will present you with what we have called a fork. Many times your discussion will begin by spotting a fork (Should I read the case narrowly or broadly? Should I read the statute literally or with purpose in mind?). But as you write your answer, you must go beyond identifying the various alternatives along the branches of what we have called forks. You must also craft arguments favoring one side and the other, and this means choosing which arguments to make on behalf of which side of each fork. As a general rule, your strategy will be to include as many persuasive arguments as possible, and we have devoted all of Chapter 10 to identifying arguments likely to be available to you.

Occasionally, however, your argument selection will link back to the legal choices you confront. This presents professors with delicious opportunities for questions with a twist. Suppose a workplace regulation requires that "all employees wear safety glasses at all times while on the premises." One employee's son is injured while dining in the cafeteria when a freak explosion causes flying debris to hit him in the eye. The employer, charged with a violation for failing to ensure glasses were worn, may rely on a literal reading of the statute to exclude the son ("not an employee"). Yet the employer may also consider arguing that the cafeteria, while literally "on the premises," is not meant to be within the rubric of the statute. (Let's say no one ever wears safety glasses in there.) Similarly, the plaintiff may argue that the statute should be extended to include visitors, since their eyes are just as much at risk. Yet the plaintiff may argue that the phrase "premises" should be read literally to include the cafeteria. You'll score a lot of points with your professor if you notice that each party is being pushed to make seemingly contradictory arguments—we'll call them "conflicting styles"—on different points. We appreciate the added layer of complexity that attention to this sort of detail involves, but, if it's any solace, lawyers often make arguments of conflicting styles in the same case without anyone's noticing.

Some areas of law, however, like constitutional law, demand that special attention be paid to the style as well as the substance of each argument. Tough questions in constitutional law almost always require discussion on at least two levels. You must analyze the particular problem at hand in light of constitutional text and existing precedent. And you may need to invoke more general arguments about the appropriate style of reasoning. This will include reference to topics such as whether the document should be read through the lens of original intent or more as "a living, breathing document."

Consider the litigation that will almost certainly reach the Supreme Court (and in the meantime will be tested on scores of exams) concerning the constitutionality of racial preferences in admission to universities. Both supporters and opponents of preferences have strong arguments referring back to constitutional text, history, and precedent. Supporters of preferences can cite *Regents of the University of California v. Bakke*, 438 U.S. 265 (1978) (seemingly upholding some preference on grounds of diversity) and can also rely on the general purpose of the Fourteenth Amendment to improve the situation of African-Americans. Opponents can point to the literal language of the equal protection clause and to many cases casting a pall on all kinds of race discrimination.

Yet supporters and opponents can also rely on arguments that sound more like interpreting the Constitution in light of the times. Supporters of racial preferences can stress the disastrous resegregation of universities that might result from a constitutional ban on racial preferences. Opponents of preferences may stress the progress society has made in overcoming racism and the present need to move quickly toward color-blindness.

In quickly writing an exam answer about racial preferences it would be tempting, and in many ways satisfactory, simply to include both sets of arguments—the appeal to text, history, and precedent (on the one hand) and the appeal to the current needs of the Nation (on the other)—on both sides. But constitutional law is argued best by stopping to consider whether one kind of argument you assert will ultimately undermine another. As a preference opponent, for example, if you want to rely heavily on the literal language of the document, you may not want also to rely on recent progress. Making the latter argument may hint that you don't think the literal language point is sufficient and open the door for others to disagree on how much progress really has been made. And as a preference supporter, you may worry that an emphasis on the consequences of desegregation may detract from your own efforts to find help in the constitutional language and history.

This last twin fork, then, forms a perfect transition into Part II of this book. For it illustrates that law (especially as it is tested on law school exams) is always as much about crafting arguments as it is about spotting issues. You can't make arguments *until* you spot the issues, but there's plenty left to do once you have.

Part II

Strategies for Issue-Spotting, Analysis, and Argument: Heart, Brains, and Courage

Chapter 8

Taking Exams Seriously: A World Full of Wicked "Whiches"

Part I's description of the multiple issues you may find buried in exams is merely one of many accounts of legal reasoning techniques available to law students and practicing attorneys. We have chosen to emphasize the way in which complex facts often present a set of decisions that lawyers and judges must make in considering how to resolve disputes. That's because this skill is heavily tested. What we want to stress with equal force in Part II is that spotting issues is simply not enough, either to ensure good exam performance or to make yourself into a good lawyer. Your professors are looking for you to push through the ambiguities you find and testing your ability to analyze real-world disputes.

Many people we know (ourselves included) spent a good deal of time in law school decrying the importance of grades and exams. No doubt legal education would be improved if students received more feedback and grades were based on multiple exercises rather than just one exam at the end of each course. We think there are reasons, however—even apart from mere professorial inertia—that the standard law school exam has changed very little over the last 50 years. Exploring those reasons may help you understand why we persist in putting you through all this torture.

Consider the following story. You are an associate in a large Texas law firm, attending a meeting with several other associates and a senior partner, whom we'll call Karla. Karla has called you all together to listen to a problem presented by a long-time client, Fred, the owner of a medium-size, real estate development company. Fred explains that he wants to launch a substantial excavation project in the remote Dallas suburbs. Fred tells you he plans to pump enormous quantities of water from beneath land he owns. He's afraid, however, that all this pumping may cause subsidence of neighboring lands, and that this might even cause damage to homes owned by the many suburban neighbors. Fred tells you that if he has to pay for this damage, the project will become economically infeasible. He wants advice on what to do.

Notice first that this story sounds very much like something that could happen to you in law practice. It also looks very much like a law school exam question. This is no coincidence. It has become fashionable at today's law schools to criticize traditional law school classes for failing to incorporate the performance skills necessary for law practice. Thus, many schools have added required courses in negotiation, witness preparation, client counseling, trial practice, etc. We applaud these developments. From our vantage point, however, there remains a direct and important connection between actual lawyering and the skills tested on traditional law school exams. Indeed, one reason law school exams look so different from tests in other settings is that law exams reflect professors' efforts to get students to stop thinking like performers on quiz shows and start thinking like people whose knowledge can be brought to bear to help clients.

Our story may help illuminate this difference, so let's get back to it. As you read on, notice how many of the participants in the discussion are responding to Karla as if they were taking pages from a playbook written by undergraduates, the law school rumor mongers, or, if the truth be told, other guides to law school exams. See for yourself whether you find the comments of these "associates" fully responsive to the situation.

The tall associate on your left, whom we'll call College Whiz, is the first to speak. "It just so happens," Mr. Whiz pipes up, "that I've been reading a great deal about water law. One thing I have learned is that the law draws a key distinction between underground water that runs in a clear path and percolating water whose course is hard to chart." Whiz grins from ear to ear, expecting a big dose of praise from Karla and the rest of the group. Instead, Karla turns to Fred and asks, "Can you tell us anything about the nature of the water under your land?" "Oh yeah," Fred replies. "I had a geologist out there just last week. It turns out that the water under my land just bubbles all over the place. No one can predict where it will be when, but there sure is a lot of it. I can make a bundle pumping it out and selling it to those big power companies."

The next to speak is a rather quiet associate who seems to know so much about law that everyone has nicknamed him Encyclopedia. He begins inauspiciously. "I think it's important that we all put Fred's problem in the context of the broader history of water law. This past week I have read three books about the origins of riparian rights, the ways in which different communities have grown depending on what water laws they have chosen, and the need for water conservation. I thought I'd tell you all what these books have to say." Two sentences later, Karla asks Encyclopedia to go get coffee, and Fred breathes an audible sigh of relief.

A young woman associate, whom we'll call Ms. Issue-Spotter, chimes in next, thinking she's going to score big. "I think it's pretty clear," she says, "that Fred came here for help with whether he can pump out the water, and he's probably not interested in a long lecture about water law." Fred smiles and the other associates nod gently in approval. Karla, however, is not impressed. "That certainly *is* pretty clear," she says, casting a withering look over at Ms. Issue-Spotter.

Your best friend at the firm, whose parents oddly named her IRAC, is the next to venture into the discussion. "Issue-Spotter is right," she says, "that the **issue** is whether Fred can pump without paying for the damage. The **rule** in Texas is that, as long as you aren't intentionally and maliciously out to hurt your neighbors, you can pump as much percolating water from underneath your land as you would like. **Applying that rule** is simple because Fred is engaged in legitimate commercial activity. So the **conclusion** is plain that Fred can pump without paying for the damage." IRAC is so happy she expects the meeting to be adjourned and a letter written for her promotion file. Karla asks, however, if anyone has anything else to add.

"I sure do," pipes up Mr. Real-World Experience, an older associate whose stint with the firm began only after several years working for his dad's real estate company. "I don't care what the legal rules are," he opines, "for in the end some loose-cannon judge is going to stick it to Fred because courts are going to favor smug suburbanites over risk-taking business folks every time."

"I agree," echoes Ms. Policy. "But it's not a matter of favoritism. It's a matter of weighing costs and benefits. Courts won't want to encourage development that damages the surrounding community, and so I'll bet they'll find a way to hold Fred responsible."

Karla turns to Fred and adds the following: "I think what my colleagues are trying to remind us is that even if the rules initially appear in your favor, we can't expect courts to reach results that defy common sense. Can you dig your wells in such a way that you won't cause any damage?" "I suppose I might be able to," Fred replies, "but that would cost a fortune and might spoil the deal altogether. Is that what you are advising?"

"You'd better at least do that," adds the firm's best-dressed associate, whose parents oddly named him IRAC as well. "I agree the **issue** is whether Fred can pump without paying for the damage. The **rule** in Texas, though, is that an owner is responsible for damage caused by land subsidence. **Applying that rule** means our earlier discussion of underground water is irrelevant. This leads me to the **conclusion** that because Fred knows he's going to cause the subsidence, he'll certainly be liable if he could prevent it easily and might be liable even if there's no way to dig without causing subsidence."

Karla now turns to you and says, "So, where do you come out on all of this?" Every instinct in your competitive body is telling you that you need to take sides. Are you with IRAC your friend, or IRAC the good-dresser, or what about Ms. Policy? If this were Final Jeopardy, you'd either pick the right one or go home empty-handed. But Fred is not a game show host, and

Karla doesn't want your vote—she wants your analysis. You might say something like the following:

"Fred, before we go any further, I'll spend a day in the library trying to discover if there is any case like yours decided in the Texas courts. But since no one here knows of one, I'll probably come up dry. What this means is that if you go ahead and dig, and damage does result, you are likely to be sued by the victims. After all, they will have suffered considerably and are unlikely to accept that without a fight. You will have a strong legal argument that you should not have to pay. Many judges will see this as an open-and-shut case in which you have simply exercised your right to withdraw water from your own property. As you have heard in the discussion, Texas law recognizes that right.

"But, as you also heard, Texas has a different rule that applies to land subsidence cases. These cases normally involve owners who remove soil from their land, but there's no logical reason why they might not be extended to cover withdrawals of water. If your neighbors push this argument, some judges will see them as mixing apples and oranges. But other judges may see a legitimate clash between two valid rules. That clash will be resolved through a combination of gut judgments and careful consideration of social policy. If you want, we can try to put percentages on our estimation of your chances of prevailing. Rough guesses today may give way slightly to more thoughtful judgments after some additional research. For now, however, it seems safe to say that there is a non-trivial risk you'll have to pay even if you dig with the utmost care, and a substantial chance of liability if a court concludes you could have accomplished similar goals by digging more carefully."

Karla says she's heard enough, adjourns the meeting, and asks you to stay behind with her and Fred so that the three of you can go to lunch.

Hard Cases Make Good Exams

We're sure you can tell that our little story, based on the case of *Friendswood Development Co. v. Smith-Southwest Industries*, 576 S.W. 2d 21 (Tex. 1978), was carefully selected to show how even simple questions can lead to a range of conflicting approaches. In the terms we presented in Part I, this legal problem is one of "competing domains." Lawyers often disagree about what percentage of problems in day-to-day practice actually raise such thorny issues. Certainly, there will be times when clients will walk in and ask questions like, "Will I have to pay income tax on money my employer gives me, even though it's not part of my regular salary?" All things being equal, a simple "yes" might suffice here, although further probing might allow you to suggest techniques like company-provided automobiles for business travel that might reduce your client's tax burden. But almost all lawyers agree that clients frequently present issues where the judicial result is in doubt and a great deal of thought is necessary to consider how to proceed. And, what's even more important, virtually all law professors agree that it's the thorny problems that make the best exam questions.

Putting Part I directly into the context of exam preparation, then, allows you to see all our "forks" as answers to the following questions. Where do all those thorny issues come from? What is it about law that generates so much opportunity for argument and thus requires law professors to train students to consider both sides of every question? Who put all those wicked "whiches" into the Wonderful Land of Laws? You should now have a better sense of why law is about issues as much as it is about rules. And so we will proceed in the rest of this Part to discuss techniques for improving your ability to spot issues on your exams and to handle them well when you find them. We want to close this chapter, however, with a few more observations about the connection between the constructed world of the law school exam and the real world of the practicing lawyer.

Return, then, to our story about groundwater. The easiest point to see is that the legal story begins not when Fred decides he wants to pump, but at the moment it occurs to him that his neighbors might be damaged and might seek legal redress. It's conflict like this, actual or potential, that is always the root of legal problems. As you read through many exam guides, ours included, you'll note recurring advice about how an important way to organize your answers is to pay careful attention to the various parties named or adverted to in the question. This is a useful technique to develop, but it's important not to forget where it comes from. Pairing one party against another to assess whether there are grounds for legal redress is not an artificial performance enhancement for exams but a logical outgrowth of the nature of legal practice.

Remembering that law begins with conflict is also a useful antidote to the overly formulaic approach to rules that we cautioned against in Part I. Fred's lawyers must start from the point that there are neighbors out there who may be harmed by what Fred wants to do. No rule Fred can cite, or law he can pull from a book, will make their loss or potential anger disappear. They may be able to hire their own lawyers who will devote all their intellectual energy to figuring out some way to translate their actual injury into a legal cause of action. Our example is tailored so that the well-dressed IRAC is able to pull out the subsidence rule as a counter to the water rules. As we have seen, such rule conflicts often make good issues for exam analysis. They also show how sometimes the issue in a case is which of two bodies of law should be applied, an issue that might be lost if you are blindly following the IRAC method. Like our hero in the story, what you need to do on exams is move rapidly and aggressively in linking issue recognition to what your "client" wants to do.

But even when rules aren't paired so neatly, the lawyers for the neighbors are unlikely to give up without finding something in the law to support their case. Conflicts like that between Fred and the neighbors pit one person's right to do what he wants on his property against another's right to be secure in hers. Since American law values and protects both rights, it's only natural that the law will contain provisions that point in both directions. And the number of conflicting values we treasure — things like liberty/equality, free speech/fair trial, or efficiency/due process — make conflicts in the law unavoidable and give law professors ample opportunity to invent problems that will pull you in both directions.

Keeping in mind the human dimension of legal conflict will also help prevent you from getting stuck on only one issue. Notice that Fred comes to his lawyers wanting to know whether he'll have to pay if he pumps out the water. A blizzard of studying and cramming categories into your head may help you to recall that there's an issue of whether Fred's withdrawal of the groundwater was done negligently. And if you read back through our story you'll see that this issue, as much as the one Fred originally posed, eventually became important to the discussion. But if you imagined Fred in a room with the injured neighbors, this issue would quickly leap out at you. When Fred says to the neighbors something like, "I made a good profit selling that water, and after all I only took water that was rightfully mine," you just know some neighbor will shoot back, "Yeah, but did you really have to pull the water out like *that*?"

In sum, the vast panoply of disputes that form the core of law school exam questions are no more than a formalized representation of the variety of human conflicts that occur in our complex society. Think back over your own life and ask yourself how many serious conflicts you have had that could readily be resolved with a simple yes-or-no answer. That's all it takes to begin to understand why most law school exams are about *Getting to Maybe*.

Chapter 9

How To Spot Issues, and What To Do Once You Spot Them

Now that you have seen what issues—or what we have called "forks"—look like, there are only two questions you need to answer to ensure your place at or near the top of your class. First, what can you do to learn to recognize "forks" when they appear on your exams? You know, and so do we, that it's not enough for you to sit and read someone else's description of "forks" in the comfort of the library; you need to know how you can learn to spot them on actual exams. Second, and equally important, you need to know what to *do* with the "forks" when you find them. Once again, it won't be enough merely to tell the professor you have "spotted" an issue.

We're going to tackle these two crucial questions over the course of the remaining chapters. But if we used the same detailed style that we used in Part I, this breezy, "how-to" book would read more like a 19th century treatise. So we are going to proceed along the following lines instead. In this chapter we will concentrate our energy on two key areas. First, what lessons can we draw from our chapters on forks that will help you tailor your studying with an eye toward exam preparation? It stands to reason that the study techniques you developed as an undergraduate are sub-optimal from a law school exam standpoint, since your earlier exams were very different. Second, what are the crucial components of writing exam answers that help you move forcefully from spotting forks to analyzing issues and suggesting results? We think each of these topics is large enough to deserve more than what we say in this chapter. That's why we include in Part III a set of "Test-Taking Tips" that will provide illustrations and extensions of the key points we make here. These Tips alone can take you a long way toward better performance.

Two myths, however, are particularly pernicious and deserve special rebuttal in this chapter. First, many people believe there is no way to learn to spot issues. As we will show, this is utter nonsense. Second, many people speak as if exam writing involves little more than the application of rules to a given set of facts. If you've stuck with us this far, you already know that this can't be true. There is so much ambiguity in any rule structure that rote application will seldom get you anywhere. Indeed, we hope that after reading our criticisms of what is known as the IRAC method, you will never let anyone around you say something so foolish again.

But, if spotting the issues isn't enough and rote application won't work, what will? In a nutshell, we want you to see every issue-spotting problem as really asking two questions. The first asks you to identify the forks we have described so extensively. This chapter—together with what you've learned from the book so far—should give you the tools necessary to become adept at that. The second question asks for an analysis of which road the court should follow. The challenge is to make the transition from noticing, for example, that a case might be read broadly or narrowly to arguing that it *should* be read broadly or narrowly. We introduce that topic in the second half of this chapter. The multiple array of "should" arguments, however, is so important to top performance that we leave a complete analysis to the next chapter; you'll need to read what it feels like to be a "Czar of the Universe" before you are ready to tackle your next set of exams.

A. Issue-Spotting

1. What the Course Will Tell You If You Listen

a. Classnotes and outlines

You have heard from your professors and countless other sources (and you'll hear it again from us) that you cannot prepare adequately for exams merely by reading commercial outlines or even outlines prepared by other students. You are now in a position to understand why.

Part of the reason, of course, is that no outline can tell you how to be creative in responding to the new situations your exams present. The real problem with most law school outlines, however, is that they are organized solely around topics and rules. Your Contracts outline will tell you about formation, breach, and damages. Your Property outline will discuss types of ownership. Your Torts outline will teach you the difference between strict liability and negligence, between directness and foreseeability as tests for proximate causation. Your Criminal Law outline will review types of intent. You need to know all these things. But as should be clear from "fork proliferation," they are not enough.

You need to know not only the rules. You also need to know all the places where the rules don't yet settle all the questions likely to arise. There's no reason to expect someone else's outline to answer these questions. That's not what outlines are intended to do. Students often think professors are being elitist, pretentious, or worse when we tell you that commercial outlines aren't the answer to your prayers. That's because you are reading our criticisms through old lenses. We don't mean to imply that you can't often trust commercial outlines to give you accurate statements of the law (although clearly some are better than others). Nor do we mean to suggest that the outlines don't sometimes do a better job than even some of us can in presenting the existing material in an organized fashion. The big problem is that if you think *learning* the material is all you need to do to perform well, then you haven't been paying attention so far.

We recommend an additional (not a substitute) approach to outlining your classes. Rather than simply passively accumulating the information presented, you should employ the techniques we have described in Part I. Some ideas for such outlining might include:

- Find some statutes discussed in the course and identify the underlying purposes of the statutes. But don't stop with a list of purposes; that's what other outlines do. Instead, force yourself to invent situations where the multiple purposes compete with each other and consider how a court might resolve these situations. Put those examples into your outline.

- Find those areas of your course that are organized in what we refer to as the "gantlet" structure — as a series of elements that must be satisfied before one party can prevail. Put in your outline examples where it's not clear whether each of the elements is satisfied.

- Read over your cases and include in your outline not only what they settle, but what they leave open. This is a fundamentally different strategy from what you'll find in almost any other discipline. You want to study what you *don't* know as much as what you do.

- Outline your course around foundational "forks in the law" and recurring "forks in the facts." Any respectable Torts outline would describe the differences between strict liability and negligence, perhaps the crucial "fork" in the course, and would also detail some of the underlying policy arguments that might push courts toward one doctrine or the other. But in your *Getting to Maybe* outline, you would go beyond the definitions of strict liability and negligence — which you would have already learned by heart, along with virtually all your other classmates. You would identify the strict liability vs. negligence fork as one of the key *choices* the tort system faces. You would then list the places where that system appears to have chosen one or the other and attempt to see where ambiguities still arise. Can you broaden the "lead case" on strict liability to cover handguns or snowmobiles? And what are the key "forks in the facts"? If there's strict liability for "products," for example, is a genetically engineered vegetable a "product"? How about a cloned sheep?

• Finally, the best advice we can give for outlining is to think of yourself not merely as responding to but inventing hypotheticals. Those long exam questions from prior years that you should be poring over may appear daunting. Whatever are you to do with all that ambiguity? You know now, however, precisely where all that ambiguity comes from. If you practice writing some questions of your own, you'll put yourself in the mind-set where rules that seemed clear may suddenly seem more ambiguous and open-ended. This will mean you are surely on the right track.

A similar point should be made about classnotes. When you sit in a lecture during undergraduate school, your vision of the professor may be of someone who has information to impart. If class discussion digresses from the professor's main points, you may find yourself nodding off, or in any event not taking notes any more. Law professors too have information to transmit, but that's not really the point of a law school class. Instead, the class discussion is designed to highlight ambiguities and alternative perspectives. As each student raises yet another possibility, the professor will keep pushing for more. It's not crucial that you take down every word. But, as you are taking notes, one thing to look for is how ambiguities in the material opened the discussion in the first place. Why wasn't the case you are discussing open and shut? Why does the professor think it worth considering an alternative point of view? The places where the law is unclear are as important for your studying as—even more important than—the places where the law is clear.

There is also every reason to believe that class discussion will provide hints about the nature of your exam that will help you spot issues. One common class technique will be for a professor to ask whether two cases decided by the same court are inconsistent. A long discussion may then ensue in which some students argue that the cases can be reconciled. Other students will suggest no reconciliation is possible. Many students are then annoyed if the professor fails to adjudicate between the student camps. If the professor doesn't tell the class whether the cases are or are not inconsistent, many students feel the class had no resolution and nothing was learned to go into notes or an outline. The contrary, however, is true. Emphasis on this particular inconsistency means the professor believes it's a pressure point for future legal development. If the professor is astute, the tensions she identifies may eventually give rise to actual disputes you'll confront in legal practice. But if you are astute, you'll watch for this inconsistency to show up even sooner—on your exam.

b. Themes and "issues"

As former college students ourselves, we have enormous sympathy for a certain sense of shock that strikes people as they move from undergraduate to law school. University courses often focus on big themes—the shift from classicism to romanticism, the clash between fiscal and monetary policy, the People's Congress vs. the Imperial Presidency. There's a sense of loss in giving these up for a narrow-minded focus on the exact provisions of the U.C.C. or the Internal Revenue Code.

A good law school course, however, quickly restores a student's faith in the intellectual challenge of her chosen profession. There she'll hear discussions of themes every bit as large as those encountered while an undergraduate. Criminal law may involve deep questions of free will and determinism. Contract law may pit notions of paternalism against a so-called free market. Tort law may match spreading losses against notions of individual responsibility.

The pain is thus perhaps doubly great when you turn from your class discussions to your exam preparation. You may say to your Property professor, "All semester long we had this great conversation about the balance between protecting investment and encouraging competition. And now you want me to tell you whether some silly covenant 'touches and concerns the land.'" More generally, you may legitimately wonder why so many of your classes focus on big themes, yet your exams are mostly fact patterns that require "only" issue-spotting and analysis. And if you wonder too much, you may begin to tune out discussion of themes altogether, so as to focus on what you think you need for top performance. We urge you not to make this mistake.

The broader themes your professors build into your courses are directly relevant to issue-spotting and analysis. You just need to know where to look. The whole point of our discussion of forks is to illustrate how many places the law leaves room for argument about the right result. And what makes the law so grand is that once the argument has begun, it's impossible to keep the themes out.

Even the "silly" question about whether a particular covenant "touches and concerns the land" may directly invite a discussion of the very theme, investment vs. competition, that our hypothetical student felt was the best part of the class. Suppose the covenant placed on the land by the seller requires the new owner not to use the site as a research facility. Assume that such facilities are unlikely to produce more noise or traffic than the other uses of land in the area, and that the seller's sole purpose for including the restriction was to foreclose competition with his own research facility on an adjacent lot. An exam analysis of whether the covenant "touches and concerns the land" might start with familiar interpretive issues like whether enforcing the restriction must safeguard the seller's land from physical consequences or whether any effect on the market value of the seller's land is sufficient to meet the "touch and concern" test. But you'll miss the whole point of the question if you don't see how this interpretive issue is linked to the broader theme. A pro-competition court will want new research facilities to be built and thus may look skeptically upon the seller's efforts to satisfy the "touch and concern" requirement. But a court eager to protect seller's original investment will be much more open to arguments that the "touch and concern test" has been met.

And this Property example is the norm, not the exception. Nitty-gritty disputes about doctrinal issues that appear on exams are almost always connected to the big themes of the course. Whether an actor in a movie possesses a criminal intent when he strikes the victim and causes harm during a scene is the kind of question you might find on an exam. Yet you can't answer it fully without grasping broader themes of Criminal Law. A Torts exam, as we've noted before, may ask whether a landlord is responsible for burns caused when the lack of hot water leads a tenant to boil water and accidentally spill it. You can't answer questions like this without knowing rules like "the doctrine of proximate cause." But your answer will also suffer if you don't see that determining whether the landlord should pay raises the issues of fault, loss spreading, and responsibility that have been the larger themes of your course.

If you simply write an essay on those themes when responding to an issue-spotter, you will do poorly indeed. And, in that sense, law school *does* ask for different responses than an undergraduate essay on classicism vs. romanticism. But the themes you study are nonetheless crucial to top performance on issue-spotters. Indeed, you might use them to help predict the particular issues the professor finds worthy of treatment on the exam. Above all, pay attention when your professor or your classmates try to link doctrinal issues to the larger themes and issues you came to learn in the first place. That's what a first-class legal education is about, and that's what you'll find tested at exam time.

c. Old exams and study groups

The kind of outlining and study of themes we describe above is not easy. But here we have not just good, but very good, news. In many cases, your professor will have done a great deal of the work for you. That's because you'll often find copies of old exams on file in the library. If you care about your performance at all—and we know you do or you wouldn't be reading this— you simply cannot pass up the opportunity to review carefully your professor's old exams. You'll hear this from others (and, because it's so important, you'll hear it from us again). But here we want to make the case explicitly in terms of our "forks" approach.

Your professor may have taught the course several times before. In each old exam she will have had to invent problems that present precisely the kinds of "forks" we identified in Part I. It's good practice to learn to identify these "forks" simply because it will help you learn to hunt for issues rather than merely spinning out rules. But, even better, *it's more than likely that some of the "forks" you find on old exams will show up again on yours.* Most professors have particular "forks" they find especially interesting or at least useful for writing exam questions, and they are not shy about repeating them. So when you read over old exams, it's not merely to get practice in the abstract but also to teach yourself some of your professor's patterns. In writing this book, each of us read over several exams given by the other. We're sure we could do a lot better on another of those exams now than we might have cold turkey. Even the most energetic and creative professors, who think they are doing something new every time, in fact tend to fall back on old habits—like a poker player who can't help making a certain expression every time he has a good hand.

We urge you to bring along *Getting to Maybe* when you sit down with your old exams so that you can explicitly look for the kinds of forks we describe. Don't worry. Like Waldo, they are in there somewhere. But we urge you to bring along something else as well: your classmates. Once you see that exam preparation is as much about hunting for things you don't know as memorizing things you do, you can see much more clearly why studying alone may not be enough. Finding those forks is difficult the first time through. If you do it with friends, each of you will find some forks the others don't. So by the time you get to the exam, you'll have seen enough of them so that the ones actually tested will either be ones you have encountered before or sufficiently similar that you'll be likely to recognize the pattern.

2. What the Exam Will Tell You If You Let It

No matter how well prepared you are, and no matter how many times you have read *Getting to Maybe*, the exam setting is likely to present unforeseen issues and difficulties. In Part III we provide some practical tips on how to handle the experience. Here, however, we want to offer more substantive advice on several general techniques that will help you find and organize the forks.

a. Map the parties' claims and conflicts

We know you have read countless exam guides that have told you to pay special attention to the parties described in the question and who has what claim against whom. You are now in better position to understand why that's so important. It's the conflict between parties, like the conflict between Fred and his neighbors in the previous chapter, that creates all the forks in the first place. There's only a fork in the law, like a dispute over which of two rules to apply, when it's in one party's interest to apply one rule and another party's interest to apply a different rule. Paying special attention to the parties and the nature of their conflicts will thus almost always help get you started on issue or "fork" identification.

We recommend thinking through your exam problems from the perspective of each party. If the plaintiff says this about the law, how will the defendant respond? If the defendant characterizes the facts this way, how will the plaintiff characterize them? This will get you into the right frame of mind for aggressively identifying and analyzing the relevant issues.

There is also a role for good old-fashioned "black-letter law" in all of this. In most of your courses, you will learn the "gantlet" of conventional elements of various claims and defenses. The classic example is the doctrine of adverse possession—that old chestnut from the Property course—the seven elements of which (open, hostile, continuous, etc.) are memorized and forgotten by generation after generation of law students.

Most students enter law school under the impression that what they're going to have to do for three years is memorize lists of this sort and, dull as that may sound, many are more than a little disappointed when they find out that their professors want them to focus instead on cases and hypotheticals that test the meaning of this element or that one and its application to exotic facts. (Does mooring a sailboat at a seemingly abandoned dock near your beach house for eight summers constitute "continuous" use? If the farmer waves and smiles at your kids as he blithely plows a portion of your land, is his incursion "hostile"?)

Accordingly, it won't get you very far on an exam if you simply copy a list of elements into your bluebooks. But what your list *can* do is provide you with a useful map as you search for issues buried like treasure in your exam questions. To continue our example, an excellent way to go about identifying the issues in an adverse possession hypothetical is to work your way carefully through the list of elements as you sort through the facts presented, looking for forks and ambiguities. The list may also provide you with a good way of constructing a roadmap for your reader. ("First, I will discuss whether mooring the boat during the summer constitutes 'continuous' use. Then I will consider whether the use was 'open,' etc.") The point, then, is not to regurgitate the list, but to *use* it.

b. Don't stop with the first issue you see

Apart from finals, perhaps the most anxiety-provoking experience for the typical law student is the first-year orientation party. A common strategy for coping with this peculiar rite-of-passage is to cruise the room looking for a familiar face in the sea of strangers — ideally someone you knew from undergraduate or high school, but desperate times call for desperate measures, so even someone you just met earlier that day will do. This "start with the familiar" strategy can provide some comfort — and, as you are introduced to your friend's friends and then to their friends, a base from which to begin "working the room" — but it can also be self-defeating. Thus, if you spend all evening sticking like Velcro to the one person you already know, it's going to be a mighty dull party for you as well as for the object of your anxious embrace. When we were in law school — a thousand years ago — we called such persons "cling-ons," and we learned to watch out for them at social functions.

You may be surprised to learn that the anxieties of law school finals drive some students to adopt a strikingly similar strategy on their exams. Faced with the daunting task of analyzing a dense one-and-a-half- to two-page single-spaced hypothetical involving (for example) a multi-vehicle disaster and a cast of dozens, these students panic and quickly scan the question for something, *anything* they might recognize. They focus like a laser beam on the first familiar issue they see ("Aha, there's a contributory negligence vs. comparative negligence issue!"), and embrace it to the exclusion of a veritable glut of other issues lurking in the facts (*e.g.*, issues involving negligence *per se*; inviting rescue; proximate cause; multiple causes; damages). Like the social "cling-on," the exam-taking "cling-on" is only searching for security in an extremely discomfiting setting. But the exam-taking "cling-on" isn't any likelier than his social counterpart to be happy with the results of his efforts.

c. If the answer seems too easy, it probably is

Assume you encounter a hypothetical on your Contracts final that goes something like this: Seller agrees to supply widgets to buyer for $500,000; seller breaches the contract and refuses to part with the promised widgets; buyer purchases the widgets elsewhere for $600,000 to meet her pressing needs. What are buyer's damages? Under U.C.C. § 2-712, buyer is entitled to the difference between the "cost of cover"—*i.e.*, the cost of purchasing replacement goods—and the contract price. Accordingly, the answer here appears to be pretty straightforward: $600,000 – $500,00 = $100,000.

But what's wrong with this picture? In a nutshell, it's this: Law exams almost *never* test anything as easy as the ability to subtract $500,000 from $600,000, so if you think that's the "answer," chances are you haven't yet fully grasped the complexity of the question. We appreciate that you may be tempted to stick with "$100,000" despite this warning; after all, simple subtraction is something even the most math-anxious among us can handle, while the rules governing (for example) a buyer's remedies under the U.C.C. may seem utterly confusing in contrast. But when an answer seems that easy and straightforward, there is almost surely an issue lurking in there somewhere that you missed the first time through. Here are three specific ways you might go about spotting it:

(1) *Retrace your thinking step-by-step*. One of the most effective strategies for spotting issues is to think the problem through once again and undertake a careful, "step-by-step" audit of your initial analysis. To continue with our widget-sale example, your re-thinking might go something like this:

> Under § 2-712(2), Buyer is entitled to the "cost of cover" less the contract price. The facts state that the contract price is $500,000; what's the "cost of cover"? Sub-(1) of the provision defines "cover" as a "reasonable purchase" of substitute goods. Buyer bought substitute widgets here for $600,000; is that a

"reasonable purchase"? Well, we don't have many facts about the purchase; all we really know about it is the price Buyer paid, which is $600,000. Is that a "reasonable" figure? How would *I* know? There's nothing in the facts—like a market price—to compare it with. Wait a minute: I can compare it with the contract price, and it is a full $100,000 more than $500,000—that's 20% higher. That's a lot; maybe the issue is whether the price is just too high to be a "reasonable purchase."

Chances are, the ability to spot and grapple with this "reasonableness" issue is the "fork in the facts" that the professor was attempting to test with her question, and retracing the analysis in this step-by-step fashion is a good way of finding it if you missed it the first time.

(2) *Force yourself to argue the "other side."* Another effective strategy for "figuring out what you missed" in a question is to imagine that you are the lawyer for the party who has the most to lose from the seemingly "easy" answer. Suddenly, what seemed to be a virtue in your original answer (*i.e.*, that it is easy to subtract $500,000 from $600,000) is outweighed by a vice (*i.e.*, your client stands to lose $100,000!). What can you do to reduce or minimize your client's loss? Just as retracing your steps can reveal questionable assumptions, *attacking* an answer from the "other side" can achieve the same purpose. Seller's lawyer is likely to react skeptically to buyer's claim that a figure 20% in excess of the contract price was a "reasonable" cover, and that is precisely the sort of skepticism that the professor is looking for—and likely to reward—on your exam.

(3) *Work out your analysis on paper.* Don't let the way we've divided up this chapter fool you: Spotting issues (on the one hand) and dealing with them in an answer (on the other) are not always discrete phases of exam writing. Indeed, the first two suggestions for ways to spot additional issues—*i.e.*, retracing your thinking step-by-step and forcing yourself to argue the other side—are approaches that may yield better results if you do them on paper than in your head, for many of us need "to see whether it writes" in order to figure out what we think. Moreover, there's no better place to do hard thinking about an exam

question than right there in the bluebook where the professor can see it and reward it. To continue our example, an answer that begins with a frank admission that "$100,000 is too easy" and proceeds to discover the "reasonable purchase" issue, either by re-examining the initial assumptions or by attacking them from the other side, is the law school equivalent of the Return of the Prodigal Son. Since most law professors care more about the quality of your analysis than the accuracy of your answers, you may well get more credit by showing the professor how you "found your way back" to an issue than would an answer that simply spots the issue and moves on.

d. If you finish early, "check your work"

One of the most common characteristics of law exams is that they ask you to do about a week's worth of analysis in four hours or less. We don't defend that tradition—indeed, we think there's a lot to be said for using the extended (eight-to-48-hour) "take-home" exam instead—but the point here is that, with the rarest of exceptions, your professor won't give you anywhere near the time that even an experienced lawyer would need to offer a thoroughgoing and competent analysis of each question. Accordingly, if you finish an exam early because you think you've said all there is to say, *you are almost surely wrong*. Once again, you may be attempting to transplant undergraduate test-taking habits to the law school setting, and, once again, you would be making a serious mistake.

The point of re-checking your answers on the "memorize-and-regurgitate" college exam is to make sure that your answers are *right*; once that is accomplished, there is little to be gained by sticking around for yet another read-through. But the point of re-checking your answers on a law exam is not so much to make sure that they are "right"; once again, there is frequently no "right" answer to a law school exam question, and, even when there is, most professors are more interested in how you got there than in your doctrinal accuracy at the bottom line. What you should be doing instead is carefully re-reading the questions and your answers—and, if time and exam instructions permit, going back through your course outline—to see whether there is some issue, some argument, some angle, some complexity you missed in your analysis.

On the basis of the thousands of exams we've graded, we'd say that the odds are better than even that you missed a lot the first time around and about 100-to-1 that you are missing at least one issue or argument that the professor thinks is extremely important. Wouldn't you rather figure that out before the grader does?

B. What To *Do* with Issues Once You Spot Them

1. You Already Know More than You Think You Do

Here's more good news. Although mere issue-spotting will seldom be enough for an "A," top-notch issue identification will persuade most professors to look more favorably on your answers. That's because issue recognition has been a key factor in exam grading since long before we had the pleasure of enduring our own exams as students 20 years ago. As a senior colleague put it to us early in our teaching career, "You've *got* to test issue-spotting. How else can you tell how smart they are?"

We were skeptical then, and we aren't persuaded now, that issue-spotting measures intelligence. We think it's more likely that the skills for identifying issues are poorly taught in many law school settings, leaving most students to the luck of their own devices. That's one reason we wrote this book. Indeed, doubts about issue-spotting as a measure of performance have led some professors to write exams that emphasize analysis and argument instead. Be that as it may, however, issue-spotting remains the *sine qua non* of successful exam performance, if only because in most exam questions seeing the issue is the first step toward knowing what it is you are supposed to analyze or to argue about.

So your tour through Part I has already taken you a long way toward the finish line. The patterns we identify there will make you better at "hunting for Waldo." Better still, we hope, is that the "forks" lexicon you have been learning will help usher you down the road of analysis and argument. That's because virtually every fork we describe begins with a conflict in which you can safely anticipate that the arguments for the two sides will flow nicely out of the issues you spot. To see how and why, let's go back to our tried-and-true tricycle in the park. Consider the following two answers to whether it's banned under the "no vehicles" statute:

> Answer # 1. It's not clear whether the tricycle is prohibited since the terms of the statute could be read to cover it or not.

> Answer # 2. Determining whether the tricycle is banned from the park depends on whether we stick to the statute's "plain meaning" or delve more deeply into statutory purpose. On the plain-meaning view, the tricycle would seem to be banned, although even that's not clear because some meanings of the term may require things like "carrying passengers" that a trike might not do. If we look to the rule's purpose, we need to examine further which of the many potentially competing purposes a court may find decisive.

We're sure you see that Answer # 2 is superior. But let's focus for a moment on why that is so.

First, by sticking to a general description, Answer # 1 comes up with only one issue, whereas Answer # 2 spots at least three: "plain meaning of the rule vs. its purpose"; "competing meanings of vehicle"; and "competing purposes of the prohibition." (By the way, did you see the "linked" forks?) So, on issue-spotting alone, Answer #2 is miles ahead.

Answer #2's second advantage, however, is even more decisive. You've heard repeatedly since you entered law school that your professors want analysis and argument, not just issue-spotting. Answer # 1 doesn't advance that endeavor at all. By contrast, Answer # 2 is aimed precisely at providing a blueprint to construct the analysis and arguments your professors are looking for. That's because stating issues in terms of "forks"—like plain meaning vs. purpose—tells you right away that each party (presumably, the government vs. the tricycle rider's parents) has an argument available to promote its side of the case.

2. From Issue-Spotting to Issue Analysis

Thinking of issues as "forks in the road" will help you improve your analysis in two ways. First, you should ask yourself, "What caused the road to split in the way it is?" Second, you'll want to know, "Where will I end up if I go one way or another?" Keeping those questions in mind is key to good exam writing, as we hope a return to our familiar Artiste/Patron example will make clear.

Recall that Paul Patron offers Arlene Artiste $10,000 to paint a portrait of the Patron family and, in response to her unwillingness to commit to a completion date, states that he wants "a portrait, not a commitment." After Artiste spends numerous hours doing preliminary sketches, but before she has put brush to canvas to begin the actual portrait, Patron advises her that he has changed his mind and is revoking the offer. Your exam asks, "What legal rights does Artiste have against Patron?"

> Answer # 1. Whether Patron can revoke his offer will depend on whether we apply the common law rule or the rule provided by § 45 of the Second Restatement. If we apply § 45, there will then be a second issue about whether Artiste's work so far counts as having begun performance.
>
> Answer # 2. Patron can revoke if the old common law rule applies or, even if § 45 of the Restatement governs, if a court can be persuaded that Artiste has yet to begin performance. Patron's right to revoke under the common law is based on the fact that his offer seeks a performance (painting a portrait) rather than a return promise (he says he doesn't want a commitment); thus it constitutes an offer to form a unilateral contract. At common law, such offers can be revoked any time until performance is complete, and Artiste has not yet finished the painting. Section 45 of the Restatement replaces the common law rule with one more favorable to offerees in this context. It will prohibit revocation once Artiste has begun (as opposed to completed) performance. Patron will contend that since there's "no brush to canvas," performance has not yet begun. Artiste will counter that the preliminary

sketchwork counts as the beginning of performance and is more than "mere preparations."

Once again we're sure you'll see that Answer #2 is superior. To be sure, Answer # 1 has the virtue of spotting the central issues and, as we've explained, "that's not nothing." But Answer # 2 is better because it addresses the two questions that are the keys to a successful analysis.

First, Answer # 2 explains *why* there's a fork—why the road is split as it is—and it does so both for the "fork in the law" and the "fork in the facts." At the "fork in the law," Answer # 2 identifies the facts and reasoning that trigger the rule vs. counter-rule situation: Because Patron's offer sought a performance rather than a return promise, it may be characterized as an offer to make a unilateral contract, and the common law rule governing the revocation of such offers (revocation permitted until acceptance is completed) differs from the rule under the Restatement (revocation prohibited once performance is begun). In short, understanding the "fork in the law" not only helps you "identify the issue," but it also permits you to explain why there's an issue in the first place.

At the "fork in the facts," Answer # 2 does the same thing once again: It identifies the facts (Artiste has done sketchwork but has not begun work on the portrait itself) that could lead down one road (sketchwork as the beginning of performance) as well as another (sketchwork as mere preparations).

The second successful strategy of Answer # 2 is that it carefully explains what will happen in the dispute between Patron and Artiste if each of the issues is resolved in a particular way. If we resolve the "fork in the law" issue one way (common law), then Patron can revoke; if we resolve it the other way (§ 45), then it depends on whether Artiste has begun performance (Patron can't revoke) or undertaken mere preparations (he can revoke). Such a focus on ultimate outcomes is so important we will return to it again later. For now, however, notice how Answer # 2 takes the reader carefully through all these steps and links. It's simple and straightforward when you read it. But you need to learn to do it on your own, which you can if you remember to explain why the road we take at the fork matters to the parties.

3. The Recipe for Argument Construction: Just Add Reasons

On law exams, analysis is good; good analysis is even better; and argument is better still. Let's take it to the next level, then, and talk about what it takes to move from "mere analysis" to "argument construction." One way to describe the difference is to say that an argument is an analysis that attempts to *persuade*. That's an extremely useful definition for our purposes, since persuasion — of opponents, of judges, of juries — is what most lawyers do for a living and what most law exam questions are designed to test.

A concrete example may help you see vividly the difference between mere analysis and argument. Imagine once again that you're an associate in Karla's Texas law firm and that, as a reward for your brilliant handling of Fred's land subsidence case, she has asked you to work on a case for one of the firm's oldest and most important clients: Arlene Artiste. (Actually, you were hoping for a raise, but you're happy with the vote of confidence the assignment seems to represent and with another opportunity to impress the firm's number-one rainmaker.)

The case, of course, is *Artiste v. Patron*, and an hour ago you gave Karla a memo that reads just like Answer # 2 from the previous section (*i.e.*, the answer that analyzed the issues in the Artiste/Patron case rather than merely spotting them). You've been waiting nervously when the intercom on the phone emits a loud buzz and Karla summons you to her partner-size office with a partner-pleasing view.

"This is fine work," she says as you walk in and sit down. "Your memo is very helpful. But you forgot something. Something big, I'm afraid. As I understand it, we have a bit of work ahead of us if we're going to win this one for Arlene. First, we'd have to persuade a court to go with the Restatement approach rather than the old common law rule. Then we'd have to argue successfully that Arlene's sketchwork was 'the beginning of performance.' Do I have it right?"

"Yes, that pretty much covers it," you respond, wondering what on earth she thinks you left out.

"So, how are we going to do that? You got cases? *Texas* cases? *Arguments?* You know, they don't let us pay the judges for ruling in our favor anymore," she teases. "We gotta convince 'em just like everybody else." She seems slightly amused by your obvious embarrassment at the lapse, and you retrieve the memo and scoot quickly from her office, heading for another long night in the firm library.

* * * * *

But if Answer # 2 doesn't tell you how to go about persuading a judge, it certainly does have the virtue of telling you exactly what it is that you have to persuade the judge *of*. In the same way that identifying the forks in the road offers you a blueprint for an analysis of the question, it also offers you a blueprint for your arguments as well. Your job (if you choose to accept it) is to make arguments for choosing the path of § 45 at the fork in the law, and to make arguments for choosing the path of "sketchwork = beginning of performance" at the fork in the facts, and that's not Mission Impossible. But you'd better get started right away, for there's almost surely a young associate burning the midnight oil on the other side of town trying to figure out how to persuade the court to go the other way at each of those forks.

a. Keep in mind who the real judge is

The kind of persuasion that lawyers do for a living and the persuasion that students are supposed to do on exams are alike in more ways than just the one suggested by this story. When you think about it, a lawyer is typically attempting to persuade at least two audiences at the same time. Her primary task may be to persuade some decisionmaker (the judge, the jury, etc.) to see the case her way. But for a host of reasons, she's also trying to persuade her client that she's a competent lawyer. On law exams, students are also pitching to two audiences, yet here the priorities are reversed. The question may ask them to persuade a judge or a senior partner or opposing counsel of this or that proposition, but the real point of the exercise is to persuade the *grader* that you are doing a good job of persuading the hypothetical decisionmaker.

We can think of no better way to begin that task than by making the arguments that the law professor taught you in the course. If she assigned a series of articles that offered economic arguments on both sides of the contributory vs. comparative negligence debate, then if you get a question on the exam involving a negligent plaintiff, for heaven's sake use the arguments she's taught you. Similarly, if you spent several classes discussing the virtues of various approaches to interpreting statutes (*e.g.*, a purpose-based approach will further the legislature's aims in cases it hadn't foreseen, but a plain-meaning approach will encourage the legislature to draft more carefully in the first place), then use those arguments when you encounter a competing-interpretations question on her final.

If the professor hasn't rehearsed specific arguments on a question, consider the larger "themes and 'issues'" she emphasized in the course. If, for example, throughout the semester your Contracts class explored the conflict between the importance of protecting reliance (on the one hand) and the importance of promoting freedom of action (on the other), then don't be afraid to draw your arguments from that resource. To continue with *Artiste v. Patron*, § 45 has the advantage over the common law approach of protecting the reliance of an offeree who is vulnerable to revocation during an extended performance; but the common law rule has the advantage of protecting the offeror's freedom of action until the last possible moment.

b. Once again, you already know more than you think you do

(i) Patterns of argument for forks in the facts

Yet another advantage to the "forks in the road" approach is that many of the patterns we explored in Part I lead directly to patterns of argument. This is true in particular of the patterns we explored in Chapter 6 on "forks in the facts." Let's look at a concrete example by focusing on the second of the two issues presented in *Artiste v. Patron*—the fork you encounter if we follow the path of Restatement § 45 at the fork in the law—and watch what happens when we make the jump from mere analysis to argument:

Answer # 1. Under § 45, Patron may not revoke once Artiste has begun her performance. Patron will contend that since there's "no brush to canvas," performance has not yet begun. Artiste will counter that the preliminary sketchwork counts as the beginning of performance and is more than "mere preparations."

Answer # 2. Under § 45, the offer may not be revoked once the offeree begins performance, and it's not clear whether Artiste has met that requirement. On the one hand, Artiste can argue that she began the performance when she did the preliminary sketchwork. To an artist, such sketches are as much a part of portraiture as the brush strokes on the final canvas, and from that standpoint she "began the invited performance" at the moment she started work on her first sketch. But Patron can counter that he asked for a family portrait — not a series of sketches — in exchange for his promise of $10,000. From the customer's standpoint — and the customer is always right! — the "invited performance" is *the actual painting of the commissioned portrait*, and the preliminary sketches were "mere preparations" for that performance.

Answer # 1 tells us a lot: It spots the issue (is the sketchwork the beginning of performance?); it tells us why it's an issue (because the sketchwork might be the beginning of performance or it might be mere preparations); and it tells us what difference the issue makes to the outcome of the case (if the sketchwork is the beginning of performance, Patron cannot revoke; if it's mere preparations, Artiste is out of luck). But Answer # 2 looks like Karla got hold of it and, impatient with a mere description of the parties' conflict, began to do what lawyers do and to make arguments for why the conflict should be resolved one way or another.

Note that Answer # 2 draws on the differing standpoints of an artist (on the one hand) and a customer (on the other) to develop the arguments for the parties. In Chapter 6, we cited "differing standpoints" as one of the common patterns of factual ambiguity that law professors use to create "forks in the facts" on their exams. As we've said before, if you learn to recognize those patterns, it will be much easier for you spot issues on exams. But the point we want to make here is that these same patterns can also help you construct legal arguments. It is a short step from recognizing an issue (depending on your standpoint, Artiste's sketchwork might or might not be the beginning of performance) to beginning to develop the arguments that lawyers would make for the respective parties (an argument based on Artiste's standpoint vs. an argument based on Patron's). To put it another way, it's an "issue" precisely because there are arguments on each side of the point, so once you've spotted the issue, the arguments aren't far behind.

* * * * *

Just as issues can lead you to arguments, arguments can lead you to other arguments as well. Let's continue with your saga as the associate working on *Artiste v. Patron*, and let's assume that Karla has just read the handiwork you came up with in Answer # 2. "I like this," she enthuses. "'Standpoint!' Is that what they're teaching y'all in law school these days? Never knew there was a name for it, but it really does sort out the conflict, doesn't it?" Your confidence returning, you shake your head in agreement and are just about to speak when she continues. "But you know, back when *I* was in law school — back before they used fancy-pants terms like 'standpoint' — they used to tell us that we ought to start by reading the contract. And if we're tryin' to figure out whether sketchwork is part of Arlene's 'performance,' perhaps it wouldn't have been such a bad idea to start by seeing whether the *contract* has anything to say on the matter."

"Well, there isn't a written contract in this case," you reply somewhat defensively.

"I know that," she snaps. "But oral agreements have terms too. What did Paul Patron *say* when he hired Arlene?"

You rifle the papers in the file, pull the memo detailing the intake interview with Artiste, and read from it: "According to Client, Patron said: 'I will pay you $10,000 to paint a portrait of my family.' There was no discussion of sketchwork at that time or at any time before Patron called client to say that the deal was off."

"Well," Karla drawls, "if *I* were representing Paul Patron, I'd be sayin' that I didn't ask for any damn 'sketchwork,' I asked for a 'portrait,' and she ain't begun that yet. How are we going to respond to *that*?"

You return to your office, wondering whether your college roommate who went on to medical school has days like this. Karla's right about what Patron said, you muse, and what can you say in response to an argument as strong as that? Suddenly you remember that somewhere you saw an entire list of responses to arguments like that and you reach for a book you hadn't looked at since law school. You locate the chapter titled "Forks in the Facts" and begin to thumb through the patterns of issues that had helped you so much on your law exams. You hit an entry in the "Linguistic Ambiguity" section—"literalism vs. reasonable expectations"—and a light goes on. *That's it!* you think. If Patron argues that he said "portrait," we can argue that that's just too literal. After all, he's not buying a portrait from an art gallery; he's hiring an artist to *paint* one for him. And if you "read between the lines" of the agreement—rather than just focusing on the words Artiste says Patron used—the reasonable expectation is that he wasn't just asking Artiste to deliver a product, but rather asking her to embark on a process that begins with sketchwork.

Once again regaining your confidence, you read on looking for further inspiration and another light goes on. You hit "multiple sources of meaning" and are reminded of the "baker's dozen." *Wow!* you think. When you order a dozen loaves of bread from a baker, you shouldn't be surprised if you get 13; so if you order a portrait from an artist, you shouldn't be surprised to get sketchwork first. So even if we're stuck with the word "portrait"—and we can't "read between the lines"—maybe "portrait" has room in it for sketchwork.

Exhilarated by your insights, you click on your word processing program and start another memo to Karla. "Patron can be expected to argue that he contracted for a 'portrait,' not for sketchwork. But careful analysis suggests at least two arguments in response," the memo begins.

* * * * *

The forks in the road approach thus helps your argument-construction efforts in a second way. If the point of our earlier discussion was that a fork can provide a blueprint for developing opposing arguments, the point here is that the same blueprint can help you see a counterargument—and hence an issue that could be resolved in more than one way—when at first you see only one side.

To be sure, when you're taking an exam you won't have a Karla looking over your shoulder saying, "But the contract *says* so." But we'll let you in on a little professorial secret: Most exam questions are written so that the argument on one side is pretty obvious, for that's how we separate the merely good answers (they see the obvious argument and know exactly where to go with it) from the excellent ones (they figure out a way to respond to the obvious argument). And we think that the key to seeing the counterarguments—to knowing that you can respond to a "literal" argument with a "reasonable expectations" or a "multiple meanings" response—is a thoroughgoing familiarity with the patterns we explored in Part I of the book. That is why we've offered so many concrete examples and illustrations drawn from different topics covered in different courses. You need to make these patterns "your own" by learning to recognize them when you see them in operation in a new setting; indeed, your ultimate goal—to ensure success in law practice as well as on law exams—should be to learn to recognize *new* patterns when you encounter them as well.

(ii) Patterns of argument for competing interpretations of statutes and cases

The "forks in the road" approach is likewise very helpful in dealing with competing interpretations of statutes and competing interpretations of caselaw, for once again the patterns we studied in Part I lead to patterns of *argument*. So it is typically the case that merely by identifying the issue you have also produced a blueprint for your argument.

Indeed, in one sense, developing arguments in this context may be even easier than it was with our forks in the facts, because the positions taken by lawyers in this setting are so familiar that they typically present themselves as arguments (*e.g.*, "plain meaning"; "broad holding"), and all you have to do is apply them to the particular context.

There's the rub, of course, because *applying* these arguments to a particular context will typically require a detailed knowledge of the language and structure of the statute or of the facts and reasoning of a case or a line of cases. You can't make a plain-meaning argument if you don't know what the statute says, and you can't argue for either a "broad" or a "narrow" interpretation of a case you haven't studied carefully. No matter how good you get at these arguments, you can't deploy them effectively unless you first have a solid grasp of what it is that you're arguing *about*.

c. The crucial role of policy arguments

There is a vitally important dimension to argument construction that we haven't focused on yet—"policy argument"—a dimension so important that we have devoted all of the next chapter to the topic. Law students frequently make the mistake of thinking that policy arguments should be made only in the context of questions that present themselves as "policy questions." (*E.g.*, "You are a legislative aide to Senator Smith, and she has asked you to prepare a memorandum discussing the pros and cons of a bill that would amend the National Labor Relations Act to add the following provision . . . .") But in fact, policy arguments have an incredibly important role to play in each of the kinds of issues we've been exploring. Indeed, in the typical rule vs. counter-rule problem discussed in Chapter 3—where, for example, the facts are set in an imaginary jurisdiction that has not yet decided whether to follow the traditional common law or the Restatement position on some issue in Torts—policy arguments are frequently the only arguments available, since you can't rely on a statute, or a precedent, or "the facts" to resolve the parties' conflict.

And when you confront forks in the law that involve issues of interpretation—of either a statute (Chapter 4) or of caselaw (Chapter 5)—you'll find that you need policy arguments more often than not as well. Recall, for example, that many issues of statutory and caselaw interpretation are really arguments about how to further this or that policy—or how to deal with competing purposes or policies—in other words, *policy* arguments.

Finally, even the application of statutes and cases to facts involves an important element of policy analysis; recall, to take only the most dramatic example, our "hidden forks" problem from Chapter 7, where the question presented was whether the result (the family loses its farm to the corporate tenant) was consistent with the policies that prompted the legislature to enact the landlord/tenant statute. The family had nothing to go on *but* policy, so if you'd ignored that dimension of the problem, you would have had no "issue" to discuss.

4. Where to Focus Your Fire

In the general Test-Taking Tips appearing in Part III, we devote substantial attention to the problem of dealing with time constraints and credit allocations on a law exam. But because the issue-spotting questions we've been discussing raise special difficulties in this connection, we thought we'd take a moment to address them here.

a. Focus your fire on points in conflict

Assume you encounter an exam question involving the application of a state whistleblower statute to a complex fact pattern. You whip through the pertinent section of your course outline and are thrilled when straight-away you see four different points implicated by the facts. First, there is a provision requiring would-be whistleblowers to notify the employer in writing before disclosing illegal conduct, and the facts reveal that the employee in this case gave firm officials only a one-page photocopy of the statute the employer has allegedly violated. (Is that a "notice in writing"? you wonder.) Next there is a provision stating that notification must be made to a "supervisor"—and a related provision defining that term—and the facts reveal that the whistleblower gave the photocopy to the firm's general counsel, who may or may not be a supervisor under the statute's definition. ("A fork in the facts!") Then there is a section prohibiting discharges in retaliation for whistleblowing but permitting employers to fire employees "for cause," and the facts suggest that the employer here was motivated both by the whistleblowing and by the employee's terrible record of tardiness. ("Didn't the professor call that a 'mixed-motive' question?") Finally, there is the jurisdictional requirement of the statute—a firm must have 10 or more employees to be covered—and the facts state that there are 25 employees. ("*Gotcha!*") You have an hour to draft an answer—45 minutes, now that you've read and re-read the facts and worked your way through your course outline—so where will you begin?

We've read enough exams over the years to know that the first instinct of some will be to lead with the jurisdictional requirement. Even though most law students profess to suffer from math anxiety, it's amazing how much they love to write answers carefully explaining that 25 is *much* larger than 10.

To be sure, there's nothing wrong with addressing the jurisdictional requirement in these circumstances. For one thing, meeting it is crucial to the application of the statute; for another, the professor gave you a fact in the question that satisfies that requirement. But resist the temptation to expand your treatment beyond a sentence or two at the most—*e.g.*, "The requirement of 10 employees under § 101(4) is easily met by the fact that the employer has 25"—in a misguided effort to "rack up points" on a topic about which you feel confident (*e.g.*, the difference between 25 and 10; the history of jurisdictional requirements; the successful efforts of the small-business lobby to exempt its members from various employment statutes) in order to put off addressing topics with which you feel less comfortable (*e.g.*, the notification and "mixed motive" issues). To put the point in terms of forks in the road, the professor is almost surely testing your ability to address the issues in the question about which there is genuine dispute and arguments to be made on both sides—and not your ability to tell whether 25 or 10 is the larger number.

b. Focus your fire on points that make a difference

Let's continue with our whistleblower example, and assume that, upon carefully re-reading the facts, you realize that the whistleblower gave photocopies of the statute to both the company president and the general counsel, who happened to be in the president's office when the whistleblower dropped by. You've still got a fork in the facts: The general counsel may or may not be a supervisor under the statute's definition of that term. But before you're off on a lengthy disquisition about the facts pointing each way, force yourself to ask *what difference does it make* whether the general counsel is or isn't a statutory supervisor?

If the general counsel were the only individual to whom our whistleblower gave the alleged notice, then the general counsel's status would obviously be a vital issue. But on these facts, since the whistleblower gave a copy to the company president as well — and there's no question that's *she's* a supervisor within the meaning of the statute — the general counsel's status will make no difference to the outcome.

To be safe, of course, you might devote a sentence or two to identifying the issue and even the key facts that create the ambiguity; that way, you're sure to get any "issue-spotting" points the professor is giving out. Far more important, you should briefly explain why the general counsel's status doesn't matter; chances are, that will get you more points than any discussion of whether lawyers are supervisors. But any more than a few sentences and you're twice a loser: You lose once because you've wasted time better spent on issues that *do* make a difference, and you lose again when the professor reads your answer and wonders why you gave extended treatment to an issue that wouldn't affect the outcome no matter how it was resolved.

c. Focus your fire on issues emphasized by the professor

The good news is that you've figured out that the jurisdictional requirement isn't really an issue, and that the general counsel's status doesn't really matter. The bad news is that your answer so far consists of two extremely short paragraphs making these points, and you've now got only 30 minutes left on a one-hour question that's worth 25% of the exam grade. There are two issues left — the notification issue and the mixed-motive issue — and you estimate that you could easily spend an hour writing on either of them. *What will you do?*

Whatever else you do, you should start out by writing a "roadmap" paragraph that briefly describes the two analyses you plan to give. The professor can't give you credit for insights that don't appear in your bluebooks, and by proceeding this way you offer yourself some protection against the prospect of running out of time before you reach the second issue.

But which issue should you tackle first? To resume a theme mentioned earlier, remember who your *real* judge is and that chances are she is trying, as most law professors do, to test what she taught you. So what did she teach you? If she devoted a substantial portion of the course to close and careful statutory interpretation, and if the notification question requires an involved analysis of the sort she repeatedly forced students to undertake in class, then you'd be wise to use the opportunity to "show your statutory stuff." On the other hand, if a major theme of the course was the problem of "mixed motives" in employment law, then perhaps the exam question is the perfect vehicle for bringing that theme to a close analysis of particular facts. Either way, the point is to let the professor—rather than the luck of the clock—be your guide in making your triage decisions.

d. Write till the facts run out

We close with a very important point, but one we offer more as a caution than a finely detailed prescription. On most exams, you simply won't have time to discuss every ambiguity you see. Indeed, *Getting to Maybe* has prepared you to find ambiguity everywhere you look. If you understand that the twin fork is the basic technique in almost every exam, then you see that it's a short step to long questions that involve multiple forks. If there are three relevant statutes and two relevant cases for your problem, then even if each has only two plausible interpretations you have already 32 different combinations to discuss—trust us on the math! You are sure to tie yourself in knots if you go down every path. Accordingly, you need strategies to ensure that you aren't discussing an ambiguity that the professor won't find relevant to the test.

We've just suggested several strategies for accomplishing this: Focus on disputed issues; focus on issues that matter; and focus on the points emphasized by the professor in the course. But we have one more suggestion for "keeping on track": Use the fact pattern as your guide. Although some facts are in there for "color," and some professors throw in extraneous facts (we call them "red herrings"), the exam question will mostly contain facts that are in there for a reason. So, if you find as you write that you are considering additional issues that are raised by particular facts, you are probably on the right track, and you should keep writing until these facts have been thoroughly analyzed. By contrast, if you are turning to new issues merely because they are prominent in your course outline or, worse still, if you find yourself continuing to invent issues based on "what ifs," chances are you are tying yourself in knots. Stop. Take a deep breath. And turn your energies elsewhere.

C. What *Not* To Do With Issues: Herein of "IRAC"

Cards on the table: In our combined quarter-century of law teaching—and in the thousands of bluebooks we've read over all those years—neither of us can ever recall seeing an exam answer organized around the so-called IRAC method ("issue-rule-application-conclusion") that was truly first-rate. Not a one. Indeed, a former colleague puts the matter well when he warns his first-year law students that those who use IRAC tend instead to come up with IRAN ("issue-rule-application-*nonsense*") and that this makes the grader IRATE. And the last thing you want your answers to do to the person faced with the formidable task of grading 100 or more sets of bluebooks is to make her irate!

We readily acknowledge that we may be dealing with a skewed sample here: Since we urge our own students to avoid IRAC like the plague, it may well be the case that the IRAC-based exams the two of us encounter are written by individuals who have ignored other important things we've said as well. Moreover, there is nothing wrong in principle with an approach to exam taking that encourages students to organize their answers around issues and to take the pertinent legal rules and principles they've studied and apply them to the facts presented in the question. (Indeed, in broad outline, that's roughly analogous to the approach we've recommended here.)

If students drew *those* lessons from IRAC, we'd have no quarrel with the notion of using the method as a base from which to develop even better and more sophisticated exam-taking skills. But judging from the many applications of IRAC we've actually encountered over the years, most students seem to learn two other far less salutary lessons instead.

The first one is that IRAC is the law school equivalent of the Veg-o-Matic: There is no exam question, no matter what its shape or size, that you can't "slice and dice" with the help of this handy-dandy little tool. But in point of fact, IRAC is designed for a particular kind of exam question, albeit a very common and important one: the "issue-spotter." And deploying it in the context of one of the many kinds of questions that don't follow the issue-spotter format almost invariably leads to unmitigated disaster. We're going to address this aspect of the IRAC problem at some length in the Test-Taking Tips appearing in Part III.

We'll focus here on a second lesson that IRAC unfortunately seems to impart: the belief that you can reduce legal analysis to a simple four-step formula. But that dog just won't hunt, for even in the context of the traditional issue-spotting question for which IRAC is designed, the formula is as likely to mislead you as it is to enable you to construct a quality response.

For one thing, following the order of operations suggested by the acronym—(1) spot the issue; (2) identify the rule; (3) apply the rule to the facts; and (4) offer a conclusion—can get you into serious trouble. Thus, many "issues" appear only *after* you've first identified the pertinent legal "rule."

For example, an oral contract for the sale of goods at a price of $500 raises an issue under the Statute of Frauds, but identifying U.C.C. § 2-201 as the applicable rule may itself raise many more questions than it resolves. (Although there is no written contract, is there a check or a letter or some other writing sufficient to indicate that the parties have a contract? Did the disappointed party send the reneging party a confirmation of the deal prior to breach? Are the goods "specially manufactured"? Have any of them been delivered or paid for?) Similarly, IRAC identifies the "conclusion" as the final step in your answer, but often it is only the beginning. Thus, when the "application" of a "rule" to the facts brings about a "conclusion" that is utterly at odds with legislative purpose— recall our "hidden forks" about the corporate tenant trying to take over the family farm—the professor may well be testing to see whether you are able to make a lawyerly argument for *circumventing*, rather than merely "applying," the rule at issue.

An even more fundamental problem with IRAC is the unstated premise that there is but one "rule" and but one way to "apply" it once an "issue" is spotted. The whole point of Part I of this book is that many exam questions raise issues that could be resolved different ways under different rules (*e.g.*, contributory vs. comparative negligence); under competing interpretations of the same rule (*e.g.*, plain meaning vs. purpose-based interpretation of "vehicle"); or under competing interpretations of the same case (*e.g.*, broad vs. narrow readings of *Hawkins v. McGee*). And even if we are able to settle on a single rule or a single reading, the task of "applying" it to the facts is similarly complex; indeed, we devoted an entire chapter to examples of problems that would come out different ways under competing factual interpretations.

In the same way that the parties may disagree about the "rule" or about its "application" to the facts, they can—and in the real world they frequently do—disagree about the "issue" presented by the problem. As suggested in the section on "competing domains," law exams frequently test your ability to see that more than one body of law—and hence more than one issue—might be implicated by a single problem. (Recall how useless IRAC was in the debate among the associates discussing the land subsidence case in Karla's Texas law firm.)

Disagreements and conflicts such as these are the heart of most exam questions, and you are likely to miss them altogether if you read the questions through the distorting lenses of IRAC.

Chapter 10

Czars of the Universe (Otherwise Known as "Policy Wizards")

Phillip Areeda, Harvard's late, great Antitrust and Contracts teacher, had an unmistakable style. In overcrowded yet reverentially hushed classrooms, the acknowledged master would zero in on individual students to ask, without warning, his favorite question: "Ms. Jones, if you were Czar of the Universe, how would you have decided today's case?" The question served as a powerful wake-up call for anyone still clinging to the idea that law school was principally about learning rules.

In its own way, virtually every law school exam question also asks you to reflect not only about what the law is but upon what it *should* be. Thus far, we have been focusing on only one kind of exam question, albeit the kind of question that appears on virtually every law exam given in U.S. law schools: the issue-spotter. At first blush, Professor Areeda's Czar would seem to have little role to play in the analysis of such questions. Assume, for example, that you encounter a problem on your Property final in which a group of struggling musicians attempts to invoke the warranty of habitability against the landlord who rents them their loft space. Some facts suggest that the tenancy is a commercial one—that's what the lease says, and the loft is in a decidedly commercial district—in which case the warranty would not apply. But other facts suggest a residential lease—the musicians live as well as work in the loft, and this is known if not acknowledged by the landlord—which would make the warranty claim a winner.

The problem thus presents a classic case of "concurrent forks," for the road taken at the "fork in the facts" (commercial vs. residential lease) determines the path the case will take at the "fork in the law" (warranty of habitability applies to residential but not commercial leases). As we discussed in the previous chapter, you'll get a lot of credit with most professors for simply identifying and analyzing these issues, but you'll get more points still —as Karla stressed to her young associate—if you present sound and persuasive *arguments* on behalf of the respective parties.

The point of this chapter is that behind every successful Karla is a Czar: Many of the most effective arguments available to lawyers representing clients—and, more important here, to students answering exam questions—are *policy* arguments. To return to our struggling musicians, the student who identifies the commercial vs. residential lease issue; explains its significance to whether the warranty of habitability applies to the parties' lease; and carefully marshals all the facts that support the competing characterizations will surely do well on her exam. But the student who does what a first-rate lawyer would do—who offers reasons for *why* a court should choose one characterization or the other—is on her way to an "A."

Thus, the professor is likely to reward the student who points out that extending the warranty to tenants who knowingly use rental property for purposes that violate the spirit and perhaps the terms of their lease will create an incentive for tenants to ignore the obligations of private agreements they freely and willingly enter. The professor is also likely to reward the student who argues that it will encourage subterfuge if landlords can escape legal responsibility even when they know they have residential tenants. And the professor is likely to save the biggest rewards of all for those students who mobilize Czar-like policy arguments such as these on both sides of a case that began as a traditional issue-spotter.

Every now and then, however, borrowing from Professor Areeda's playbook, law professors will cut to the chase and ask questions directly about what sort of policies the legal system should adopt. Should the Congress pass a statute requiring that government pay compensation when its actions reduce the value of an owner's property by more than 20%? Should gun manufacturers be held liable for injuries to gun victims even when "fault" lies with the criminal who misused the gun? Should Congress abolish the Independent Counsel statute? Such questions isolate exam-taking skills somewhat different from those we have already described.

One way to grasp the more traditional issue-spotter is to understand that you must simultaneously argue issues of characterization (is the studio a residential or commercial space?) and issues of policy (what happens when we expand or contract the warranty of habitability?). Professor Areeda's question allows us to isolate the policy components for purposes of exposition. But whether you are talking "big picture" or attempting to resolve a nitty-gritty dispute within a classic issue-spotter, you need to be prepared for the particular wrinkles involved in your brief reign as a Czar of the Universe.

A. To Know and Not To Know— That Is the Answer

The first trick to conquering policy issues is to get past two wholly natural reactions. On one hand, there's a way in which policy questions provoke the kind of panic you might feel sitting down to dinner with your fiancée's parents for the first time. "So kid," your prospective father-in-law chimes in, "what position do you think the United States ought to take toward NATO expansion?" What you want to say, of course, is, "How the heck should I know?" But you understand that somehow that would be inappropriate.

So, too, the policy aspects of law school exam questions strike many students as somewhat unfair. We came here to have you teach us the law, the student thinks, and now here you are asking us to tell you what it should be. What was the point of all that studying if now all you want are our opinions? The answer, of course, is that professors don't want just your opinions. We want considered analysis based on what you have learned in the course. Your initial reaction to questions like whether diversity jurisdiction should be abolished may quite honestly be, "I don't know." After all, if you actually did "know," we wouldn't think of this as much of a question. But when you sit down to write, you will discover that although you can't provide a foolproof answer, you "know" a lot more than you thought.

The second natural reaction to policy questions is merely the opposite side of the same coin. A student who is also a landlord may feel very strongly, for example, that rent control is a bad thing. A question asking whether a particular jurisdiction should abolish its rent-control laws won't give this student pause over whether she has anything to say. To the contrary, what will strike terror in the student's heart is that the plenty she has to say won't square with her professor's not-too-well-hidden liberal views. The professor may have said repeatedly that answers will be judged not on which position the student takes but on how the student argues the case. But since it's unlikely the professor has taken the time to explain carefully what is meant by a well-argued case, the student's understandable feeling is that a good answer will be one that agrees with the professor's position. Yet as understandable as this feeling may be, *it's just not true.*

Every professor can say for sure that she has often given sterling grades to essays with which she strongly disagrees. And all will likewise tell you of the dismally mediocre performance of students who guess at the professor's basic views and parrot them back devoid of all nuance or thoughtfulness. We don't mean to deny that at the margins some subtle biases may affect professorial reactions to student answers. But far and away the best answers go not to those who take "the right side," but to those who take sides "the right way." In short, you can take any side you want, as long as you temper your enthusiasm with an intelligent appreciation of the alternative point of view.

Nor is there anything metaphysical or mysterious about what makes up a good answer. As this chapter will explain, good answers to policy questions typically consist of the following components: 1) considering the problem from different perspectives, or what we will call different "dimensions"; 2) explaining arguments within each dimension that support opposing outcomes; 3) finding something about the problem that's more complicated than it originally appears (often, this complicating factor can be identified by considering the relationships among the various arguments you developed in parts 1 and 2); and 4) above all, not despairing when your analysis does not achieve either a clear resolution of the problem or even a clear identification of a simple trade-off between values.

We have organized this chapter to shed light on these components of good policy analysis. In "Touching All Parts of the Policy Kingdom," we describe argument "dimensions" in ways we hope will prove useful in linking policy issues to our earlier description of "forks in the road." Just as the law often presents different directions in which the lawyer's argument can travel, policy argument offers many different reasons you might want to head in one direction or another. We'll show why that's the case. In "Head and Tails You Win," we use the argument dimensions to show how you can mix and match them to enrich your exam answers. Finally, in "Find the Fun," we explain how no amount of memorization can prepare you for all the different combinations that exams (or law practice, for that matter) will throw at you. We offer examples of some of the more familiar twists you can expect, so you won't be surprised to find them and so you can watch for countless others your professors are sure to invent.

The techniques you'll find here will enable you to extend your discussion and analysis to make persuasive arguments of the sort we described in Chapter 9. You won't find any advice here on how to reach the "right" conclusions. Your task, after all, is to argue for one case and against its opposite, not to prove that there is an unequivocally correct solution. Indeed, if upon reflection actual resolution of the issue appears difficult to you for a whole variety of reasons, you should rejoice in the fact that you are probably getting the point. Even for Czars of the Universe, it's *Getting to Maybe* all over again.

B. Touching All Parts of the Policy Kingdom

One of our favorite definitions of a good law student is someone who will always have three or four intelligent sentences to say about any topic thrown her way. She may not be able to put together *more* than three or four intelligent sentences, but, as we'll explain, this won't necessarily be crippling on law school exams.

The reason three or four sentences will quickly leap to mind is that there is a standard set of perspectives from which almost any policy issue can be viewed. If you go through your class notes, you will discover these same perspectives mixed intermittently throughout. We'll begin by introducing these different perspectives to emphasize the need to consider most or all of them in a good policy answer. (We'll show how this works in practice in Chapter 15, when we take you through some sample exam questions.)

1. "Shaping" Society

First and foremost, policy issues ask students to consider the future consequences to affected parties of a decision one way or another. Who will gain and who will lose if the issue is resolved a certain way? *What* will each side gain and lose? How will the gains and losses occur? One way to think about this approach is in terms of simple cost-benefit analysis. As we shall explain, there's more to it than such simplicity implies. But it would be perilous, if not foolhardy, to tackle a policy issue without some consideration of winners and losers.

Indeed, lawyers often differentiate between "law" and "policy" based simply on how much emphasis is placed on the consequences of the outcome. Run-of-the-mill legal issues often raise most directly the question of what the law has said before, via either statute or precedent, about a particular issue. By contrast, policy questions often begin with the assumption that the law is unclear and that the decisionmaker should resolve the dispute by turning to broader considerations, especially the future impact of the decision on these and similarly situated parties.

For the sake of convenience, we'll label arguments about a policy's impact "SHAPING" arguments, to remind you of the need to think about the shape of society after a particular rule is put into effect. So, to take one example, if your hypothetical exam question asked whether landlords should be held strictly liable for tenants' injuries, one obvious line of analysis would evaluate how landlords might be affected by such a rule and what this would do to the supply of housing in the future. In short, how would a rule of strict liability shape the overall housing market?

2. Administering Policy

It should be immediately clear that law students may not be the people best trained to answer questions about how a particular policy will shape actual events. Wouldn't an economist or a political scientist know better how to study the likely landlord reactions to a rule imposing strict liability?

Perhaps so. But two crucial points about exams are in order. First, law professors quite properly believe that only a very poor advocate would push for a particular legal outcome without giving serious consideration to market and other societal consequences. Economists might do better research studies, but they are less likely to find themselves in court. So professors relentlessly test for students' ability to consider the consequences of rule-choices.

Second, the good law student will make up in breadth what she may lack in understanding of (say) regression analysis. Above all, one aspect of rule-choice will remain close to the law student's heart. How will the legal system actually administer the chosen rule? Like cost-benefit analysis, this question is more complicated than it might appear.

For now, let's focus on the two ways in which ADMINISTRABILITY is most likely to affect policy decisions. First, as every parent knows, the mere fact that there is a rule prohibiting something doesn't mean people won't do it anyway. So part of administrability just reminds policymakers to pay attention to whether the announced rule will actually work in practice. If landlords are strictly liable, for example, will tenants know their rights and bring lawsuits for injuries? Will tenants sign leases that contract away their right to sue? (And then the follow-up: Will such waivers be held valid?) There's no point in adopting a rule that would create enormous economic benefits only if it worked as intended when we can predict in advance that the rule can't be effectively applied. And this means that your discussion of how a particular policy will create winners and losers (or similar kinds of SHAPING arguments) must consider how the policy will be enforced. In your courses, you may hear this problem referred to as the relationship between the "law on the books" and the "law in action."

Second, every policy choice has an impact not only on the people being administered, but on those doing the administering. For most law school exam questions, courts are the anticipated administrators of legal rules. So an analysis of whether State X should adopt strict liability for landlords should include a discussion of how courts might find it easier to resolve cases if the complex and fact-intensive issue of landlord fault is removed from judicial evaluation. A streamlined litigation process will almost always count as a sound argument on behalf of a particular policy. Indeed, policy issues will often present you with an opportunity to compare the pros and cons of a "rule-like" formulation (if these three circumstances are present then the defendant is liable) with the pros and cons of a more flexible "standard" (negligent landlords must pay). Many of you will discuss the significance of the choice between rules and standards explicitly in your Contracts or Property courses.

It's important to see, though, that bright-line rules don't always reduce judicial workload. In our example, injured tenants would presumably bring more lawsuits if it were easier to recover. Not having to prove fault would provide a strong incentive for injured tenants to take their cases to court. It might ultimately be a good thing if there were more such lawsuits. Landlords might be more careful, and tenants might receive what they deserve. But taxpayers will have to pay for more judges and court space to handle the extra load. Of course, when you're sitting alone in a room with your exam book, you will have no meaningful way to determine whether more judicial resources will be freed as a result of streamlining than will be required to take up the extra caseload. But you'll sure score a lot of points with your professor for raising the administrability dimension of the problem and for noticing that both landlords ("the floodgates will open") and tenants ("cases will move faster") can make use of it to help their cause.

3. Doing the Right Thing

By the time you sit down to write your exams, it's a safe bet that you have become a bit shy about introducing concerns of fairness or morality into your professional discussions. For one thing, you came to law school to learn new ways of thinking. So you want to sound like a trained lawyer rather than an uninitiated moralist. Moreover, virtually every law student has an early experience in which a professor appears unimpressed (sometimes that's putting it mildly!) with a classmate's comments based on personal conviction. Most often, the professor is only trying to show that the issue at hand is more complicated than the student's remarks suggest. Too often, however, a sharp exchange is misread by the class as a message that the law has no place for instincts about fairness or personal views of morality. Indeed, the professorial no-nonsense attitude will sting particularly hard for students who found law school attractive precisely because of its connections to deeper ideas about politics and justice.

We have many reasons to urge you to resist suggestions that you sever notions of justice from your understanding of law. It's not good for the country for law schools to produce an army of technocrats, and it's not good for your psyche to ignore your own instincts. For our purposes, however, we will focus on only one point. Ignoring justice will be disastrous for your grade point average. The trick for law school exams is not to forget about justice and morality, but to learn to present them in the right way. Every policy question, indeed every law school exam question that hinges on ambiguity in the decisionmaking process (*i.e.*, all of them), not only leaves room for, but demands that you consider the underlying fairness of competing outcomes.

Consider again an exam question about imposing strict liability on landlords for injuries suffered by tenants. Your concerns about sounding unprofessional are certainly well-founded. No teacher will be satisfied by answers concluding that landlords should be held strictly liable because "it's not fair for tenants to have to pay." You'll do only slightly better with the converse suggestion that "it wouldn't be fair to make landlords pay since they aren't at fault." The improvement is that you have provided a modicum of content to your notion of fairness by invoking a principle, "no liability without fault." But you still have a long way to go. After all, the whole point of strict liability is that it involves liability without fault. Courts sometimes adopt it and sometimes don't. So the issue is which way to go here.

Your discussion of fairness will become much richer and much more appealing to your grader if you work your way through the following points. Remember how we showed in Chapter 5 that every exam question that asks about application of caselaw has hidden questions of policy? To determine whether fixed precedents require home sellers to disclose a fight at a nearby school, to take our earlier example, courts will consider the policy rationales supporting and opposing disclosure requirements. Our point in this chapter is that every exam question about policy has hidden questions of fairness—or, if you like, consistency—that will enable you to frame multiple arguments about the fairness of opposing outcomes.

a. The unfairness of change (consistency over time)

The exam question may make you Czar of the Universe, but if you choose to adopt any policy different from current law, you need to consider the effects of transition. If applicable law now holds landlords liable only for negligence, then landlord attorneys will challenge any shift on grounds that landlords relied on the old rules. Specifically, landlord lawyers may note that landlords would have paid less for buildings, charged higher rents, and taken out more insurance had they known strict liability would be in effect. Reliance alone will then be put forward as a reason to maintain the status quo. (Note, by the way, that the ubiquitous nature of transition issues proves the silliness of believing that policy questions are somehow softer and less rigorous than purely legal ones. You can't address the transition issues without knowing what the current rules are. So there's no faking here, either.)

Moreover, change will also be resisted with the straightforward argument that it's not fair to treat one group of tenants (those who couldn't recover under the old negligence rule) differently from a second group (those who would be permitted to recover if we switched to a strict liability rule). Of course, this argument is so general it would defeat any effort to change any rule. But it is used anyway by lawyers arguing against a change in the legal rules, and the fact that it has any appeal at all should remind you that some notion of "consistency" lurks behind virtually all ideals of fairness within legal argument.

b. Treat like cases alike

When the exam writer first appoints you Czar of the Universe to decide a policy question, it's tempting to believe that you may restrict your thinking to produce the best possible outcome using what we call "shaping" arguments. But your reader will properly test any result you reach against similar results reached by other decisionmakers. If you argue for strict liability, but everyone else who has considered the issue disagrees, your contrariness alone many count as an argument against you, as the following sections suggest.

(i) Consistency over space

Suppose that the vast majority of states apply a negligence rule for cases involving suits against landlords. No formal rule prevents your state from reaching a different conclusion. Indeed, many would argue that one reason for our federal system is to permit legal experimentation by individual states. If you want your state to go it alone, however, your position will be stronger if you point out why you believe the legal system can easily cope with different rules in different places. You might say, for example, that land ownership implies a significant commitment to a particular locale, so that it would be fair to ask landlords to learn the rules of every state where they hold property. Different landlord liability rules, for example, would be easier to manage than differing rules governing property that moves easily and frequently from jurisdiction to jurisdiction—*e.g.*, regulations requiring safety equipment on your automobile. Alternatively, if you are arguing that your state should stay in line with others by sticking to a negligence rule, you can always stress the desirability of uniformity, but this will be particularly powerful if you can offer reasons why uniformity is especially important here. (Perhaps it will be easier to teach landlords and tenants what insurance to buy if the rules don't change as they move from place to place.)

Notice how your ability to generate discussion will spring from having identified a point of comparison (rules in other states). This technique can be replicated for virtually any policy proposal. When you recommend a solution, you can always ask yourself how this solution will fit into the broader set of legal rules that you know. Describing the fit is not only a sound analytical perspective; it will also serve you well in writing your essay exams.

(ii) Consistency across social categories

When you actually read through judicial and other discussions of the strict liability issue for landlords, you'll often encounter rhetoric about the dangers of transforming landlords into "insurers." At first glance, this may seem a bit mysterious. What do landlord interests hope to gain by tossing around such phraseology? If the issue at hand is whether landlords should be strictly liable, then policymakers are obviously trying to decide if there is an insurance aspect to being a landlord. How can it help the argument to decry being "an insurer?"

The law's emphasis on consistency helps unravel this mystery a bit. Landlord lawyers opposing strict liability can seek support from the way the commercial world has in the past divided certain responsibilities. They paint a world split between value-creating business ventures, responsible for damage only when at fault, and risk-taking insurance ventures whose business is to pay for damages across the board. (Landlords, according to this line of reasoning, fall into the first category.)

One reaction to such landlord rhetoric is to note that the legal world need not follow pre-existing commercial categories. After all, as Czars of the Universe, courts and legislators are free to set the rules that best serve society, not those that slavishly cater to established interests. Such reform rhetoric, however, is itself overblown. A rule that departs too drastically from existing understandings is likely to be unpopular and ineffective. So yet another vision of fairness you must confront is the landlord claim that to be consistent across groups the law should take seriously categories that are already in place.

Fortunately, if you are arguing for strict liability, you have a ready counter here. You might note, for example, that the law already imposes strict liability on manufacturers of defective products. Accordingly, existing law does not maintain a rigid distinction between business ventures and insurers. Landlords may respond that the kind of strict liability sought by tenants would go well beyond product liability and cover situations in which the apartment is not even defective. Note again, however, that what started as a seemingly open-ended discussion of the best rule ends up including the kinds of comparisons one finds in the traditional application of precedent to particular cases.

(iii) The distribution of wealth (consistency across economic class)

Lest you think we have forgotten, let us close our discussion of fairness with the issue most likely to drive opinions about political matters. American legal thinking is deeply committed to two views about the allocation of economic resources. Its *meritocratic* aspects accept the increasingly unequal distribution of wealth and income as a necessary, perhaps even desirable, by-product of individuals' differing abilities to contribute to the social good. From this perspective, landlords might be painted as hardworking entrepreneurs struggling to make a profit while providing a vital service. The last thing they need is to have additional costs heaped upon them to pay for injuries that aren't even their fault.

Tenant interests, however, will counter by stressing the *egalitarian* component of American legal thinking. Housing could fairly be characterized as a basic need. Plus, all things being equal, odds are that tenants will have fewer resources available to them than landlords do. Accordingly, tenants may offer a straightforward leveling argument that stresses how landlords are in a better position to afford the loss. As beneficiaries of a legal system built to protect the rights of property owners, landlords should have no grounds to object when asked to bear a few costs.

There's plenty of room to spin out this story and link it to the shaping and administrative concerns described earlier. If additional costs are initially placed on landlords, they may ultimately be passed back to tenants through higher rents. But even so, costs will then be spread among all tenants rather than falling entirely on the injured (and hence relatively poorer) ones. An uninsured tenant who can't cover medical costs might find herself on the street. The debate need not end there, but the point we want to make is that the clash between meritocracy and egalitarianism is another theme you can watch for in a high percentage of policy questions. Discussing the issue in these terms will redound to your credit, provided you are responsive to concerns that will be expressed by both sides.

What won't work, however, will be global statements about fairness divorced from the context of the question. Suppose, for example, that as a true Czar of the Universe you would outlaw the landlord/tenant relationship as an anachronistic throwback to the feudal period. If you spend all your time explaining such "progressive" views, you will probably receive a very poor grade. Your mistake, however, won't be that you have taken an unpopular position. Rather, you will have committed the single most common sin of all exam takers. You will have failed to answer the question. Your professor wants to know about strict liability for landlords, and you have to discuss this—whatever your view of the underlying relationship.

To be sure, you might try to combine your deep hostility for the landlord/tenant system with a direct answer. You may argue, for example, that strict liability should be imposed because adding costs to landlords will make the system more expensive and hasten its demise. (Leave aside here the point that the cost is already there, and the courts really are only talking about who should bear it.) Few professors will penalize you directly for such a broad-scale political attack, and virtually none will for the direction of your views. But the task you have undertaken for yourself is enormous. The traditional answer will assume that the system as a whole will remain unchanged, with only this one issue up for grabs. As you can see from the arguments already described, a thorough analysis of even this more modest point will keep you plenty busy in the time allotted.

If you prefer to tackle the question by using it as a springboard to re-imagine the entire system, your professor will legitimately expect a well-worked-out explanation of how housing will work under your new scenario (SHAPING); how the new rules will be implemented (ADMINISTRATIVE); how transition issues will be covered (CHANGE AND FAIRNESS); how the new rules with fit with other rules in society (TREAT LIKE CASES ALIKE); and how the new system will resolve the clash between meritocratic and egalitarian views (FAIRNESS ACROSS INCOMES). We think that's a lot to tackle in the course of one exam question, and our view wouldn't change whether your direction is left (a progressive attack on ownership) or right (a conservative attack on the idea of tort recovery — all those plaintiffs' lawyers standing in the way of justice). If you think you can pull off a comprehensive defense of an entirely different legal system and link it to a resolution of the particular question at hand, we doubt that you'll have much to fear from a professor who disagrees with your position. Otherwise, even as a Czar of the Universe, you are better off sticking to the question asked.

4. What Kind of Czar Are You?

Another dimension that demands discussion when responding to straightforward policy questions grows out of the role you have been assigned. You may have noticed that Professor Areeda's colorful phraseology glosses over the fact that it's judges, not Czars, who are asked to resolve particular cases. In the exam context, the key point to remember is that American law includes a familiar set of concerns over which decisionmakers should get to decide which issues.

Return one more time to the issue of strict liability for landlords. Your professor may have phrased the question, as she may phrase virtually any policy question, in a number of ways. You might be asked whether, as a Supreme Court Justice in State X, you would be willing to embrace strict liability. You might be asked whether, as a legislator, you would vote for a statute imposing strict liability. Or you might be asked whether strict liability is a good idea without any explicit identification of how it might be adopted. And remember, you might even be asked that question—at least implicitly—in the context of an old-fashioned issuer-spotter, in which policy arguments about the choice between strict liability and negligence would figure prominently in a high-quality analysis of a problem involving those "competing domains."

All the forms of argument we've discussed (SHAPING, ADMINISTERING, FAIRNESS) are relevant no matter how the question is formulated. But if you are placed in the role of a state Supreme Court Justice, you would be wise to add comments about your position as part of a supposedly less political branch of government. Here again you can't perform well without knowing about the rules currently in force. If you are considering a particular proposal, like strict liability for landlords, you may have a very different reaction if what's called for is a shift from a well-circumscribed negligence regime. Judges, you may argue, should leave such dramatic changes from the status quo to the legislative branch. Moreover, there's a standard line of argument that legislators are better-positioned than courts to respond to what we have called here "shaping" concerns. Finally, if the question doesn't specify what your role is, you may score points for noting how you might reach a different conclusion if you were voting as a judge or as a legislator. Not all professors agree on the limits of the judicial role, and some don't see a sharp divide between legislating and judging. But virtually all professors will expect you to write something about your institutional role. So don't get carried away with being a Czar for too long.

5. Government Non-Interference and the Prime Directive: Even Czars Have Limits

If today's pop culture contains an image of a figure more powerful than an ancient Czar, surely it would have to be that of *Star Trek*'s StarFleet Captain crusading through the universe at many times the speed of light. *Star Trek*'s creators, however, captured an important part of our legal culture when they adopted the "Prime Directive" and banned our science fiction heroes from interfering with other civilizations, no matter how clearly it appears that interference is the right thing to do. In one stirring episode of *Star Trek: The Next Generation*, for example, Captain Jean Luc Picard refuses even to inform an entire planet that the so-called medicine they are receiving is nothing more than a vicious narcotic, let alone to take affirmative steps to change the practice. Those of you who watch the show will appreciate how many interesting situations the writers create to illustrate the difficulty of defining what counts as "interference." But all of you stepping up to your next set of law school exams can use *Star Trek*'s Prime Directive to help you remember another basic dimension of law school policy questions: Americans are suspicious of governmental interference.

Your favorite color in the whole world might be green. Yet, if you were made Czar of the Universe, it's unlikely you would suddenly order everyone to use nothing but green for all decorative designs. For one thing, if you keep issuing crazy orders, your tenure as Czar is unlikely to be a long or happy one. More important, however, you would have reason to believe that each citizen is a better judge of what color to paint her house, for example, than you are. Indeed, you might even see it as unethical for you to use your coercive authority to reach into that aspect of your citizens' lives to impose a mandatory color. Despite your role as Czar, you keep saying to yourself that America, after all, is a free country. And what this means to many people is that there are certain zones of freedom where the law, and especially the Czar, should heed the unwritten rule: "Keep Out." This is one way, for example, to think about the U.S. Supreme Court decision in *Griswold v. Connecticut*, 381 U.S. 479 (1965), invalidating laws against birth control. And it's one way to think about a whole host of questions you can imagine finding on your exams — questions about gun control, abortion, assisted suicide, mandatory air bags, motorcycle helmets, etc.

Here, too, policy arguments are likely to come in matched pairs. Laissez-faire proponents will typically stress the importance of individualized decisionmaking (I should decide for myself whether to trade money for safety by buying an air bag). Advocates of regulation may stress effects on third parties (insurance costs for everyone will rise unless air bags are mandatory). Regulation's opponents will paint a picture of a private realm from which government should be excluded ("this is a family matter" or "let the market decide"). Government interventionists will stress the dangers of tyranny within the so-called "private" sphere itself (government staying out of the family means the powerful man can dictate terms to the less powerful woman; government staying out of the market may mean the powerful boss can steamroll the less powerful worker). As Czar of the Universe, even you can't resolve these dilemmas. But by remembering this dimension of legal problems, you can chalk up still more points on almost any policy question.

C. Heads and Tails You Win

Our account of SHAPING, ADMINISTERING, FAIRNESS, INSTITUTIONAL ROLE, and NON-INTERFERENCE arguments is not meant to be exhaustive. We readily admit that sophisticated policy argument and legal reasoning are more nuanced than anything we can capture here. Our concern, however, is preparing you for the task of writing your exams. If you look at other study guides, you will find instructions on writing checklists for various substantive courses. In Contracts, for example, you might analyze questions looking for whether an offer is extended, whether it was accepted, whether consideration was paid or promised, whether a breach has occurred, and what damages should be. Our list of policy perspectives can't substitute for a sound grasp of your courses any more than a checklist can capture all of Contracts.

Instead, our emphasis on multiple dimensions takes a crucial step toward resolving a paradox you may have spotted within the limited guidance others provide about exams. "Argue both sides," your professors repeatedly tell you. But when you do, sometimes an exam comes back with red writing saying, "Draw conclusions. Don't be wishy-washy and indecisive." In such cases, you may wonder just who it is who can't make up his mind.

It turns out, however, that your professors aren't asking the impossible. You *can* simultaneously be decisive and argue both sides. The first step is simply to recognize the psychological bind. Your exams often demand that you carefully articulate the strongest case for at least two opposing resolutions. Should there be strict liability or not? This will push you emotionally toward seeing the merit in both outcomes and may lure you away from your initially strong feelings one way or the other. Yet your exams may also demand that you choose one outcome as better than another, and this may push you toward repressing the complexity and conflict that your professor wants you to expose.

As you sit down to write, the best way to avoid the oversimplification error is to remember the kinds of arguments we have described above. Bring as many as you can to bear on the problem, and you will likely generate doubts about how the dispute should be resolved. Once you have generated doubt, however, you have to bite the bullet and actually choose one route as preferable. You may be unable unequivocally to refute the opposing viewpoint, but it's enough merely to explain why you were more persuaded by one side than the other. Pushing through doubts to a resolution is part of what judges do every day, and exams are as good a place as any to start learning to do this yourself.

1. Getting Past the Obvious

We're sure you've noticed how participants in hotly contested political conflict have a tendency to reduce debate to one argument per side. This may be done through battling slogans (right to life vs. right to choose) or by seizing on your side's strongest point (affirmative action means no color-blind society vs. affirmative action gave us Colin Powell). Exam questions, however, don't call for the same TV skills now demanded by contemporary politics. As you begin writing, you are interested in building a multi-faceted argument on each side of an issue. There's plenty of time to encapsulate the essence of your position at the end of your answer.

For many students, policy questions offer your first meaningful chance to discuss the kind of issue that brought you to law school in the first place. So it's not surprising that you are tempted to summarize debate the way we so often hear it during political discussion. Moreover, many arguments just seem to present themselves as one really strong point versus another. If your exam question asked whether the law should require people to wear motorcycle helmets, for example, you might choose to write about "helmets save lives" versus "legal mandates reduce freedom."

Using the terms we've introduced in this chapter, this version of the dispute pits the ultimate shaping argument (the world will be a better place if fewer people die) against a classic non-interference argument (keep the government out). A moment's thought, however, reveals that there's much more to the motorcycle helmet dispute. Proponents of a helmet law might appeal to some of the other dimensions we've been exploring and bolster their argument by analogizing to seat-belt laws already in place (fairness as consistency across groups); by noting how insurance premiums might fall (another shaping argument); by noting how police officers can more easily tell whether a helmet is on than whether a cyclist is driving recklessly (administrative issue); or by citing health-care costs for injured cyclists (interference is warranted because losses will fall on third parties). Helmet opponents might emphasize our culture's tolerance for all sorts of dangerous activities like skydiving or snowboarding (fairness as consistency across groups). Drivers without helmets might actually see better and drive more carefully—with the result that there may be fewer accidents, even if those there are tend to be more severe (another shaping argument). Helmets may be easy to detect, but there are countless motorcyclists and it might be more cost-effective to have police officers pulling over speeders than breeze-loving riders (administrative issue).

Non-lawyers might react to this lengthy litany with a certain amount of disdain. "You're making a federal case out of it," is how some might put it. "The crux of the matter," they'll say, "is whether you are willing to restrict freedom to save lives, and the rest is just fluff." Perhaps. But as budding lawyers your job is to begin considering multiple angles precisely when other people are rushing to the bottom line. That's why the key to top performance on a policy question is not to get stuck on any particular formulation of a problem. Think of two kids on a schoolyard yelling at each other "Will Too!", "Will Not!", "Will Too!",

"Will Not!", and you'll have an image of how a one-dimensional answer will sound to your grader. Your multi-dimensional answer won't necessarily make solving the problem easier. (That's why result-oriented people may shy away from it.) We promise, however, that you'll do better on policy questions by following this approach.

2. One Good Argument Deserves Another

Breaking down policy questions into multiple dimensions also helps with a second important component of the exam answer — responsiveness. One of the hardest things about lawyering strategy is knowing when to meet an argument on its own terms. Let's say your opponent contends that a rule you propose is too complicated to be readily administered. If you think the rule is manageable, you can tackle the argument head on. You may, however, conclude that any explanation of the rule's supposed simplicity will be so complex that the more you say the worse you will look. As a matter of argumentative strategy you could easily decide not to address the administrability issue at all, preferring instead to focus on the fairness of your proposed rule. You just have to decide whether the judge will think you are ducking a key point (not good) or sticking to your main issue (good).

Law school exam tactics, however, are different. If you fail to raise a particular argument, your professor won't know whether you are displaying argumentative savvy or whether you just missed a key point. Some professors will give you the benefit of the doubt and will explicitly authorize you to stick to the strongest points on each side. Do what they say on their exams! Our experience, however, is that most professors will be impressed if you can both respond to a strong argument on its own terms (meet one SHAPING argument with another) *and* demonstrate how shifting the ground of the discussion may strengthen the other side (switch from SHAPING to FAIRNESS or ADMINISTRABILITY concerns).

Let's start with a simple example that may stir memories of your earliest days in law school. Suppose your unimaginative Property professor decides the exam is a good place to re-visit

Pierson v. Post, the famous case involving the capture of a fox. If you were on the New York Court of Appeals, he asks, what rules of ownership would you think should govern wild animal captures today and why? Odds are that you will recall the opinions in the case and be able to construct arguments based upon them.

Your first hurdle requires basic knowledge of examsmanship. Note how the question calls for a conclusion and doesn't say anything about "arguing both sides of the case." Although some professors will explicitly instruct you to consider counterarguments, the formulation in our example is typical of many policy and other sorts of questions. It's tempting, then, to announce a result, put forward an argument to support it, and move on. So you might start with something like, "I see no reason to depart from the longstanding rule of *Pierson v. Post*, because I agree with that court that requiring actual possession, trapping, or mortal-wounding-with-continued-pursuit is the easiest rule to administer. Who wants uncertainty in the law of wild animals?" If you were answering a friend's question, that might be the end of the matter.

Few professors, however, will be happy with such a summary conclusion. Why would you be asked to discuss any policy issue if it weren't perplexing enough to raise doubt about the appropriate resolution? So you know, even before recalling anything about the actual case, that there must be a strong argument on the other side as well. And, of course, *Pierson v. Post* finds its way into so many Property casebooks because the majority opinion is met by such a vigorous dissent. Policy questions, even if they don't say so, almost always require you to confront the best arguments for the opposing side.

In his *Pierson v. Post* dissent, Justice Tomkins supported a rule whereby a hunter chasing a wild animal would be awarded ownership if he had a reasonable prospect of capturing the animal. Tomkins wanted to discourage intruders from interfering during the hunt. Otherwise, Tomkins fretted, hunters won't find it worthwhile to make the necessary investment in the enterprise (buying and training hounds, getting up early, etc.). By now you should recognize this as a classic shaping argument. Tomkins urges us to choose the rule that he believes will generate more hunting and thus more dead foxes. If you never mention

Tomkins's point, your teacher is likely to assume you overlooked it and grade you down accordingly.

So the next step in actually answering a policy question is to combine opposing arguments into a conclusion. Consider this still relatively simplistic response. "I would continue the rule of *Pierson v. Post*, because the certainty gained from a clear rule is more important than the incentive effect of a more flexible approach." Notice first the improvement over the wholly conclusory first try. This answer recognizes points on both sides but comes down firmly on one side. Yet an obvious problem remains.

Any curious reader, and surely your professor, will want to know *why* you concluded that certainty outweighed incentives in the wild animal context. It's one thing to say so and quite another to say so convincingly. And it's at just this spot that we suspect many students begin to experience some confusion. How, sitting in the cloister of an exam room, can one meaningfully measure certainty gains against incentive losses for purposes of a valid comparison? As long as you limit your answer to what appear to be the strongest points on each side, you risk producing arguments that seem to be talking past each other with no obvious scale upon which to weigh alternatives.

This phenomenon of arguments that cross but don't meaningfully clash is a familiar part of contemporary partisan bickering. Consider, for example, the debate over campaign finance reform in which proponents stress the dangers of large contributors "buying elections," while opponents emphasize threats to "free speech." Each side has a strong point, but neither political camp focuses sufficiently on how best to respond to the other side's strongest point. For your law school exam purposes, you can't afford to sink to partisan levels. In short, you not only need to "argue both sides," but to "argue both sides responsively."

3. When in Doubt, Just Say No

You can further improve your *Pierson v. Post* exam answer even if the only arguments that occur to you are an administrability argument on one side (requiring capture promotes certainty) and a shaping argument on the other side (flexibility will spur investment). The simplest technique is just to find some way to minimize or devalue the argument that you ultimately reject. So your answer might read something like, "I would continue the rule of *Pierson v. Post* because the need for certainty remains strong while the need to encourage killing wild animals has diminished in light of demands for conservation"; or "I would continue the rule of *Pierson v. Post* because the need for certainty is powerful, while people are likely to hunt even if there is a risk the prey will be snatched at the last minute." The common theme here is that all you need to render your answer somewhat more thoughtful is a bit of brainstorming about how to explain the other side's position and then undermine it. Notice that now you have considered both sides, reached a conclusion, and, at least preliminarily, explained why you chose one argument over the other.

4. Learning to Mix and Match

Whole new vistas will open for you, however, if you keep in mind the argument dimensions we have described. You should ask yourself whether the arguments that appear the strongest in favor of each side are arguments along the same dimension, or whether they appear to be talking past each other. You can then turn any difficulty created when your initial views pitted different types of arguments against each other into another opportunity to excel. All you have to do is figure out whether you can fill in what might be understood, in the *Pierson v. Post* example, as the missing boxes in the following chart:

	Pro-Plaintiff (hunter)	Pro-Defendant (poacher)
Administrability	?	Clear Rule Promotes Certainty
Shaping	Encourage Investment	?

You now have two obvious questions to ask yourself. First, can you invent any arguments in favor of the dissent's pro-hunter position that directly respond to your conclusion embracing the long-standing rule of capture? Put more concretely, are there any rejoinders to the idea that *Pierson v. Post's* capture rule will promote certainty and ease of administration? Second, can you invent any arguments supporting the capture rule that respond to the dissent's shaping argument—*i.e.*, that a more flexible approach will encourage hunting? Of course, you never know in advance whether such arguments will occur to you. But by noticing the way in which the two sides are arguing along different dimensions, you give yourself a chance to score points by developing responsive arguments.

In case this still seems a bit abstract, think about a family fight over what restaurant to dine at one evening. Your brother pushes the Chinese place around the corner because it's close. Your sister wants to go to the one across town because it's cheaper. Like the exam-taking student, you are asked to "decide the case" and give reasons. It's not easy to assess, however, whether proximity or economy should be the deciding factor.

Think how much more effective you could be if you could respond to each sibling on his or her own terms. If you choose the closer place, you might remind your sister that the portions there are larger so that the leftovers could serve as a second dinner later in the week. Having met her concerns over cost head-on, you may now find it much easier to emphasize the overriding importance of reducing travel time. Or, if you want to go across town, you might remind your brother of three other errands the family needs to do near the farther restaurant. Since the trip needs to be made anyway, you say, why not get good food for less money? Our experience in such family disputes is that such reconciling views often occur to people only after a good deal of yelling and a decision by fiat. On law school exams, however, keeping in mind different dimensions of policy argument can buy you some precious time to multiply considerations before you turn in your bluebooks.

Return, then, to the *Pierson v. Post* example. The judicial opinions appear to pit an administrability argument on one side (certain rule) against a shaping argument on the other (protect investment to spur hunting). Your challenge is to invent an administrability argument supporting the flexible approach and a shaping argument favoring the court's insistence on actual capture or its equivalent. Like most things, once you have clearly identified the challenge, it's quite easy to accomplish. Consider this greatly improved answer: "I believe the courts should continue to adhere to the longstanding rule in *Pierson v. Post* because it provides certainty to judges and hunters and because in the end it will produce the most successful hunting as well. Critics of the rule have long argued that permitting last-minute intruders to snatch prey will discourage necessary investment. But this argument actually cuts both ways, because if we really want to ensure that the most foxes are killed, we should reward the people who actually catch the foxes, not those who spend money to chase them. Protecting the investor is just another name for discouraging competitors, and in the end a rule that keeps foxes up for grabs until caught will promote the most aggressive hunting." Notice here that not only do you consider the other side, and not only do you respond to the other side, but you do so directly on the other side's own terms. This is the beginning of a fully developed answer.

Similarly, if you decided to defend the dissent's position, you might write something like this: "I think the time has come to embrace a more flexible approach to the rule of capture. Not only will this give hunters greater security to invest in the necessary hunting equipment, but it will actually prove easier to administer as well. The apparent certainty of the longstanding rule is an illusion. First of all, even the famous case of *Pierson v. Post* itself carved an exception for a hunter who mortally wounded an animal and remained in pursuit. This means that when a wounded animal is taken by another, the wounder might need to resort to litigation to prove, apparently via autopsy, that the animal actually would have died from the wound. But even more than that, the blatant unfairness of the rule will mean that quarrels on the hunting fields will continue. Hunters deprived in the middle of the chase won't give up merely because the intruder claims to rely on some legal rule. They will lie, cheat, and invent stories to pursue a prey they believe rightfully theirs. So litigation, and thus uncertainty, will continue—all at the cost of a dangerous drag on valuable hunting."

Notice here how a third dimension, the element of fairness, is deployed not for its own sake but in service of an administrability argument. In short, nothing will remain certain if it's not fair. This is a standard technique that presents yet another opportunity to show your stuff. And in this answer, too, you have not only considered the other side, but responded on the very terms that the other side treated as dispositive. Such replies won't always be available, but your exams are a good place to start hunting for them.

5. Accentuate the Multiple

By now, our next recommendation should be obvious. Recognizing the multiple dimensions of policy argument provides an immediate technique for finding more in the question than what initially comes to mind. If, as in our rule of capture example, the main battle appears to center on administrability and shaping arguments, there's still plenty of room to expand the discussion to consider more of the dimensions we described earlier. Indeed, a fully complete answer to any policy question is likely to consider many of these dimensions and not just the one or two that appear most immediately relevant. You need not worry if you can't think of an argument for each side that corresponds to every dimension we describe. Not all policy questions implicate all types of argument. And, we cannot stress enough, you may construct many other creative and valid arguments beside those we describe. Our goal is to get you rolling by getting you to think like law school's version of a Czar. We have no doubt you'll have plenty to add to the story.

Completing our rule of capture example, then, might involve the following arguments on each side. Maintaining the rule of *Pierson v. Post* might be defended on the ground that it's been the law a long time and change would be needlessly disruptive. (DO THE RIGHT THING—Consistency Over Time.) If you are imagining yourself on a court, you might want to endorse maintaining the rule unless and until the legislature decides to change it. (WHAT KIND OF CZAR ARE YOU?) You might stress the desirability of having hunters feel free to chase any animal without worrying that someone else will come along and claim he

was chasing it first. (SHAPING TOWARD EXPANDED FREE-
DOM.) And you might tack on rhetoric about keeping the government out of hunting disputes unless absolutely necessary,
such as when there is theft of an already captured animal.
(NON-INTERFERENCE.)

By contrast, if you want to argue for switching the rule, you
might defend change on the ground that property law has often
abandoned clear rules, like the common-enemy rule for surface
waters, in favor of reasonableness standards. (DO THE RIGHT
THING—Consistency Across Social Groups.) If you imagine
yourself a judge, you might point out that, since judges invented
the original *Pierson v. Post* rule, courts should be free to modify
it. If the legislature prefers the old rule, nothing will prevent a
statute from restoring the old status quo. (WHAT KIND OF
CZAR ARE YOU?) You might stress the desirability of hunters
feeling secure when chasing an animal that no one else will come
along and beat them to the kill. (SHAPING TOWARDS EX-
PANDED SECURITY.) And you might note that once disputes
between hunters arise, resolving them either way will necessitate
government involvement so that there's no way to take a hands-
off approach. (NON-INTERFERENCE COUNTERPOINT.) In
the end, you might imagine the problem producing an argument
chart like the one below:

	Keep Capture Rule	Pursuer Earns Ownership
Shaping	Encourage Competition	Reward Investor
Shaping	Promote Freedom	Protect Security
Administrability	Clear Rules Reduce Quarrels	1) Old Rule Not So Clear 2) Unfair Rules Breed Disputes
Do the Right Thing	People Have Relied on Rule	Trend toward Flexibility
What Kind of Czar	Change is for Legislature	Courts Change Common Law
Non-Interference	Keep Government out of Hunting	Dispute-Resolution Role Inevitable

From your perspective as an exam taker, the important components of this chart are the two alternatives identified in the top
row and the argument dimensions listed in the left-hand column.
It hardly matters whether you find our discussion of *Pierson v.
Post* a convincing analysis of the rule of capture, nor even whether
you agree precisely with our characterization of the dimensions of
argument. Many law teachers, for example, would choose to re-
characterize what we have called a shaping argument for freedom
as an argument about rights. They might say that the party who
first chased an animal could claim ownership by alleging "a right
to security." How dare someone come along and steal the fox that
the defendant worked so hard to capture? In contrast, the party
who actually caught the animal could assert "a right to act freely."
If no clear rule forbids it, then people should be able to do as they
please, including grabbing an animal already being pursued.

The advantage of rights rhetoric is that it seems less political
and open-ended than forthright policy analysis. The discussion
about what the rule should be is recast as a battle about what the
law already is, even when there's no clear guide to that determination. The emphasis on decisions taken in the past serves judges'
interests in pretending not to have as much power as the Czar-
image suggests. They can feign powerlessness by justifying results
based on "rights" that parties supposedly have prior to the beginning of a dispute. We find this reliance on rights rhetoric somewhat mystifying, since you never really know which party has a
"right" (*e.g.*, to the wild animal) until after the question has been
resolved. Accordingly, we tend to avoid "rights" rhetoric when
talking about policy questions. Again, however, you should be
reading us not to mimic our style preferences, but to develop your
skills of talking about problems in as many different ways as possible. On your exam questions, you will be rewarded as much for
presenting multiple arguments as for characterizing the problem
exactly as your professor would.

Perhaps, then, one way to tackle your exam questions is to
draw a chart like ours. A policy question, unlike an issue-spotter,
may make it clear what the two likely policy alternatives are. For
issue-spotters, you need to identify the forks and then present arguments pushing one way and the other. Once you have isolated
the policy issue, such as whether the landlord should be held

strictly liable for the tenant's injuries, you will once again be presented with a choice between policy alternatives. (Obviously courts could invent all kinds of sub-rules — such as yes for bodily injury but no for property damage — but the great thing about an issue-spotter is that you may limit your analysis to the facts presented in the question.) In either case, you want your basic alternatives across the top of your chart. You want the various dimensions of argument we have described and others you may identify along the left-hand column. Your job, then, is to fill in the boxes.

	Alternative A	Alternative B
Shaping (Cost-Benefit)	?	?
Shaping (Rights)	?	?
Administrability	?	?
Do the Right Thing	?	?
What Kind of Czar	?	?
Prime Directive	?	?

But, you ask, perhaps disappointed with our suggestions so far, how are we supposed to know what arguments to put into the boxes? Our answer is twofold. First, we have been telling you all along that *Getting to Maybe* is a tool to be added to hard work, not a substitute for it. You will have had to think carefully about the course from the beginning to be able to ace the exam. Second, and perhaps more helpfully, if you know that filling in boxes like those in the chart is part of what you need to learn, you can organize your course studying along lines that will better prepare you for the moment of truth.

D. Find the Fun and *Snap* the Test's a Game

Now comes the fun part. We believe that most students on most exams will do pretty well with a relatively routine application of the kinds of argument we have described in this chapter. We promised at the outset, however, to try to go beyond straightforward student techniques to offer some insight into the process professors use to construct exams. You may find that insight particularly helpful when you try to tackle straightforward "policy" questions. On issue-spotters, you'll get loads of credit simply for unearthing the policy conflicts hidden in the fact pattern, and often you'll be too busy dealing with multiple forks to take the policy analysis beyond an argument or two on each side. But on "policy" questions, the nature of the policy conflict is usually made clear, and you must therefore be creative in showing how problems are not as simple as they first appear. If the grading curve is stiff, it may not be enough to do well at demonstrating the skills described in our tour of the Policy Kingdom. Moreover, to be fair, the argument dimensions presented here don't come close to a complete picture of the complexity you will encounter in practice. So, when they can, professors add to the level of difficulty. Fortunately for you (at least for those of you reading this book), professors do so in familiar and predictable ways, most of which are variations on a theme.

1. Trade-Off vs. Paradox

Here's the theme. Law school exam questions often require you to discuss policy questions in terms of a trade-off between competing values *and* in the less familiar terms that Deborah Stone has eloquently described as "policy paradox." Many students miss this because it is so seldom explained. Once you see it, however, you'll never again look at policy questions in quite the same way.

Let's start with a very simple example from outside the law. You are thinking about which of two houses to buy. One house is close to your workplace. The other is farther away but a little larger and more comfortable. All of us have a bottom-line-oriented friend who would be happy to sum up your decision as convenience vs. space. It's a tough choice, this friend will say, but life is full of tough choices. We have already discussed the technique of enhancing a discussion by considering other dimensions of a problem. Certainly you might expand the house selection discussion by bringing in other variables. So, if the goal is a good discussion of the impending choice (and exam questions almost always want discussions more than decisions), you might want to talk about other factors, such as which house will appreciate more in value or which will take more time to maintain. We all, however, can hear our friend's voice shouting in our ear to free our mind of minor distractions and focus on the main trade-off at hand.

If you want to drive your bottom-line friend nuts, however, consider the following potential wrinkles on choosing a house. Suppose that the house that's farther from work is actually close to an express bus stop. If there's a special traffic-free lane for buses, the bus commuting time might even be less than the driving-plus-parking time from the closer house. Consider the following statement: "The house that's farther away is more convenient." At one level, this appears to be an obvious paradox. Yet, a moment's thought reveals that, in other ways, this conclusion makes perfect sense. If we stopped here, you might say, "Great, the farther house is bigger and more convenient so I should pick it." Alas, real-world decisions aren't likely to be so simple.

For one thing, to push the point, the paradox may come at you from the other side as well. Suppose your family work pattern has always been that you and your spouse take turns using your downtown workplace on weekends for long-term work projects. There's plenty of room there for your spouse to store work materials. It turns out, however, that the express bus does not run on weekends, and the long drive appears daunting for both of you. You can deal with this in the larger house by setting up home offices for each of you. Subtracting these two rooms, however, now actually gives you less living space in the larger house than you would have in the smaller house. Consider, then, the following statement: "The smaller house will give us more living space." At one level, this appears to be another obvious paradox. By now, though, you get the picture.

Moreover, paradoxical aspects are more likely to complicate matters than resolve them. It might be that the bus will get you to work faster from the farther house, and so it might appear that this house is also more convenient. But there's convenience and then there's convenience. If you like to have your car at the office during the day to run errands, taking the bus won't work so well. If you carry large quantities of work back and forth, the bus may prove more difficult. The rooms you plan to devote to home offices may effectively shrink the larger house, so the closer house may now seem more livable. But you can probably store things in the home offices, put books on shelves, and even let the kids use the rooms for an expanded game of hide-and-seek. So there's living space and then there's living space.

All this means that for purposes of fully discussing which house to buy, your bottom-line friend's emphasis on a trade-off between convenience and space may greatly oversimplify the problem. In real life, such oversimplifications are often helpful to bring you to closure on a tough issue. But if you are going to excel as a Czar of the Universe, you don't have the luxury of ignoring the paradoxes or wishing them away.

Let's move back now to a more direct application of paradox to policy questions. Consider how many legal and ethical problems initially draw our attention to a difficult trade-off between competing values. The current debate over campaign finance reform, for example, might be seen as a contest between egalitarian ideals ("level the electoral playing field") and libertarian ideals ("candidate spending is free speech"). The debate over affirmative action is often cast as pitting diversity against merit. Mandatory AIDS testing raises issues of privacy versus public health. It is easy to imagine writing about any one of these issues as if it were nothing but a choice between such conflicting values.

Each side could be defended along many of the dimensions we have discussed in this chapter. So, to take the affirmative action example, proponents might stress diversity because we will be better off building a multi-cultural society (SHAPING); because injustices of the past warrant redress (DO THE RIGHT THING); because courts should let university officials or employers make key decisions (WHAT KIND OF CZAR ARE YOU?); and because reserving a certain number of places for minority candidates is an easily administered policy (ADMINISTRABILITY). Opponents might emphasize merit because we will be better off building an efficient society (SHAPING); because today's meritorious applicants shouldn't suffer for sins of the past (DO THE RIGHT THING); because courts are charged with enforcing constitutional norms (KIND OF CZAR); and because it's hard to distinguish benign from invidious discrimination (ADMINISTRABILITY). Although this formulaic debate hardly captures the subject, it would be a good start on an exam question such as: "Affirmative action should be abolished—discuss."

To get beyond a good start, however, will require you to look past the familiar trade-off into which the debate has been pigeonholed. So, to continue the affirmative action example, supporters will often make the point that a true notion of merit requires consideration of diversity. The university applicant with an unusual ethnic background may add more to classroom discussions than would just one more person with high test scores. So we might get the seemingly paradoxical statement that the university should admit the student with lower test scores because she is more qualified. From the other side, affirmative action opponents sometimes argue that a true notion of diversity would rest on more than racial or ethnic background. Indeed, the iconoclast with high test scores might add more diversity than someone admitted pursuant to more traditional affirmative action. So we might get the paradoxical statement that affirmative action hurts diversity—often put pointedly by contrasting "Cosby kids" with disadvantaged whites. The key here is that by unsettling the standard trade-off between diversity and merit both sides have complicated and deepened the argument in ways likely to make exam graders very happy. We believe that you should keep your eyes open for such opportunities when dealing with policy issues. Of course, not every question calls for a translation of trade-off into paradox. But once you start looking, you'll be surprised how often this technique will help.

2. The Pattern of Paradox

We can already imagine readers wondering whether we haven't quite taken you far enough. After all, we promised at the book's outset to show you how law professors build questions, not merely to clue you in on what to look for. Yet, if you read through our examples of paradox in the previous section, we mostly just illustrate what policy paradox looks like. But you need to know how to *find* it. Since paradox is everywhere, we can't provide an exhaustive guide. But in this section we will illustrate some of the most familiar dilemmas and paradoxes that professors use to add complexity to policy issues.

a. The short run and the long run

The initial shift from trade-off to paradox is most obvious in cases in which short-run and long-run effects of policies are likely to be different. During our years in law school, for example, rent control was a favorite policy topic for Property exam questions. Our guess is that by now the paradoxical aspects are front and center in your Property course. At rent control's inception, its supporters often argued that decent housing for low-income people is more important than marginal profits for wealthy landlords. (DO THE RIGHT THING—Fairness across social class.) Opponents stressed the rights of landlords to do as they please with their property, noting that grocers and owners of other kinds of property don't have to lower prices to make their products affordable. (DO THE RIGHT THING—Fairness across social categories.) This approach makes it appear as though the issue is ultimately a battle between tenants (pro rent control) and landlords (anti). Along these same lines, rent-control supporters argue that abandoning rent control will force poor people onto the streets and contribute to homelessness (SHAPING).

Consider the joy in the landlord camp, however, the first time someone came up with the following formulation: "Rent control is a bad thing because it's bad for tenants. Although in the short run some low-income tenants may be able to secure housing they otherwise could not afford, in the long run no one will want to invest money in a price-regulated industry. Fewer dollars will flow into housing, so fewer rental properties will be built. The housing supply will be artificially low, and tenants will pay higher rents or become homeless more than they would without rent control." This is no mere rhetorical device; many people believe it to be true. We need not discuss that here. For exam purposes, what's important is how the rhetorical shift illustrates an important technique.

By changing the discussion from the short-run impact to the long-run impact, rent-control opponents can succeed in altering our understanding of the problem. What was once a trade-off between tenant interests and landlord interests is re-characterized as a paradoxical choice between tenant interests now and tenant interests later. (Landlords may use a similar technique by sowing division within the group allegedly aided by rent control. So they may say rent control may help existing tenants but only at the expense of younger, newer tenants seeking a foothold in the housing market.) When you do it well, this kind of problem re-characterization will fill your grader's heart with glee. It might even help win a presidential election (*e.g.*, let's raise revenues by cutting taxes). So it's worth noting some of the other ways the shift can be accomplished.

b. Intent vs. effects

Suppose your Criminal Law professor asks you to evaluate legalizing drugs, such as marijuana, cocaine, or heroin. In our day (long ago!), some drug users pushed legalization pretty hard, stressing points like "the government shouldn't tell us what we can do with our bodies" (NON-INTERFERENCE). This argument, however, was always a political loser. Drug opponents argued that only criminalization could stop the flow of dangerous drugs, and the dominant view has been that we should do whatever it takes, up to and including criminal penalties, to stop people from using and selling certain drugs.

Recent proponents of legalization, however, have shifted the ground of the debate. Rather than stressing the rights of drug users to do as they please, some decriminalization advocates have conceded that public policy should be to slow down or stop drug use. So they applaud the goals of current laws that impose stiff penalties for drug use. But goals, supporters of legalization say, are not enough. The key question, is what *effect* do our current laws have?

Perhaps criminal penalties don't work as we intend. The black market for drugs has become extraordinarily lucrative, creating enormous incentives for pushers to get customers hooked. The high cost of drugs causes addicts to commit crimes to get money for the next fix. The drug war diverts police resources from other pursuits. And the failure to stop drug use may breed disrespect for the law—particularly in areas where drug use is most rampant.

None of this means that we should necessarily legalize drugs. But it illustrates that answering a policy question should always cause you to consider whether the solution you propose will have the effect you intend. In the drugs example, you could do well highlighting the trade-off between the user's freedom to experiment on his body and the society's need to combat reckless behavior and adverse health effects. But you'll do even better by noting that no clear policy alternative follows once you decide society's interest should outweigh the individual's.

The gap between a law's intent and effect is a pervasive source of paradox. To take another example, one of us overheard several young teenagers in a multiplex movie theater considering which of several films to see. One girl proposed *Contact*, the thought-provoking movie starring Jodie Foster about how the world might react to evidence of life on other planets. "Oh, we can't see that," replied another, "it's only rated PG." The rating system, purportedly designed to guide parents and reduce the amount of sex and violence kids would see, was actually working in reverse.

Or consider the paradoxical statement that raising the drinking age may increase highway deaths. Sounds like nonsense until you hear that what happens when the age is raised is that teens drive to a nearby state with a lower limit to buy booze and then die on the road on the way home. These kinds of paradoxes are just another aspect of policy debate you can expect to find built into your exam questions. Few professors keep a list of paradoxical situations, but virtually all are happy when their policy questions have twists to separate the "B"'s from the "A"'s. And, just as legislators don't always grasp a statute's consequences, professors writing questions don't always intend the paradoxes that you identify in your answers. But we assure you that you'll be rewarded for bringing your grader up to speed.

c. Law on the books vs. law in action

The gap between law on the books and law in action is a close cousin of the gap between intent and effect, and so we won't belabor it here. For some people, however, thinking of the gap this way makes it easier to understand. Suppose your Tax professor poses a policy question such as: "Should the marginal rate of income taxation on the highest-earning taxpayers be increased?" This is a very difficult issue, and it's likely to draw you into discussions of fairness (meritocracy vs. egalitarianism) and incentives (will productive people work less if taxation levels are too high?). But if you get lost in these trade-offs too quickly, you run the risk of assuming that a higher rate of taxation "on the books" will necessarily mean more taxes will be paid "in action." Income shifting to capital gains, increased use of shelter techniques, and outright cheating, however, are all possible taxpayer reactions that your teacher will love hearing about in your response. Of course, in a theoretical discussion it would make perfect sense to say, "First let's worry about where the rates should be, and then we'll worry about how to collect the money." But successful Czars—like successful policymakers— seldom have the luxury of focusing on what *should* happen without also considering what *will* happen.

d. Categories are many-splendored things

In his 1996 acceptance speech to the Republican National Convention, presidential candidate Robert Dole tried very hard to cast his party as the party of freedom. He glorified the government's role as something more important than feeding the hungry. Government must ensure that farmers and their families are free to feed themselves and others, Dole exclaimed. Senate Minority Leader Tom Daschle responded for the Democrats in his speech before the Democratic convention. He claimed Democrats are the party of freedom; but, he said, where Republicans emphasize freedom *from* (presumably from government), Democrats emphasize freedom *to* (freedom to own a home, to pursue an education, etc.). So who really is "the party of freedom"? Well, it all depends on what you mean by "freedom."

This kind of "category ambiguity" runs throughout virtually every policy controversy you'll find on exams—and in real-world debate, for that matter. Indeed, although we have placed this section under "The Pattern of Paradox," category ambiguity is actually a far larger topic in American law, and we don't pretend to offer a comprehensive treatment here. Instead, we want merely to explain how the many-splendored meaning of terms like "freedom" or "equality" can help you improve your exam answers.

Fortunately, we have already provided some examples. The affirmative action controversy, we noted, pits diversity against merit only until you stop and think about what is meant by "diversity" and "merit." The house shopper we described was choosing between convenience and space until we showed how "convenience" and "space" could be looked at in different ways. But these are merely the tip of the iceberg. Our public schools are filled with honors classes limited to those students who performed well in earlier grades and on standardized tests. Does this square or conflict with our commitment to equality? The familiar conflict between "equality of result" and "equality of opportunity" reminds us that the right answer is "it depends on what's meant by equality." But even this formulation contains further ambiguities that prevent it from actually solving real-world problems. If we required that honors classes be open to all who wish them in the name of "equality of result," would we then further insist that each student receive the same grade? If we permitted the current selection method in the name of "equality of opportunity," would we allow public schools to exclude some students altogether based on low test scores?

We can't caution you enough, then, about avoiding categorical slogans as a substitute for detailed consideration of the question at hand. Congress is contemplating laws that would prohibit private groups from spending money for political advertisements during the final 60 days prior to an election. Does this infringe on freedom of speech? Perhaps. But a mere recitation of "free speech" as a bar to such laws is unlikely to persuade your grader that you have thought the problem through.

•

Or, to take another example, your Property exam has a question such as, "Should landlords be prohibited from imposing requirements for the number of people in a given apartment?" This is a hard issue because landlords might use such requirements as a pretext for discriminating against families with children, and at the same time landlords may also have legitimate reasons for avoiding overcrowding. But it certainly won't help your answer to say, "The landlords should be permitted to limit occupancy because restricting them would interfere with their property rights." After all, it all depends on what we mean by "property" and by "rights."

3. Paradox is an Attitude

We could extend this chapter at great length listing still more paradoxical twists professors can write into exams. For example, suppose the question is whether an administrative agency should mandate adoption of a new safety device (*e.g.,* air bags) to supplement one that's been in place for a long time (*e.g.,* seat belts). Many students may cast the problem in terms of the higher cost of the new device when compared to the safety benefits that can reasonably be expected. Imagine the grader's glee, however, when she picks up the paper that reads, "Requiring air bags may provide manufacturers with the necessary hands-on experience needed to invent ways to install them more cheaply, so that the sheer act of mandating them might indeed reduce their costs." (For paradoxes, after all, you can't do much better than the chicken and the egg!)

At this juncture, however, we want to make the broader point that as an exam taker you aren't merely looking for paradox, *per se*, as much as trying to remain open to multiple perspectives on the same issue. Democrats often support minimum-wage laws because they focus on shifting money from shareholders to those at the bottom of the working class (glass half full). Republicans often publicly oppose minimum-wage laws on the ground that some low-paying jobs simply won't be created because of the mandated wage (glass half empty). Good exam takers are free to take either position as long as they carefully consider both points of view.

But if finding comfort in paradox requires an attitude, can you really learn it from reading a book like this? Some of our most respected colleagues have told us that it's not possible to teach the kind of playfulness necessary to develop stellar exam-taking skills. Obviously, we disagree. By now we have explained the idea as best we can. Let us close this section then with one more example of how turning trade-off into paradox can be fun —or at least can pave the way for Law Review performance.

Sometimes paradox arises because a trade-off between competing values just can't capture the complexity of a situation. Imagine, for example, that you are taking a seminar about the judicial confirmation process, and the exam asks you to discuss how a nominee should handle Senate testimony. Everyone can envision urging a nominee not to be too candid. The candidate might alienate an important constituency or violate the norm against comment on cases that may later come before the court. Everyone can also envision advising the nominee not to be overly diplomatic. Otherwise, the Senate may think the candidate is ducking the hard questions. So a simple version of the problem is to navigate the trade-off between candor and diplomacy.

Think how happy the professor will be, however, to read an answer that describes the problem in the following way: "As my client gets ready for her Senate testimony I would urge her to be diplomatic, not as a way of hiding her true feelings, but as a way of communicating them more accurately. If her rhetoric is too sharp, the problem won't be that she'll be penalized for her views. It's that her views will be twisted out of context, and she'll be criticized for views she doesn't even hold. At the same time, I would urge my client to be candid, not merely to demonstrate bravery and a willingness to tackle hard issues, but to generate trust. Candor it seems to me is the heart of diplomacy, for no one can be diplomatic unless she is trusted. Rather than a middle ground between candor and diplomacy, my client must be candid and diplomatic at different times and in different ways. This is best accomplished by practicing measured responses to the kind of questions she will receive."

The student's technique here is similar to the one we described using the affirmative action example. General categories (here candor and diplomacy, there diversity and merit) are critically evaluated to see if they can be meaningfully interpreted in different ways. There's still a long way to go to write a complete answer to the question. But breaking out of the familiar description of the conflict is a great way to start.

4. When in Doubt, Write It Down

By now we imagine you've had just about enough of our efforts to stylize what good policy answers will look like. We anticipate two entirely legitimate concerns. First, you are probably thinking that it's all well and good for us to spin out multiple conflicting arguments at the leisurely pace afforded us by word processors and faculty offices. You have to answer policy questions under enormous time pressure and facing very high stakes. Second, we are sure you've noticed that we never quite get to the point where we actually take a stand on an issue and tell you which way you should resolve it. How, you wonder, will reading this book help you to write quickly and make good decisions?

We have several answers. We urge you to begin by reading this chapter over carefully while working on an old policy question given by one of your professors. We are confident that the arguments we describe here will play an important role in your efforts to draft a response. Each time you practice, the arguments will become more familiar, and you will get faster at adapting them to new situations. We never said exam-taking was easy. We also urge you to continue on to Part III, where we provide many concrete tips for how to cope with time pressure and the other challenges that the exam process presents.

Above all, however, the key ingredient we are trying to provide is confidence. When you sit down to write an answer to any question, it's human nature to seek a simple, straightforward response. As thoughts pop into your head that cause you to wonder whether there may be more to the question than your first reaction implies, there's a tendency to fear your doubts or to want to banish them. But those doubts are your friends. Write them in your answer. They may not in the end lead anywhere, and, if they don't, say that too. Remember that your professor can't know what you were thinking unless it's written on the page.

What should be clear from reading this chapter is that almost any policy conclusion, no matter how sound, will be legitimately subject to reasonable doubts. As a military general or company CEO, you might choose to hide such doubts to create a commanding image. By contrast, a true Czar of the Universe would confront these doubts head-on, confident that doing so would confirm his wisdom more than it would undermine his authority.

Likewise, as an exam taker, your job is to explain all the angles before coming to rest on a conclusion. Your challenge is to organize the angles into a coherent, readable answer, not to leave them out. Take heart. Those of you who work through this book know everything you need to accomplish that mission. When in doubt, tell your grader why.

Part III

Test-Taking Tips — Your Very Own Ruby Slippers

Introduction

Congratulations! You've completed the most difficult portion of *Getting to Maybe*. By contrast, we think you'll find the material in this part of the book—a series of "tips" on Preparing for the Exam (Chapter 11), Writing Exam Answers (Chapter 12), and Mistakes to Avoid (Chapter 13), as well as answers to a number of Frequently Asked Questions (Chapter 14) and a set of Sample Questions and Answers (Chapter 15)—relatively easygoing. Indeed, if you are short on time (say you've picked up this book in a moment of panic the night before your first law school exam!), we'd suggest focusing on these tips for now and turning to the rest of the book when the dust settles.

But don't let the breezy style and accessible format fool you. Like dieting advice, these tips are much easier to explain than they are to follow—especially in the high-pressure context of the typical law school exam. Although even a quick read might help dispel some of the misunderstandings you may have picked up from other sources, you'll get much more out of these tips if you learn how to *use* them, and for most students that will take considerable practice. A good way to start is to work your way through the tips very carefully, paying special attention to the examples and illustrations we offer throughout. After that, we suggest that you give Tip # 4 a try ("Review the Professor's Old Exams") and attempt to translate your understanding into action.

Finally, if you find yourself stumped at any point, you can access the hypertext version of these tips on-line through our Web site at *<http://www.getting2maybe.com>* and on the *Lexis-Nexis for Law Schools* Web site *<http://lawschool.lexis.com>*, where you will receive guidance on how to e-mail questions to us. Obviously, we can't answer every one, but we plan to respond to a representative sample of "frequently asked questions." We bet that if something is bothering you, it will trouble enough others that we'll be addressing it sooner rather than later.

Chapter 11

Preparing for the Exam

The tips that appear in this part of the book are designed as a supplement to good old-fashioned studying, not as a substitute for it. You aren't going to do well if you don't attend class, read the assigned material, and struggle to understand it—case closed. Often, however, students who spend what should be adequate time preparing for exams don't study as efficiently as they might. And once you've read all the cases and reviewed your classnotes until you just can't look at them anymore, what should you do then? Try these tips as a way of studying smart while you are studying hard.

Tip #1. Exam Preparation
Takes All Semester

Here's the part where we tell you to prepare diligently for class, to attend class regularly, and to take good notes. We understand how tempting it is to ignore such advice; *of course* a couple of law professors are going to tell you that you need to go to every class well-prepared and to write down every word we say! But consider the possibility, however remote it might seem, that the reason we want you to do these things is not to torture you, but because we have reason to think that this is the best way for you to succeed in your legal studies. Indeed, when it comes to excelling on law school exams, we think this advice is second in importance only to Tip #7 ("Read Each Question Carefully, and Answer the Question Asked"). Here's why:

Regular class attendance is crucial to exam performance.

It's a common perception among non-lawyers that law is a body of "rules" that law students must memorize and be ready to regurgitate on demand in law school and, ultimately, in legal practice. But if you've been a law student for more than a week, you've no doubt begun to figure out that rule memorization and regurgitation are of very little use in class discussion and that the emphasis is far less on what the rules *are* than on how lawyers and judges *use* rules to analyze and solve problems.

For most students, this represents an abrupt departure from their undergraduate studies, where teachers frequently use class time to convey and perhaps clarify the same information contained in the reading for the course. By contrast, in law school the assigned readings are typically only the starting point for the analysis the professor pushes her students to undertake in class, and you can be sure that it is the analysis developed in class that will be carefully tested on the final. As a result, class attendance is generally *the* key to preparation for the typical law exam. (If you have to miss a session, we recommend that you seek permission from the professor to have someone tape-record it for you. A classmate's notes may do in a pinch, but—even assuming you can read the writing and decipher the abbreviations—the best they can be expected to offer is only a glimpse of what you missed.)

The better your preparation, the more you'll get out of a class.

Most law students quickly surmise that the cases and rules they are supposed to study in preparation for class are only the starting point for the analysis and discussion that actually take place in the classroom. But some students take this logic a step further: Since you can't learn the law's lessons simply by reading the assigned materials on your own, they figure, why bother reading those materials at all? Why not simply go to class and wait for the professor just to tell you exactly what you need to know?

The problem with this thinking is that it assumes that the point of the law school classroom experience is to teach you what the cases and materials "really mean," rather than to help you learn how to analyze, interpret, and argue about those materials and how to do so on your own. To be sure, if a particular class discussion is focused on a short and simple phrase (*e.g.*, "a benefit previously received by the promisor" under § 86 of the Second Restatement of Contracts), you may well be able to keep up with that discussion even if you are reading the phrase for the first time right there in class. But if the focus of the discussion is much broader than that—like a complex statutory provision, or a court's opinion, or a line of cases—you're in deep trouble. Like the blindfolded man who mistook the elephant's trunk for a snake, you're unlikely to get the details right and are even less likely to grasp "the big picture."

Attendance and preparation may be even more important at the end of the semester than at the beginning.

The end of the semester is invariably serious crunch-time, with paper due-dates, makeup classes, and professors rushing to get through their syllabi. Yet this is no time to let class attendance and preparation slip, since the material presented during the last several classes of the semester is quite likely to appear on the final. For one thing, many professors teach their courses so that concepts and issues unfold in cumulative fashion, and as a result the final two or three topics may well "bring together" various themes and problems that the professor thinks are especially important and hence worth stressing on the exam. For another, most professors draft their exams at the end of the semester—partly because we're procrastinators (just like our students!) but partly because we don't know what we'll test until we see what we've actually taught. In any event, it is only natural for us to focus our questions on the topics that are freshest in our minds, and the topics covered at the end of the course are likely to loom large in just this way.

Tip #2. Focus Your Exam Study on Your Classnotes

The reading period is coming to a close, and you're pulling another late-nighter in the library. On one side of the desk is a beautifully printed, carefully organized commercial outline summarizing the main points of the topic you are studying. On the other side rests the virtually indecipherable chicken-scratch that you call classnotes. Although it's tempting to focus your flagging energy on the easy-to-read work of the so-called experts, don't do it. For at least two very important reasons, your classnotes are your best bet.

Most professors test what they teach.

Despite the widespread suspicion that your professors are out to trick you, most of us endeavor to test exactly what we've tried to teach. Thus, while a high-quality commercial study aid may offer a useful overview of a particular area of the law, nothing will provide a more accurate guide to the particular topics and issues that your professor thinks are most important—and is therefore most likely to examine—than what she actually emphasized in class. Moreover, quite apart from the variety of course content, different professors focus their teaching on different lawyerly skills. Some will emphasize rule application and argument; some will focus on policy analysis; some will embrace a theoretical perspective; some will stress fact-sensitivity; and most will do some mixture of all four. Whatever your own professor's approach, you can be sure that it is not captured in any study aid—unless she happens to be the author! As a result, your classnotes are likely to be among your most valuable resources as you prepare for your exams.

Your classnotes can help you predict questions likely to appear on the exam.

Many—perhaps most—law school exam questions are simply variations on hypotheticals and problems discussed in class; so carefully working your own way back through those hypos and problems is an excellent approach to preparing for the final. Indeed, some professors will signal their intention to draw explicitly from a particular class discussion by warning the students that "a problem like this will almost surely appear on the final"; obviously, it is a good idea to highlight such predictions in your classnotes and to focus your study efforts accordingly.

But your notes may contain subtler hints as to what will be tested as well. For example, it may be a good idea to pay special attention when the professor has gone back over particular material a second time—perhaps in response to a particularly insightful question from you or one of your classmates—and has done so in a way that suggests she has developed a new way of looking at the topic in the course of teaching it to your class. In our experience, it is more likely than not that she will focus on such "second thoughts" somewhere on the final, since she may well have experienced her own rethinking as one of the highlights of the course.

Tip #3. Prepare Your Own Outline of the Course

For virtually every law school course, there's a 1000-plus-page casebook; a statutory and/or new-case supplement; and an extraordinary number of hornbooks and other commercial study aids. If you were the publisher of all that material, you'd be rich; on the other hand, if you were the tree that generated the paper—not to mention the legal pads and notebooks that students fill to the brim with their casebriefs and classnotes—you'd be dead.

As a law student, you are likely to spend a lot of time feeling more like the tree than like the publisher. For one thing, you've got to lug the stuff from class to class. For another, you've got to find some way to master the cases, the rules, the outside materials, and your accumulated class and reading notes in time for the final. And while there are countless more or less equally effective approaches to the former task—we've seen everything from backpacks to shopping carts—we can think of no better way to "pull it all together" for exams than to prepare your own outline for each course. Here's why:

Law exams test rule application, not memorization.

Let's start with the good news. No law school exam question we have ever seen or heard about asks students to quote back from memory an even moderately lengthy passage from a case or a statute; accordingly, you don't have to worry about memorizing all those cases and rules and notes you have before you. What our exam questions test is not your recollection of the rules but what you can *do* with them: that is, your ability to make arguments about how to interpret and apply the rules and concepts you've studied in a variety of real-world contexts.

Thus, for example, you are highly unlikely to encounter a question that asks you to regurgitate from memory the definition of "goods" offered in U.C.C. § 2-105(1). Instead, you are likely to be asked to *apply* that definition to a variety of transactions. Sometimes the application will be straightforward (*e.g.*, to the book in which you are reading this); sometimes the application will be tricky (*e.g.*, to the software program we used to produce it). Obviously, you will need to have a pretty good idea of "what the rules are" in order to apply them in either setting, but you can safely leave the task of memorizing vast quantities of text for regurgitation-on-demand to the interns and residents on *ER*.

Don't mourn . . . Organize!

You're right if you are thinking that we've just delivered the bad news as well: Even though you don't need to memorize all those rules, you *do* need to master them well enough to be able to use them to analyze real-world fact patterns, and that is no easy task. We think that the best way to do this is to prepare an outline for each course—an outline designed to help you remember the rules you've studied and, even more important, to help you to understand those rules; to recognize the difficulties you're likely to encounter in interpreting and applying them; and to see where they fit in the "big picture" of the subject matter your professor is attempting to teach. We've devoted a substantial section of Chapter 9 to the art of outline-writing. What we've said there doesn't easily reduce to "tip" form, so we encourage you to work your way through that material if you wish to develop or improve your outlining skills.

Write the outline yourself.

The real point of an outline is not to have it but to *make* it. In our experience, the very process of outlining—of working your way back through the mass of course material and organizing it in a way that helps you make sense of it all—may be the most valuable part of your legal studies. In fact, we boldly predict that the more time you spend drafting and redrafting an outline, the less time you'll spend actually referring to it during the final. Of course, if you're taking a closed-book exam, you'd better not refer to your outline—or to anything else, for that matter—at all! But even on the far more common open-book exam, you are likely to find that the outline has already done the job by helping you to learn the material in the process of organizing it, thus freeing up precious exam time for reading and re-reading the questions and writing and refining your answers.

Commercial study aids are a poor substitute.

Although most law professors tend to sneer at hornbooks, canned outlines, and other commercial study aids, we concede that such materials can provide a useful supplement to your legal studies, provided you use them properly and recognize their limits. (See FAQ #8, "Should You Use Commercial Study Aids?") But one terribly important thing a commercial outline cannot do is provide you with the experience of organizing your *own* outline for a course; as we've said, we think the "pulling it all together" process is one of the most effective vehicles students have for learning the law. Moreover, a commercial outline is likely to fail you in a second, equally important respect: While a high-quality publication may well offer a useful general overview of a particular area of the law, your final exam is highly likely to focus on those topics and skills that your professor emphasized in class. As a result, an outline that draws on your own classnotes is likely to be infinitely more useful than the one-size-fits-all version you can buy in a bookstore. Finally, commercial outlines emphasize what is clear and what is settled about the subject matter, whereas your professor is far more likely to test the unclear and the unsettled. If you organize it well, your outline can thus be a far better guide to *your* exam than a commercial product ever could be.

Outlines prepared by other students are only marginally better.

In our experience, the value of outlines prepared by fellow students runs the gamut from marginally useful to downright dangerous. Most law professors update, re-organize, and even rethink the material they teach often enough to make it far too risky to rely on an outline from earlier renditions—even very recent ones—of the course. Indeed, an exam answer that draws on material the professor taught last year—but has taken the trouble to modify or transform for your class—is very likely to irritate her a lot, and that's something you never want to do to someone faced with the formidable task of grading a mountain of bluebooks.

Outlines of the current course are obviously better, but their utility depends almost entirely on your personal role in their preparation. Thus, if your study group develops an outline through a genuine collective effort—discussing and analyzing the entire course as a group, but perhaps divvying up topics for outlining among the individual participants—both the outline and the process of making it can be of genuine educational value. Even here, however, you are sure to find that your mastery of the material you outline yourself greatly exceeds your grasp of those parts of the course outlined by others; once again, it is the process of outlining, and far less the product you produce, that makes a difference to exam performance. Indeed, preparing for the final by using an outline or a part of an outline that you did not write yourself—even if it is authored by someone you consider to be the class "star"—is like attempting to make the NBA by reading about Michael Jordan's practice regimen. To paraphrase the famous athletic shoe commercial, when it comes to the law school outline, it's not enough to have it or even to study it. The point is to *do* it.

Tip #4. Review the Professor's Old Exams

We believe that reviewing exams your professor has given in previous years is one of the most effective ways to prepare for finals. Prior exams, especially recent ones, are likely to reveal the issues the professor finds significant or interesting enough to examine, and they may offer clues as to format (*e.g.*, lengthy issue-spotters vs. short-answer problems vs. policy questions) as well as content. Simply put, nothing else—not the most thorough studying; not the most popular commercial outline; not even the best book on exam-taking (this one!)—can provide you with this kind of insight into your own professor's approach.

We understand that looking at old exams can instill panic if done too early, when the questions will almost surely seem unimaginably difficult. Accordingly, you'll need to pick a time for this somewhere near the end of the course—though given the importance of the task, don't wait till the last minute either. But whenever you do it, by all means don't pass up your best opportunity to find out how your professor goes about the task of examining students!

Gather knowledge about your professor.

As much as we pride ourselves on the universal value of the advice offered in this book, it is no substitute for learning as much as you can about the way your particular professor gives and grades exams. Many professors make this easier by holding review sessions in which they describe in advance the format (if not the content!) of the exam, and many more help you out by placing previous exams on file. If such exams are available, get them and go over them carefully, for you'll have no better guide to what this year's exam will be like than the questions that appeared on prior exams. Law professors are even less likely than leopards to change their spots.

Don't wait until you are finished studying to look at an old exam.

It's incredibly dispiriting to read a series of questions on topics you've never even heard of, so there's much to be said for waiting until you are well into a course before you start working your way through old exams. (For upper-class electives, the counterpoint is that looking at old exams may be one way of deciding whether you are interested in the course in the first place.) But we urge you not to leave this important task to the very last minute. Law school exams aren't meant to be easy, and even the best students will often feel at a loss until they actually begin working through an answer. Looking at old exams at some point early in your exam review will give you time to incorporate the professor's particular way of thinking into your studying. Also, if an old exam raises issues that appear unfamiliar to you, you'll have time to determine whether the surprise is the professor's "fault" (*i.e.*, she has changed the content of the class since last year) or your own (*i.e.*, you missed something important in the course).

Simulate the exam experience at least once.

Let's face it, taking exams isn't anyone's idea of fun. One reason is that a lot is riding on your performance. But it's precisely because a lot is at stake that we think it's important to practice taking an old exam. You wouldn't dream of giving a piano recital without sitting down in a quiet room and playing the piece all the way through several times prior to the big day. Neither should you go into an exam without putting yourself through the daunting and even intimidating experience of being alone with your questions and your blank pages—and bluebooks aren't necessary! (Doing this will also give you an opportunity to practice budgeting your time among questions of varying difficulty and format; see Tip #15, "Watch Time/Credit Allocations.")

Go over old exams with your friends as often as you can.

We can't stress this enough. In our experience, many hardworking students who've been disappointed with their exam grades have turned out to be solo studiers. To be sure, working alone should play a crucial role in your legal studies. But once you feel confident about your basic understanding, group sessions reviewing old exams are perhaps the best way to test your facility with the concepts. As most law professors and more than a few lawyers have learned over the years, there is no better way to discover the holes in your own thinking than by being forced to communicate your views to others.

Moreover, studying old exams is one of those experiences that confirms the old adage two heads are better than one—and more heads better still. Thus, no matter how good you think you are at "seeing all the angles," you're sure to encounter many more if you work your way through a question from last year's exam with a small group of classmates who have varying perspectives on life and law.

We understand "study group" sessions can become needlessly competitive if each person insists on showing that his or her approach is the right one. But the way to deal with that problem is to talk about this danger in advance and agree collectively to avoid it; indeed, you can "vote with your feet" and change study groups if you find you just can't make yours work for you.

Tip #5. Consider What Questions *You* Would Ask

It's often said that there is no better way to learn a subject than to teach it. After a combined quarter-century of teaching, we're convinced that the most learning of all occurs when we sit down to write the exam. Exam writing forces you to look at the course as a whole; to identify the interesting issues; and to imagine where the law is headed.

This is exactly the kind of thinking that can prepare you to *take* an exam as well. Here are some helpful hints for thinking about your courses from the "top down," almost like a CEO would think about her company. We suggest you try them after you've spent a good deal of time mastering the course material from the "bottom up"!

Pull the forests out of the trees.

There is no substitute for knowing the material covered in your courses. But don't let a blizzard of detailed knowledge substitute for some quiet reflection. As the exam approaches, try to identify a small number of major issues that the professor has covered; three to six would capture the typical law school class. Have dinner with a friend unfamiliar with law and, focusing on those issues, explain the course in broad strokes—or try to before your friend falls asleep!

For example, from this perspective you might conclude Constitutional Law is about protecting individual rights from government intrusion; about dividing power between the national and state governments; and about allocating governmental power among the President, the Congress, and the Courts. (Crucial as they are, it is easy to lose sight of these broader themes when you are bogged down in the details of smaller points— *e.g.*, the rules governing the relationship between the privileges and immunities clause and the market-participant doctrine.) Then, force yourself to outline the major points the professor has tried to make about these recurring issues and about how these issues are implicated in individual cases. (Which theme or themes are at stake, for example, in deciding whether a particular plaintiff has standing to challenge a government action?)

A related exercise is to put yourself in the position of a professor who wants to see whether his students have grasped the principal themes of the course. You might imagine a conversation with one of your classmates; what questions would you ask her if you were trying to test her this way? Even if you can't predict the professor's questions with great precision, you'll find that this kind of thinking will help immensely in your preparation for the exam.

Look for important cases pointing in opposite directions.

Try to identify leading cases you have studied that take differing approaches to the same question of law. Based on similar facts, for example, one case might hold that a federal statute pre-empts state law while another case rules that there is no pre-emption. Now see if you can invent a fact pattern that contains some elements of the first case and some of the second case. For example, your hypo and the first case might both deal with a problem requiring a uniform national standard (a factor favoring pre-emption), but your hypo and the second case might deal with statutes whose wording suggests a less imperial congressional intention (a factor cutting against it).

Such hybrid fact patterns form the core of many exam questions. If you do enough of them, you might even be able to approximate the questions you will actually encounter on the final. But even if you don't get that lucky, you'll be developing one of the key skills you'll need for top performance, because you'll know exactly what to look for on the exam.

Identify underlying conflicts.

Every body of law is aimed at solving real-world problems. If the solutions were easy, we wouldn't need much law and there wouldn't be a whole course devoted to the subject. What makes the problems hard is that there are often two or more important goals that are in some tension with each other.

In property law, for example, we want rules that will make owners feel safe and secure in their investments, but we don't want rules that will ban all new competitors. In contracts, for another, there is the tension between rules that promote freedom of action and rules that protect reliance on promises. In torts, for yet another, there is the tension between limiting liability to actors who are "at fault" and expanding it to cover any and all harms one person causes another.

Before the final, try to identify the key conflicts from your course and the situations you've studied where it's particularly difficult to reconcile those conflicts. It's a safe bet that your professor will be doing the same thing as she drafts your exam.

Look for trends and limits.

Law professors frequently identify "trends" in the topics they cover, priding themselves in their forecasts of issues that are likely to arise in the future and the direction the law may take. Don't be surprised if they ask you to do the same thing on your exams.

Courses like Labor Law may make it easy to think in terms of "pro-union" or "pro-management" trends. But every course will have some issues in which patterns and directions can be detected, even if they are not so obvious. In Contracts, for example, the cases you've studied may reveal a recent trend toward enforcing the "plain language" of the contract, rather than understandings implicit in the transactional context. Similarly, you may have noticed—or your professor may have emphasized—that constitutional decisions are increasingly hostile to efforts by Congress to regulate "local" matters.

A classic professorial ploy for gauging your grasp of such developments is to invent situations that "push the envelope"— *i.e.*, that test just how far this or that trend will go before countervailing policies or concerns are likely to limit them. In Torts, for example, you might detect an increasing tendency to hold market actors responsible for damages they cause even when they are not at "fault." Try to come up with situations that stretch the "no-fault" concept to the breaking point: Might gun manufacturers be held responsible when their products kill or cause injury, even if there was absolutely nothing wrong with the gun? Should an aspirin manufacturer be held liable if someone intentionally uses the aspirin to administer a fatal overdose? Questions like these frequently appear on law exams, and we can think of no better way of preparing for them than by attempting to come up with them on your own.

Consult your casebook as a source of questions.

During the press of class preparation, it's sometimes difficult to take time to focus on the problems in the casebook that typically appear at the end of textual material. These problems are designed to make you think hard about complex topics, and you may feel pressed to move on to the next section. As you begin your exam preparation, however, it's time to go back and look at these problems again. Many professors consult these problems as a source for writing exam questions. Indeed, if you are really ambitious you might look at some of the problems in other casebooks for your course, which are usually available in the library. Even if your professor doesn't build a question based on any of the problems you study, this exercise is nonetheless terrific practice for the challenging problems you'll encounter on the exam.

What interests you?

Last but not least, take a few moments to consider what you find most interesting about the course. What problems would you want students to grapple with if you were writing the exam? If you'll forgive us for indulging a professional conceit, much of what you know about the subject you've learned from the professor, so it wouldn't be a coincidence if the two of you have ended up on the same wavelength!

Chapter 12

Writing Exam Answers

As Chapter 1 explains, law school exams are different from those you've encountered in other educational settings: You can't guarantee success simply by memorizing and parroting back a great deal of material, nor will elegant writing substitute for careful and critical analysis.

Here, then, are some specific steps you can take to enable you to use the skills that got you into law school—and the hard-earned "legal knowledge" you've gained since—to achieve better exam performance.

Tip #6. Carefully Read the Exam Instructions and Follow Them to the Letter

In the world of law school exams, some rules are made to be broken, and some rules aren't. Learning to tell which is which may be crucial to successful exam performance.

On the one hand, a classic type of law school exam question is designed to test your ability to know when and how to "break" a legal rule you've studied by offering a hypothetical in which a seemingly straightforward application of the rule will lead to results that are utterly at odds with the rule's underlying purpose. By contrast, the rules stated in law exam instructions— e.g., page or word limits—should *never* be broken. Here's why:

The "stuffy tuffy" may actually enjoy penalizing you.

As you might expect, different professors will react to violations of exam instructions in different ways. If your professor is what we call a "stuffy tuffy"—someone who demands that each student to come to every class meticulously prepared, who conducts a relentless Socratic inquiry in a rigorous and highly formal manner, and who seems to take great delight in squeezing an extended analysis out of even the most reluctant student—chances are that he will take the same extremely demanding approach to grading your exam. Although we have always suspected that this sort of classroom style is largely a pathological by-product of "partner envy," stuffy tuffies no doubt *believe* that what they are doing in the classroom will best prepare you for the rigors of legal practice.

At least when it comes to demanding strict adherence to exam instructions, they have a point: Absent prior permission from the court for good cause shown, real-world judges and court clerks routinely refuse to accept pleadings and briefs that don't meet in every respect the applicable requirements governing (*e.g.*) page-length and format, and to our knowledge no court anywhere has ever ruled that "I didn't know about the page limit" or "I didn't have time to read the rules" or "I just forgot" constitutes "good cause shown." The stuffy tuffy who is trying to prepare you for a career in which carelessness may harm a real-world client isn't likely to accept excuses like these either.

The "nice guy/gal" may agonize over it, but will probably penalize you, too.

It would be a serious mistake to assume from what we've just said that a professor who runs a "kinder, gentler" classroom will look more kindly or gently on a failure to follow exam instructions. For one thing, virtually *all* law professors—from the most conservative curmudgeon to the most easygoing liberal; from most traditional "black-letter" teachers to the most postmodern "theory of theory" folks—take very seriously the task of preparing their students for the rigors of law practice. There is more than a little bit of the "stuffy tuffy" in all of us, and the student who fails to follow rules that are as straightforward as most exam instructions is highly likely to bring it out.

Our own experience leads us to make a second point here: Many students seem to think that, when push comes to shove, the "nice-guy/gal" won't have the heart (or the guts) to penalize a student for something as "picky" as a failure to follow exam instructions. Truth be told, they're on to something: Many professors we know—and almost all of those whom we like— would rather walk over a bed of hot coals than lower a student's grade on what seems like a technicality.

But here's the rub: For every student who just can't seem to follow our instructions, there are two dozen others who take the time—*and it takes time*—to read, to grasp, and to follow them meticulously. You don't have to be in law teaching very long to come to the conclusion that letting the few get away with careless mistakes penalizes the many who strive hard for compliance. And when it comes to a choice between excusing the careless and penalizing the industrious innocent, you'll find that stuffy tuffies and nice-guys/gals quickly end up in the same place.

Even if you don't "lose points," you'll make a terrible impression on the grader.

A law professor faced with grading 100 or more sets of blue-books is a little like a law student attending a first-year orientation party with 100 or more of his or her new classmates: First impressions make a big difference, and the stronger that impression, the less likely it is that further and closer examination will change it.

Naturally, this can cut two ways. When a professor reads an exam that begins straight off with a thoughtful and well-organized argument, she is likely to be more willing to resolve doubtful points in the student's favor later on. But when the first thing a professor notices about an exam is that it doesn't conform to the exam instructions, she is likely to get the impression that the student in question was either too careless to read them, too thick-headed to understand them, or too arrogant to follow them.

While redemption is always possible—in the end, nothing beats a good answer, no matter how it is packaged—persuading the grader you've provided a thoughtful analysis of her exam *questions* will be an uphill battle if she is already persuaded that you simply ignored her exam *instructions*.

When in doubt, go find out.

What should you do if you've read the exam instructions and you don't understand them—if, for example, you genuinely think that there is more than one way to read a particular direction that the professor has given? (*E.g.*, does the page limit for bluebook answers apply to typed exams?) Our first and best advice is for you to take a deep breath and read the instructions once again, for the answer you seek may well be right in front of you. Most experienced professors develop "boilerplate" instructions that they use on exam after exam, and chances are pretty good that any real ambiguity would have been discovered and resolved years ago.

But—shocking though it may seem!—even law professors make mistakes, and if after a second reading you still think the instructions are ambiguous or unclear, then for heaven's sake *ask* someone. The best place to start is with the proctor, but, at many schools, the professors are available during the exam precisely for the purpose of dealing with unforeseen difficulties like these. (Indeed, you may be doing both the professor and your classmates a favor by raising the point at a time when the professor is still in a position to clarify the matter for the entire class.)

If you are not able (or not permitted) to make such an inquiry, then we recommend handling the problem the way a good *lawyer* would: At the very beginning of your bluebook, briefly identify the ambiguity you see and explain why you've handled it the way you have. If you've spotted an unintended ambiguity, the professor may well be impressed by both your careful reading and your cool under fire. But even if you've merely imagined the problem, the professor will be able to see that you are trying to follow the instructions, and most will appreciate that.

An ounce of prevention is worth a pound of cure.

As we said a moment ago, most professors develop "boiler-plate" exam instructions that they employ with little change for each exam they give. As a result, there is no better way of familiarizing yourself with a particular professor's "exam rules" than by studying her old exams, particularly those she's given in recent years. (See Tip #4, "Review the Professor's Old Exams.") Likewise, some professors distribute exam instructions during the final class of the semester or during a review session and do so for precisely the purpose of clarifying unintended confusion and ambiguity in advance of the final. If your professor gives you this sort of "heads up," you should obviously take advantage of it.

Tip #7. Read Each Question Carefully, and Answer the Question Asked

When we told our friends and colleagues in legal academia that we were working on this book, 99 out of 100 of them responded that the single most important advice we could give you is this: *Answer the question!* It was tempting to reply that maybe our students prefer to do as we do rather than as we say, for it is a common complaint that professors—especially the most relentlessly "Socratic" ones—seem to take great pleasure in doing everything with student questions *except* answering them.

But given the stakes, we doubt that the typical failure to "answer the question asked" is the result of a rebellious attempt to turn the tables on the teacher; moreover, given the obvious facility of most of our students with exams—you wouldn't be in law school if you hadn't done pretty well as an undergraduate and/or on the LSAT—we also doubt that the problem lies in your ability to answer exam questions. Instead, we think that the most common problem is that students *misunderstand* what it is that our questions are asking. Here are some brief suggestions for how to avoid falling into this trap.

Read each question carefully and *at least* twice.

We've all been there before: It's the final exam in the course that's been giving you trouble all semester. The proctor reviews the instructions and then signals the start of the test. You begin reading the first question, which is a complex factual scenario that goes on for a dozen paragraphs over two single-spaced pages. You've read about halfway through the question when you are distracted by a familiar but in this context most distressing sound: 101 pens and pencils writing and scratching away furiously. "Oh no," a little voice in your head exclaims. "They're all already busy racking up the points, and you're the only one *in the entire class* who is still reading the question! You'd better stop reading and start writing right now, or you won't stand a chance!"

While the sense of panic is a common and even reasonable response to the stress of the exam setting, you simply must find a way to ignore that little voice, because the surest path to failure is to heed its advice. Simply put, you can't possibly answer the question asked unless you know what that question is, and it will take even the most gifted student two, and sometimes even three, extremely careful readings to gain the necessary purchase on what we're asking.

Of course you shouldn't overdo it; the point is to understand the question well enough to answer it, not to try to commit it to memory. And obviously you need to leave yourself adequate time to write, since grades are based on what's in your blue-books, not what's in your head.

But pay no heed to those around you who have rushed through the reading and are already filling their bluebooks: A one-page answer that directly addresses the question we've asked is worth far more than a dozen pages of unresponsive blather, and in our experience the race for superior grades is won far more often by the conscientious turtle than by the careless hare.

Not every question is an issue-spotter.

The classic law exam question is the so-called issue-spotter — *i.e.*, the extended factual scenario that broadly invites the student to "discuss the legal issues" raised by the facts. Faced with such a question, the soundest strategy may well be to "throw in everything but the kitchen sink": *i.e.*, to identify and, to the extent time permits, analyze any and every plausible legal issue that you can uncover. But many of the exam questions you'll encounter in law school are not nearly so open-ended. Even issue-spotters frequently restrict you to an analysis of the rights and liabilities of specifically identified parties — for example, a complicated Torts question may feature a cast of more than a dozen but ask you to discuss the legal rights of only Betty and Colin. Other common kinds of questions ask you to analyze a particular legal issue ("does X have a valid claim for adverse possession of Blackacre?") or to respond to a specific legal argument ("if Y claims that evidence of those prior negotiations is barred by the parol evidence rule, how might Z respond?").

Students who've learned to use the "kitchen-sink" strategy for open-ended issue-spotters may have great difficulty shifting gears to cope with narrower and more specific questions such as these. But an answer that discusses the rights of Aaron (when the question restricts you to Betty and Colin) or that analyzes the broad implications of consideration doctrine (when the question focuses on parol evidence) will persuade the grader that you didn't read the question she labored long and hard to draft; or that you didn't understand it; or that you are simply unable (or too stubborn) to answer it. When she grades such an answer, it's safe to say that she won't come up with what *you* were looking for either!

Avoid the "information dump."

If you were successful as an undergraduate, it probably means that you developed a facility for absorbing vast quantities of information and "giving it all back on the final." And since your success as an undergraduate helped you get into law

school, you might reasonably expect that law exams would require and reward a similar form of regurgitation. Indeed, that
expectation is frequently reinforced by second- and third-year
students who tell their junior colleagues that the thing to do on
the final is to "show the professor you understood the course."
But once again, the thing to do on the final is *to answer the
question asked.* And the student who ignores the question asked
and responds instead by "giving it all back"—we referred to
this in Chapter 1 as the "information dump"—will get
nowhere fast.

Don't fight the question or re-argue points already settled.

One of the first lessons you learn in the law school classroom
is to take nothing for granted, for the clever professor can take a
judicial opinion that is seemingly focused exclusively on (say)
whether a child can intend a battery and unearth a host of ques-
tionable assumptions made by the parties and the court (*e.g.*,
perhaps no one questioned whether the victim's "horsing
around" with the child just prior to the battery constituted "consent").

But this is yet another lesson that can get you in trouble on a
law exam. Thus, if an exam question states that A has established B's liability for breach of contract and asks you to calculate the resulting damages, you would be making a serious mistake if you tried to re-open the question of liability in your
answer. At best, you will waste precious time by trying to prove
a point that the question has already settled. At worst, you will
"fight the question" and conclude that B is *not* liable to A and
thus that the professor's question regarding damages is beside
the point.

To be sure, there is always the chance that you are right—
that the professor has made a mistake and will reward your
careful reading of the facts and perceptive conclusion. (See FAQ
#5, "What If You Think the *Professor* Has Made a Mistake?")
But 99 times out of 100 it is the student who has made the mis-

take by fighting—rather than answering—the question the professor has asked.

In a pinch, push harder, but don't B.S.

Of course, sometimes the reason that a student doesn't answer the question asked is that she doesn't *know* the answer to the question asked. Our advice here: Push harder and harder on the question, and resist the growing temptation to talk about something else. If, for example, you read a question on your Torts exam and you aren't sure what the issue is—let alone what to do with it—you should re-read the question, slowly and carefully, and then work your way back through your outline for the course until you figure out something pertinent to say. But the very last thing you should do is draft a lecture on the history or the deep philosophical underpinnings of tort law in the hopes that *something* you say will "stick" or impress the reader. The professor will know exactly what you are up to and is likely to give you a far lower grade for your efforts than the student who at least attempts, however unsuccessfully, to grapple with the question asked. (See Tip #22, "Don't B.S.")

Tip #8. Organize and Outline Before Writing Your Answer

It takes unusual self-discipline to refrain from writing long enough to organize your thoughts. But it's well worth the effort. Law school exams, like most mental puzzles, are easier to understand if you break the problem into steps.

Suppose you are planning a trip to three foreign cities over twelve days, and your best friend asks you for a preview. You might start out by listing your plans for each day of the trip ("Well, on Sunday we'll do this . . . on Monday that . . . etc."). But your friend would find it much easier to follow if you started by saying something like, "My trip will last twelve days, four days each in Rome, Paris, and London." Then, as you moved into describing your itinerary for Rome, your friend would have a context to understand the trip as a whole. Better still, you'd have an easier way of remembering your plans.

Precisely the same advantages stem from outlining your exam answers. You can quickly hit the main points and place sub-issues under their correct categories. This is much easier to do before you actually begin writing. We know that you're under a great deal of time pressure to begin writing and that you won't get any credit for things you consider while outlining and then forget to include in your answer. (See Tip #10, "Explain Your Reasoning.") But virtually every professor prefers an organized essay, and outlining in advance is the best way to provide one.

Outlining keeps you focused on the main ideas.

Few aspects of law school exams are more daunting than the lengthy hypothetical with many characters, many events, and even more legal issues. It's tempting to feel that unless you plunge right in, you may not have time to discuss everything. The problem, of course, is that even if you do plunge right in, you *still* may not have time to discuss everything. And you may find yourself devoting 30 minutes to the issue that happens to pop into your head first.

You simply can't afford to let the question bully you like this. Instead, take a few moments to consider the big picture. What are the three or four most important issues? Can other aspects of the question be grouped as "sub-parts" of these issues? Jot down a quick outline to this effect and then begin writing. Your outline will assure that your answer is well-organized and that you take time for the key issues.

Outlining helps you think sequentially.

A second major virtue of outlining is that it will force you to consider the proper order in which to take up the issues. Every question has its own internal logic that makes it easier to take up certain issues first. For example, if the plaintiff's standing is at issue, you might analyze standing at the beginning of your answer because the case cannot proceed without it.

Outlining your answer won't guarantee that you will find the best sequence. But you are a great deal more likely to choose well if you pause to think before writing, rather than just diving in and discussing issues at random.

Outlining helps you avoid wrong turns.

One way in which sequencing turns out to be very important is that the resolution of some issues makes other issues less pressing, sometimes even irrelevant.

On the first read of a lengthy issue-spotter on your Torts exam, for example, the causation issue may scream out at you for lengthy discussion. But careful outlining may lead you to conclude that negligence is the appropriate standard by which to judge the defendant's conduct and that the defendant most certainly was not negligent. If that analysis is correct, then the question whether the defendant's action caused the plaintiff's injury is immaterial. You should certainly still flag it, partly to rack up points for issue-spotting, but even more to hedge your bet in the event that your analysis of the negligence issue turns out to be wrong. But if you're right—and if your pre-outline focus on causation had made you miss the negligence issue—then you would have done poorly on the question, even if your discussion of causation were first-rate.

In short, outlining can help you to avoid getting sidetracked on issues that seem interesting at first but turn out to matter less when you've thought the answer all the way through.

Outlining helps you draft a roadmap.

In the end, your goal is not merely to think through the answer but to let your professor in on all that thinking as well, and your answer will accomplish that task far more efficiently if it begins with a couple of sentences explaining the major issues you will discuss and how they may fit together. Your outline, therefore, won't merely help you in your own thinking as you begin writing; it may also serve as the basis for an introductory paragraph that puts the entire question into perspective. In short, it will help you keep the forest in mind as you begin telling your professor about the trees.

Tip #9. Provide the Reader with a Brief Roadmap

There's no better way to get an exam answer off to a good start than with an opening paragraph that sets forth clearly the issues you plan to discuss. This assures the reader that the main issues will be considered and signals the order in which to expect them. Some questions will be so short that no introductory roadmap is necessary, and in that setting drafting one may even needlessly slow you down. Never underestimate, however, the power of an introductory paragraph that confidently begins, "In this essay, I will consider the following three points . . . ."

Create a strong first impression.

Suppose your professor is reading and grading an essay answer on a Property exam. The question instructs students to discuss three theories the plaintiff can use to seek access to defendant's land. One thing you can be sure of is that a regrettably large number of students will spend all their time on only one theory, and that some won't discuss the prospects for plaintiff's access at all.

Consider then how happy your grader will be when she encounters an opening paragraph that begins like this: "Plaintiff can seek access to defendant's land based on (1) the common law right of access to public places; (2) a statutory right to access on the ground that defendant has discriminated against her as a woman; and (3) a constitutional right to access for purposes of exercising her state-protected free speech rights." Whatever comes next, this student will have already established her ability to answer the question directly and to have identified three plausible theories.

First impressions like this are extraordinarily important. It's true you can make the same points by discussing theory (1) before you even mention theory (2) or (3). But consider the advantage of signaling the professor who is reading your analysis of the first theory that the rest of what she's looking for is on its way as well.

Put ideas in groups.

An introductory roadmap is even more helpful when there is a long list of things that you plan to discuss. As your professor reads through your analysis of nine different issues, she may not even remember Issue #3 by the time she finishes reading Issue #8. You can help her out quite a bit simply by listing Issues 1 through 9 at the beginning of your answer. But you can do even better than that by finding some way to break the nine items into smaller sub-groups.

Consider the fact that most people remember Social Security and long-distance phone numbers not by committing 9 or 10 individual digits to memory, but by dividing such numbers into three smaller groups. You can take advantage of this form of information processing if you can find a way to use sub-groups in your roadmap. For example:

> I will discuss (1) THE JUSTICIABILITY OF THE PLAINTIFF'S CASE—where issues of standing, mootness, and ripeness are the relevant sub-issues; (2) THE MERITS OF PLAINTIFF'S EQUAL PROTECTION CLAIM—where I'll consider in turn plaintiff's claimed loss of a fundamental right; his membership in a suspect class; and his victimization at the hands of an irrational government; and (3) PLAINTIFF'S DUE PROCESS CLAIM—where I'll analyze first the plaintiff's claim to a property interest; the supposed benefits of an earlier hearing; and finally the government's claim it needs to act with dispatch.

Note that this approach goes a long way toward organizing the ensuing argument for the reader, leaving her less likely to get lost in the details. (And little tricks like using all capital letters to distinguish the major groupings from the sub-issues may also prove helpful.)

Organize your own thoughts at the beginning and the end.

Another advantage to an opening paragraph that provides a roadmap is that it encourages you to stop and think before writing. (See Tip #8, "Organize and Outline Before Writing Your Answer.") You can't write an opening description of what you plan to say unless you have thought through your answer all the way to the end. And once you are finished writing, you can go back to the initial roadmap and use it as a checklist to see if you have covered all the points you listed as important.

You may, however, find it enormously difficult to provide a clear roadmap as you begin your essay. Only after wrestling the key issues to the ground will you know for sure what the main points are. In that case, simply leave a blank space at the beginning of your exam and draft the roadmap after you have written the rest of the answer. As it happens, this is the technique many attorneys use, adding a "summary of the argument" only after they have finished writing the body of an appellate brief. But even if you add it after the fact, drafting the roadmap will force you to think about the question from a big-picture perspective and help you present your answer as a well-organized whole.

Tip #10. Explain Your Reasoning

No matter how many rules you know or how insightful your analysis, you get credit for only what you actually write in the pages of your bluebooks. It is therefore crucial to reduce to writing the thought process that leads you to your conclusions.

In mathematics, you have a chance of getting the right answer through the wrong reasoning. In chess, you might make the correct move without understanding why. But in law, an "answer" is useful only if those expected to follow the law can be made to understand *why* that result was reached, and it is a principal function of lawyers to develop explanations to clarify the law in this way for judges, for clients, and for the public at large.

You seek entry into a profession in which explanations will form part of your stock-in-trade. Your professor will demand that you start giving those explanations now.

Explain to show what you are thinking.

Legal conclusions are often based on chains of reasoning with many "links" or steps. Even if you reach the end result that corresponds to the professor's own conclusion, your answer will be incomplete unless you show just how you got there.

Consider a hypothetical statute that you are asked to analyze on your Constitutional Law exam. After some careful thinking, you conclude the statute violates the equal protection clause. So you write, "The equal protection clause has been violated," and you go on to the next question without further explanation.

Reading such a response, your professor will have no way of knowing why you see an equal protection clause violation, and she is likely to grade you down even if she agrees with your conclusion. For one thing, she'll want to know what level of scrutiny you think the court should apply to the statute. If your answer is "strict" scrutiny, she'll want to know the basis for that argument. (Are we dealing with a suspect classification? Has a fundamental right been violated?) Moreover, she'll want to know what justification you think the government will put forth to support the statute and why you think that justification is insufficiently compelling.

This is not simply another case of professorial pickiness! If you went to court to defend an equal protection claim, the judge would ask you about all of these issues, and the bald assertion that the equal protection clause has been violated—without some further explanation—would do little to advance your client's cause. Likewise, a bald assertion on a law exam is unlikely to persuade the professor that you've mastered the course material. The more reasoning you show, the better you'll do, so go for it!

Explain to help your analysis.

A major advantage of working hard to show your reasoning is that it will help you improve your understanding of the question. Everyone has had the experience of making up his mind and then changing it after discovering problems during the course of attempting to defend the original position in writing. As you force yourself to articulate each step in the reasoning process, you give yourself a chance to question each part of your conclusion.

For example, if in defending the view that the equal protection clause has been violated you force yourself to explain in writing the government's interest in the challenged statute, you might discover a more compelling interest than you initially realized. Similarly, on a Contracts exam, if you try to marshal the facts that support your initial conclusion that a material breach has occurred, this effort might help you to spot circumstances that suggest substantial performance and thus cut the other way.

In short, explaining your reasoning is the best method you have for spotting the weaknesses and omissions in your own thinking. Best of all, as you begin to see the strength of the positions you have rejected, you're likely to feel a greater need to explain why you reached your conclusion and rejected other alternatives. (See Tip #12, "Argue Both Sides.") Only if you carefully spell out your reasoning from beginning to end will you have solid grounds for confidence in your conclusions.

Explain to counteract mistakes.

As we've said, you will do poorly if you reach the right answer but don't explain why. Imagine, then, how your professor will react if you reach the wrong conclusion and provide no accompanying explanation. Since she can't read your mind and the only thing you put in writing was wrong, you are unlikely to get any credit at all for your answer.

On the other hand, since most professors are more interested in the quality of your explanation than in the correctness of your conclusion, they're likely to give you substantial credit for even a "wrong" answer that is accompanied by a cogent if ultimately unpersuasive argument. Indeed, since most law school exam questions present issues that could fairly be decided either way, you are likely to be safe with *whatever* conclusion you reach, whereas you are sure to be penalized if you fail to explain your reasoning. That's another reason it's silly to be fearful about putting your cards on the table.

Make your assumptions explicit.

Your thinking about the facts of the question is just as important as your thoughts about the law. If you argue that a federal statute pre-empts a state statute because it would not be possible to comply with both simultaneously, be sure to explain why, as a practical matter, you think simultaneous compliance is impossible. If you conclude that a contract is voidable because one party was a minor at the time of signing, say so and explain what facts lead you to this conclusion.

Making your assumptions explicit in this way may help you spot ambiguities in the problem that you missed when you first read it. Thus, you may have initially concluded that the plaintiff was a minor because he read comic books and rode a skateboard. Yet as soon as you write this down, you'll realize that some adults do these things. Even if you don't catch mistakes, making your assumptions explicit will ensure that your professor can follow your reasoning, and that's the first step toward top-flight performance.

You have nothing to lose.

Even after reading all this, many of you will still want to hold back. After all, you figure that you are more certain of your conclusions than of the reasoning that got you there. The more reasoning you write down, the greater the chance the professor will catch a mistake and discover that you don't know what you are talking about. Why not just take the best guess you can about the ultimate outcome and hope the professor will be charitable and fill in the blanks in your favor?

Because *it won't work*. You can't get away with conclusory answers because for the vast majority of questions you will encounter in law school the professor cares far more about your reasoning than about the conclusions you draw. (See Tip #18, "Avoid Conclusory Answers.") Even a poorly reasoned answer most likely won't hurt you any more — and it may hurt you a lot less — than an answer with no reasons at all. So you might as well take a shot at providing the well-reasoned answer the professor is looking for. That's what law exams are all about.

Tip #11. Draw Conclusions When They Are Called For

Many law school exam questions end with queries like, "If Johnny sues Jill for breach of contract, who will prevail and why?" Such questions may cause a sinking feeling in the pit of your stomach. You believe Johnny has a strong case, but you see defenses for Jill that might be successful. In truth, you're just not sure who will win.

Congratulations! You're on the right track. Odds are that the professor drafted the question precisely to generate such confusion. Do not, however, let your uncertainty cow you into silence about the outcome. If your professor has asked for a conclusion, the surest route to a disappointing grade is to fail to provide one.

Our advice: Give the professor your best judgment about the right result while at the same time explaining why you are ultimately unpersuaded by arguments that cut the other way. In the end, you'll have to bite the bullet and embrace one side or the other.

Use life, not school, as your model for dealing with difficult decisions.

Many of you remember high school and college exams in which you were asked to solve a series of equations or to remember the precise date of a famous battle. Even if you couldn't quite calculate or remember the answer, you saw the need to venture a guess because there was no substitute for the correct response.

Law school exam questions that pull you simultaneously in opposite directions generate an understandable instinct not to reach *any* conclusions. After all, you have been trained to see what's wrong with each of the options that seems to be available. Such thinking, however, remains stuck on a vision of exams where you are graded down harshly for mistakes. Think instead about Hamlet's uncertainty ("To be or not to be . . .") as your model of tragic error.

You wouldn't fail to make a decision affecting your future simply because there was virtue to more than one option. You may, for example, have had to decide whether to attend a private law school or a less expensive state university. Either decision might have turned out to be a mistake. But attending neither because you weren't sure which was best would certainly have been counterproductive. Law school exams that ask for conclusions frequently pull you in opposite directions like this.

Draw conclusions to improve your analysis.

The greatest virtue of forcing yourself to draw conclusions is that it requires you to ask yourself hard questions. Your professor may have drafted a question for which there is no ready answer. On a Property exam, for example, the language of a document may suggest that the grantor intended to place restrictions on the property, but the general rule abhorring forfeitures may suggest that the document is too ambiguous to create restrictions. You'll probably do well on the exam by spotting and explaining the contradictory interpretations.

But if the question asks for a conclusion, you must force yourself to decide whether this is a case where the grantor's intent or the rule against forfeitures should take precedence. This will force you to describe the reasons behind each rule and to take a stab at which set of reasons seems more compelling under the precise facts given. (Perhaps the forfeiture would be particularly severe, or alternatively perhaps the grantor's intent should take priority because the grant was a gift to charity.) Only by pushing toward a conclusion can you get beyond mere boilerplate recitations of the competing positions.

Say yes to one, but don't leave the other behind.

The fact that a question calls for a conclusion means it's not enough to describe the strengths and weaknesses of both positions, however eloquent your descriptions. But don't be lulled into the opposite error of embracing one conclusion and ignoring the very strong points that point in a different direction. (See Tip #12, "Argue Both Sides.") A conclusion isn't well-drawn unless it adequately explains why opposing positions were rejected. So as you make your case, be sure to explain not only why you chose the result you did, but also why you rejected alternatives.

Watch your emphasis on reasons vs. results.

Any professor who asks you to draw a conclusion will be annoyed if you decide instead to merely recite pros and cons; indeed, some professors will find this thoroughly unacceptable. As always, you should pay careful attention to such preferences and thus heed your own professor's take on the need to reach decisive conclusions. (See Tip #14, "Remember Who Your 'Judge' Is.")

The same is true when it comes to emphasis. All professors will look at your reasons and your results, but what may vary is the emphasis individual graders will place on each. In general, we recommend that you never draw conclusions without reasons and that your worry more about reasons than results. But we also urge you to pay special attention to what's expected by *your* grader and determine the appropriate emphasis accordingly.

Tip #12. Argue Both Sides

Law exists to resolve conflict through peaceful means. Accordingly, every legal problem begins with an actual or potential disagreement between people. When a client walks into your office to tell you a story, you will always hear about some other person whose views and interests may differ from your client's. Good legal advice will follow only if you can grasp the problem from your client's point of view *and* from her potential adversary's perspective as well.

Indeed, the capacity to see and argue both sides of a case is perhaps the most important intellectual skill you will develop in law school, and so you can't expect to pick it up by reading a brief "tip," however brilliantly it is written! To be sure, we do have a lot more to say about this skill: Parts I and II of this book are an extended treatment of how to go about seeing and arguing "both sides" on a law exam.

But what we'll tell you here is that your professors have struggled hard to invent questions that present a real challenge, and they will be disappointed if you seize on some facts and arguments, while ignoring others, to reach a quick, one-sided conclusion. Instead, start by following these steps to ensure that your exam performance doesn't end up disappointing you as well.

Consider each person's perspective.

The best way to ensure that you argue both sides is to imagine how the loser might respond to your initial sense of how the case should come out. If your first instinct is that Johnny is liable to Jill because he obviously breached their contract, ask yourself what Johnny would have to say. Why *didn't* he deliver the widgets on time? Perhaps he thought they didn't really have a deal. Is there any basis for this view? Perhaps he thought Jill was supposed to call to confirm her order; or that they had additional details to work out; or that his obligation depended on some contingency that had not occurred.

The point is that in the real world there are almost always two sides to a story. On a law exam you can virtually count on that to be the case—and for good reason. To be sure, clients call on lawyers to help them with routine situations in which the rights and obligations of the parties are clear-cut and utterly unambiguous. But law school would be unworthy of its label as a professional school, let alone of its place in a university, if it did not also help you to confront the more complicated situations in which *both* parties may rightfully lay claim to some version of law and justice. Your task is to show just how each side would do so.

Seize on contradictory facts.

Contradictions make many people uncomfortable. If you were reading a novel and the main character is described as generous on page 27 and stingy on page 115, you might conclude the author was asleep at the wheel. We all recognize that people have contradictory characteristics, but we'd at least expect the novelist to try to reconcile them — *e.g.*, by explaining that our hero was usually generous but stingy when it came to his own children.

On law school exams, however, you should treat apparent contradictions as cause for celebration. Suppose Dennis grants his neighbor, Wilson, what the parties term "a perpetual easement" to use Dennis's driveway for Wilson's wheelchair-accessible van. This part of the document makes it look like Dennis intends the easement to last forever, and that it will thus be available for use by the next owner of Wilson's home who also wants access to the adjacent driveway. Suppose, however, that the same document begins with the words, "Because you, Wilson, are injured and need access to the driveway, I, Dennis, hereby grant you etc." This part of the document makes it look like Dennis wants the easement extinguished if Wilson moves away.

If you were drafting the document, you would do your professional best to avoid such ambiguities. But if you were drafting an exam response to the problem of whether the new owner of Wilson's home can use Dennis's driveway, you should be laughing your way to Law Review. That's because you have a fact that will help you argue Dennis's position that the easement is extinguished, and you also have a fact that will help you argue Wilson's position that the easement "runs with the land."

Facts that send conflicting signals like these are exactly what you need to do well on your exam; instead of ignoring or hiding from them because you find them confusing, you should search them out and exploit them for all they're worth. The professor struggled to invent them. She will be delighted when you highlight and illustrate the contradictions, and awfully disappointed if you don't.

Use tensions in the law to your advantage.

The way law pulls you in different directions takes some getting used to. Law embodies conflicting ideals like liberty and equality. Different jurisdictions have different rules, and sometimes it's hard to tell whether, for example, state or federal law applies. Even caselaw is famously riddled by questions of which precedent governs.

Each of these tensions may feel like an obstacle to overcome. Who wouldn't wonder which rule really does apply; which ideal should take precedence; or even simply which prior case is controlling? But on an exam, each of these tensions is in fact an opportunity to demonstrate your mastery of the topic. If it appears to you that one important case supports a decision for the plaintiff, while another equally controlling case suggests a decision for the defendant, just *say so*, instead of throwing your hands up in despair. You are far more likely to be rewarded for spotting both points of view than you are to be graded down for your failure to reach a conclusion in which you can be 100% confident.

After all, law is a human invention designed to resolve an extraordinary range of human conflict. How could we expect it to produce simple answers in such a complex world?

Find something interesting in the question.

Once upon a time you took exams that asked you straightforward questions like "name the state capital of Florida." (Tallahassee was worth 10 points.) But if a law professor were drafting that geography exam, she would be far more likely to complicate matters considerably by telling you that a legislative task force has decided that the state capital must be relocated and has asked you, as its chief counsel, to draft a memorandum identifying the most desirable alternative site.

An answer like "the capital of Florida should be Miami because it's the state's largest city" has the advantage of coherence, but it lacks depth. It would help if you were to add that it makes sense to have the capital be the state's largest city because today's global economy demands concentration of financial, political, and human resources. But your answer won't get interesting until you can identify a second theory that rivals the first. Maybe the capital should be Orlando, since it's more centrally located and citizens have a right to easy access to the seat of government. Only when two plausible rival theories have been identified can a productive debate occur and an interesting analysis emerge.

So, too, when law professors draft *law* exams. For every question you read, you should ask yourself why the professor found this particular set of facts interesting. What are the competing understandings of or approaches to the case that caused the professor to ask about *this* fact pattern rather than another?

For example, if a question about landlord/tenant law involves a live-in babysitter, the odds are pretty good that the professor is interested not only in a straightforward application of the landlord/tenant rules, but also in the "big picture" question of whether those rules should apply in this unusual setting. Most professors will be looking for you to present the case for the routine application of the rules as well as the case for a special "live-in babysitter" exception, so that you can demonstrate an awareness of the choice to be made and the pros and cons of each approach. Arguing both sides, then, is a technique that can help you to remember that law is about choices and that hard choices make the most interesting exam questions.

Tip #13. Stick to the Facts and Circumstances Presented

We know it's annoying to receive seemingly contradictory messages from your professors. "Be creative," we say. "Show some inventiveness, some imagination." And then as soon as you start strutting your stuff, we turn around and plead that you stick to the question at hand. But you really *can* satisfy both demands, as long as you keep the following points in mind.

Analogize, don't digress.

Perhaps the most common form of legal analysis is the analogy. This case is *like* that case, we argue, and therefore this case should be *decided* the same way that one was. Indeed, if the two cases are enough alike, the argument from analogy even gets its own fancy Latin name: *stare decisis*. As a result, the ability to identify analogous cases and situations is a vital skill, on law exams as well as in legal practice. Never forget, however, that the point of an analogy is to help you resolve the problem at hand, not to show off how much you know about some other situation.

Let's say, for example, that you get a Property exam question about parents who want to fire their live-in babysitter. The sitter claims that as a "tenant" she can't be evicted from the parents' home. She argues that her poor job performance was effectively a withholding of rent to protest the failure of her live-in quarters to comply with the warranty of habitability.

You may recall that the New Jersey Supreme Court faced an issue of whether to treat workers as tenants in *State v. Shack*, 58 N.J. 297, 277 A.2d 369 (1971). Your professor will be impressed if you note that the court in *Shack* found a way to permit migrant farm workers to receive visitors without granting the workers "tenant" status. This might suggest it will be hard for the sitter to succeed in making that claim here.

But your professor will be annoyed if once you raise *Shack* you spend three pages detailing the facts of that case, explaining how the case fits in with general issues involving the rights of owners to exclude, and how it illustrates a judicial tendency to avoid constitutional issues. The professor wants to know about the babysitter's rights—not about *State v. Shack*—and you shouldn't lose sight of that.

Be careful with the word "if."

Make up your mind which issues in the question are meant to be ambiguous and worthy of discussion (on the one hand) and which are presented as clearly settled (on the other). For ambiguous situations, the word "if" is important, even essential. You will often find yourself writing sentences such as, "If the grantor is found to have intended that the covenant run with the land, then the new owner won't be able to violate the restriction." Here your biggest concern is to make sure that where the question makes the grantor's intent unclear, you discuss how and why the court will be likely to resolve this ambiguity. (See Tip #10, "Explain Your Reasoning.")

In many cases, however, certain aspects of the question will be entirely clear. There may be a contract dispute between two experienced business persons who obviously fit the definition of merchant under the Uniform Commercial Code. You may be very proud of yourself for knowing the rule for non-merchants, and therefore tempted to throw in a dangerous sentence such as, "If the parties were not merchants, then the rule would be thus and so." Or the plaintiff in an equal protection suit may be a white male. You are still feeling the thrill of learning the categories whereby equal protection suits are judged differently when brought by women or African-Americans. You wonder how it could hurt to throw in sentences with beginnings such as, "If the plaintiff were an African-American." "If" phrases like these could hurt a lot. When the professor writes a question about merchants, she wants an analysis of merchants (and of course you should point out that you are applying the merchant rule). When the professor makes the plaintiff a white male, that's the situation he wants resolved. If you aren't careful, your professor's reaction may be something like, "If you had stuck to the facts and circumstances of the question, you might have done very well!"

Invent solutions not scenarios.

It is one thing, and generally a good thing, to invent multiple ways that a court or other decisionmaker might respond to the set of facts presented in your exam question. You can do this well by considering various theories of liability or different remedies a court might impose. It's entirely another thing, and one you should stay away from, to invent ways that courts might respond to sets of facts that are different from those presented in the question. You might have a brilliant theory for how a court should handle the scenario in which a tenant is evicted for engaging in union organizing. But if the tenant in your question is evicted because his kid writes on the walls, that's the scenario you should discuss.

Don't write treatises about the law.

The most common form of departure from the facts and circumstances of an exam question is the flight into generalized statements of law. Such poor answers start off on the right foot. You read the question and draw a correct view of the legal issues involved. So, for example, you might observe that a dispute between neighbors over a loud radio could give rise to a nuisance suit. At this point, however, having spotted the nuisance issue, you launch into a lengthy discussion of the definition of nuisance and a description of all the nuisance cases covered in the course. This discussion wastes valuable time and takes you away from the facts and circumstances presented. You may know a great deal of nuisance law. But the professor wants to hear only the parts relevant to the question at hand.

Tip #14. Remember Who Your "Judge" Is

Your law school exam is intended for an audience of one: the professor who will grade it. This is not wholly unrealistic preparation for law practice, where you will frequently find yourself trying to persuade a particular decisionmaker, such as a trial judge. But for better or worse, law students have only one person to please. Don't forget these tips for doing so.

Follow your professor's advice.

No matter how much time we spend writing about exam excellence, this is the most important advice we can give you. Listen carefully to every word your professor says about what she wants in an exam and try to provide it. If your professor tells you that she cares most about your listing the elements of a cause of action, then forget everything you read—either here in these tips or elsewhere in this book—and list those elements. Your professor is in charge of your course, and it's your job to prove you can play by her rules. And in case we haven't said it often enough, the clearest instruction your professor gives you on every exam is the language of the exam question itself. Pay close attention to the way the question is phrased and what the professor is looking for. Follow those instructions to the absolute best of your ability. (See Tip #7, "Read Each Question Carefully, and Answer the Question Asked.")

Think about your professor's style.

It's dangerous to leap too quickly from superficial characteristics to a professor's exam preferences. Thus, your professor might arrive every day in a suit and tie or a fancy dress yet be relatively relaxed when it comes to what's expected in terms of writing style on the exam. It makes most sense to listen to what the professor actually says she wants. There is nonetheless something to be gained by attempting to draw some exam lessons from the nature of the course. If every day's class is spent on refining the holdings of cases, it's safe to assume the professor cares a lot about your ability to do so. If the professor cares in class about mastery of detail and gives a closed-book exam, then you'd better be careful throwing around details you don't quite remember. If a professor appears very interested in policy arguments, then you should find a way to work them in. And if a professor appears to value in-class creativity, then keep your imagination humming from beginning to end on exam day.

Look for course topics and themes.

The increasing amount of material covered in law school courses makes it difficult for everything from your course to be tested on the exam. Nonetheless, if your Constitutional Law class spent eight weeks studying the commerce clause and you read over the exam and can't find it, read the exam again. It's unlikely your professor would have chosen to spend half a course on something unworthy of testing. Equally important, if your professor stresses certain themes such as the role of the states as laboratories for government experimentation, look carefully to see if that theme has resurfaced on the exam. Law school courses vary: Some emphasize a steady diet of rules, while others hunt for an organizing principle or a set of themes. Ask yourself how your professor has approached the course, and make sure to see if you can approach the exam the same way.

Disagree freely but knowledgeably.

Occasionally a professor will ask a more open-ended policy question that asks you to draw a conclusion about an issue you have studied. Suppose, for example, your Property teacher asks whether rent control should be abolished. One fear you may have is that your professor's liberal pro-tenant views may conflict with your position that rent control is counterproductive. Get over it! The overwhelming majority of professors are happy to read exams that disagree with their position. Your exam-taking concern should never be which side of an argument you are on, but only on what you have to say to support your side.

Keep the level high and the pace fast.

We can't stress enough the tedium that your professors experience in reading answers to the same questions over and over and over again. Every time you repeat the facts (see Tip #17, "Don't Repeat the Facts") or revert to stating the law without applying it (see Tip #16, "Don't Regurgitate Legal Rules and Principles") you slow the professor down and risk annoying her. Get to the point as fast as you can, and spend most of your time on the issues you find challenging. It may seem counterintuitive, but it will pay off.

A sense of humor can help.

Let's be clear. You want above all to stick to the point and stay within the bounds of propriety. If you are tempted to make a joke and in doubt about whether it's in good taste, don't do it. That said, if you find easy ways to throw in a little humor, by all means do so. Your professors often work hard to place a few amusing diversions in the exam questions. Perhaps the character names on the exam come from a recent hit movie or TV show. Letting us know you noticed or giving us a chuckle won't rescue a bad exam. But at the margins it certainly can't hurt.

Tip #15. Watch Time/Credit Allocations

Most law school exams are time-pressured, some quite drastically so. Accordingly, your professor is unlikely to be impressed if you write solid answers to two of the three essay questions and handle the third one with a big, bold "OUT OF TIME." It's virtually impossible to score well if you receive no credit for an entire question, and there's no reason this should happen to you. Here are some ways to avoid it.

Put your agony on paper.

All of you are accustomed to doing very well on exams and most are accustomed to exams in which knowing the answer is the key. Because law exams demand analysis, not answers, there's an understandable tendency to freeze. The question asks whether the plaintiff has standing, and you're genuinely not sure. You see a strong case that the plaintiff is "injured in fact," but you're not sure the defendant is the cause of the injury. Odds are that your uncertainty is the result of a question that the professor has deliberately drafted to invite more than one plausible conclusion. If you write down why you aren't sure, you'll probably be doing very well. But even if you really are a bit confused, you'll do much better writing something than nothing. The key here is that genuine uncertainty about the legal result is exactly what the professor hopes to create. If that uncertainty makes you feel bad, writing down why is your best revenge.

Adopt a speedy style.

Consider the chess concept of TEMPO that stresses executing your plan with sufficient speed to finish before your opponent completes hers. This means, for example, that if you are trying to move your pieces into the center and trying to defend pieces your opponent has threatened, it's great to find a move that simultaneously defends and develops a piece in the center.

The law exam equivalent is to learn to write with sentences that accomplish several things at once. Thus, there's little advantage to a writing style that begins by listing various components of a legal doctrine and then proceeds to analyze them. Compare a slow-style response to a fast one for a hypo involving a lawsuit by a presidential candidate defeated by a 34-year-old who fooled the public by forging his birth certificate:

> *Slow*: The Supreme Court in *Allen v. Wright* identified three factors to determine whether a plaintiff has standing: 1) has the plaintiff suffered injury in fact; 2) is the defendant's injury caused by the defendant's conduct; and 3) if the plaintiff prevails, can the court provide a remedy that will adequately re-

dress plaintiff's grievance. Under the first factor we see that the plaintiff has suffered an injury because he lost the presidential election to a 34-year-old (and hence ineligible) candidate. Under the second factor, plaintiff has greater difficulty because he may not be able to show that the fact that the winning candidate was underage caused the plaintiff to lose the election. The third factor is also problematic, because even if the court were to disqualify the underage candidate and seek to remove him from office, the court would not be able to install the losing candidate in the White House.

Fast: There's no question about the plaintiff's injury (he lost the election to an ineligible candidate), so the real problems with establishing standing involve proving causation (there's no guarantee plaintiff won the election due to the forged birth certificate) and showing redressability (the court clearly can't install the plaintiff in the White House).

The fast answer has TEMPO because it combines a demonstration of knowledge with an analysis of the problem rather than attempting to perform these tasks separately.

Force yourself to move on.

There's not much more to say than that. If you have ten more points to make about Question 2 and only 30 minutes left, do you think those ten points will help you more than spending the same 30 minutes on Question 3, which you haven't even begun? If you've been writing about Question 2 for an hour, odds are you have already covered the main points. If you haven't, spend five more minutes on a quick outline of these points, and move on.

Outline when you must.

You can't do as much with an outline as you can with a clear, crisp essay. But you can do a lot. Two good outline-answers are likely to put you much higher on the curve than one great essay and one big blank space. To outline, merely identify the issues you'd discuss in full if you had the time. One neat trick is to list the factors that might push you to one conclusion or the other. For example:

One clear issue here is whether the plaintiff has standing:

For Standing	Against Standing
injury clear	causation doubtful
clear legal question for court	hard to see court redress
plaintiff clearly not a bystander	

An outline like this may earn you some much-needed points. But beware: Some professors refuse to read answers that aren't written in prose, and virtually all of us prefer an essay. So while this strategy can be enormously useful, you should employ it only in a pinch.

Chapter 13

Mistakes to Avoid

Like all endeavors, law school exams offer countless opportunity for mistakes, from the simplest failure to read the question to the most subtle misunderstanding of complex legal doctrine. Certain errors, however, repeatedly appear, in large part because professors are asking you to do things on law school exams that are different from what you did in college and even different from what you've done in your legal research and writing courses. Here are some mistakes we have seen with great frequency in the course of grading thousands of exams.

Tip #16. Don't Regurgitate Legal Rules and Principles

If you've been a law student for more than a week, you've no doubt begun to figure out that rule memorization/regurgitation doesn't get you very far in class discussion. It won't get you very far in the exam setting either, for on the one hand "the rules" *are not enough* and on the other "the rules" *are way too much* when it comes to writing law exams. Here's how you can learn to avoid both of these pitfalls.

Rules are not enough, Part I: You get credit for *applying* the law, not for regurgitating it.

Unless you decide to specialize in handling the legal problems of first-year law students, chances are you'll never have a client walk into your office and ask, "What are the seven elements of adverse possession?" Instead, most clients will offer up "facts" — events that have already taken place or things that they think (or worry) might happen — and ask you to explain the legal implications and consequences.

Imagine, for example, that a client tells you that he and his brother have been mooring their sailboat at a seemingly abandoned dock near their beach house for the past eight summers, and that they want to know the risks of spending a substantial sum to fix up the dock. It may be useful to explain briefly the concept of adverse possession and to describe the elements, but if you stopped there, you wouldn't have helped the client with his problem. What will help him is an analysis that *applies* each of the elements to the particular facts and circumstances he has presented. (They moor at the dock only in the summer; would that constitute "continuous use"? Does merely tying the boat to the dock establish "actual possession"?)

So, too, with a law exam presenting this client's problem as a question: While a brief explanation of adverse possession and a listing of the elements may be a good starting point, what separates the superior answer from the barely passing is the ability to apply those legal concepts to the facts and, in particular, to identify the difficulties or ambiguities that might arise in the course of that application.

Rules are not enough, Part II: An ounce of analysis is worth a pound of law.

If you weren't successful as an undergraduate, you wouldn't be in law school today. Yet frequently success in an undergraduate program is the result of committing to memory the contents of lectures and readings and of parroting those contents back on quizzes and finals. It would therefore be no surprise if you found yourself tempted to deploy the same technique in law school by using the law exam as an opportunity to demonstrate to the professor that you have "learned a lot of law."

The difficulty with this kind of thinking is that it is indeed necessary to "learn a lot of law" in order to succeed in law school, but it is nowhere near sufficient. The typical law exam tests your ability to *use* legal rules and principles to analyze and argue about particular facts and problems. To be sure, you can't use rules you don't know, but merely showing that you know them—for example, to continue our illustration, by briefly reciting the elements of adverse possession—is only a start. To excel, you have to show that you know how to apply the rules, and, to do that, you've got to use them to analyze the facts and problems presented in the question.

Rules are too much, Part I: Lengthy quotations of legal rules waste precious time.

The typical law school exam gives you a series of questions that could easily take you a week or more to answer fully, but—for better or for worse—you have only three or four hours within which to complete your work. As a result, time is at a premium, and you need to use every available minute analyzing the facts presented in the questions in light of the legal rules and principles you've learned in your coursework. To be sure, brief quotations of pertinent rules (*e.g.*, the "clear and present danger" test in Constitutional Law or a "definite and seasonable expression of acceptance" under U.C.C. § 2-207 in Contracts) may demonstrate to the grader that you know precisely what is in dispute in a particular problem. But the ability to quote verbatim lengthy excerpts from cases, from statutes, from the federal rules, or from the Restatement would be useful only to a monk copying sacred scripture before the invention of the printing press; for a law student faced with the task of writing an exam, it is of no use at all.

Rules are too much, Part II: A lengthy paraphrase may be even worse than a lengthy quotation.

Some students seem to think they will get credit for merely regurgitating legal rules if they put them "in their own words" instead of quoting them verbatim. But this is a lose-lose proposition.

At best, they will succeed only in wasting the time spent rephrasing rather than applying the legal rules to the facts presented in the question. (A clever law student could, for example, come up with more than 5000 ways in which to rearrange the seven elements of adverse possession, but he won't get any credit for such efforts from the professor.)

At worst—and, given the high-pressure setting of a law exam and the formidable challenges of legal drafting, this is an extremely common scenario—the would-be paraphraser will restate the rule incorrectly. If she gets the rule wrong in a way that makes a difference in the analysis of the problem, the mistake may have a devastating effect on her entire answer. But even if she gets the rule wrong in a way that doesn't really matter, her sloppiness is likely make a poor impression on the grader. Depending on the professor, this may result in points off as well—all for doing something for which she wouldn't get any credit even if she'd done it properly!

Tip #17. Don't Repeat the Facts

In your first-year legal writing course, you may have learned that the best way to begin a legal memorandum is by restating the facts of the problem you've been asked to research. Although this is a useful format for memo writing, it's a bad way to organize an answer for most law exams. Here are the reasons:

You get credit for *analyzing* the facts, not for copying them into your bluebooks.

Clients want their lawyers to help them make legal sense of facts that the clients know all too well. So as law students you can expect to be rewarded for your ability to "make legal sense" out of the facts you're given—*i.e.*, to analyze and argue about them in light of the legal principles you have learned in your courses. By contrast, the ability to "parrot back" facts is useful mostly to a parrot.

Thus, for example, if a hypothetical on a first-year Property exam explicitly states that "Sally holds a vested remainder," the student who begins his answer with "Sally holds a vested remainder" or even "The legal interest that Sally holds is a vested remainder" is getting zero credit and going nowhere fast. At the same time, his classmate who starts straight-away by discussing the significance of the fact—*i.e.*, by explaining what difference it might make to the legal analysis of the problem—is already miles ahead (*e.g.*, "*Because* Sally holds a vested remainder, she faces no problems under the Rule Against Perpetuities . . .").

Repeating the facts wastes precious time.

We make the same point here that we made about regurgitating legal rules: On law exams, time is at a premium, and you need to use every available minute *answering* the questions. Any time spent merely *repeating* them is a complete waste.

Repeating the facts conveys uncertainty and annoys the grader.

Deep down most students already know that fact-regurgitation won't get them the grades they desire. So why, it is fair to ask, do so many students nevertheless fall into parrot mode when they come face-to-face with their bluebooks? Here's one answer we hear from students, particularly those who are unhappy with their exam performance: "After reading the question, I was so confused and stressed out that the only thing I was sure of was the facts. So I figured I couldn't go wrong by repeating them and getting at least *that much* right."

But here's the rub: We professors were law students once, and in any event we've read enough bluebooks to be hip to this trick. Thus, when a student begins an answer by restating the facts, he is sending the message loud and clear that he isn't sure what to do with the question, and that makes a poor first impression on the grader. What's worse: The grader *wrote* those facts; indeed, she probably spent a lot of time developing them and working out the details. Faced with the prospect of reading 60, 80, 100, or 120 bluebooks, she is likely to be extremely annoyed if she has to read them again (and again and again).

Attempts to paraphrase are likely to get you in trouble.

Once again, you can't solve the regurgitation problem— whether you are regurgitating law or facts—by paraphrasing rather than quoting. At best, you will succeed only in wasting the time spent rephrasing rather than analyzing the facts presented. At worst, you will get the facts wrong in some small but significant way that can undermine your entire answer. Consider, for example, a Contracts hypothetical in which some facts suggest that Ollie has made an "offer" and other facts suggest that he has only invited one; a paraphrase of the hypothetical that even inadvertently emphasizes one view and ignores the other is a deadly error, since the professor is undoubtedly testing to see whether the student can argue the facts *both* ways. In sum, you gain nothing—and stand to lose a lot—by attempting to paraphrase the facts.

The facts are already written down.

If you pull into a tollbooth and ask directions to the George Washington Bridge, the attendant might well repeat your question back to you: "So, you want to get to the bridge?" Your kids in the back seat might crack wise ("Duh, how did he ever guess?"), but the toll collector is no doubt making a legitimate attempt to ensure he heard the question right before trying to answer it. Unlike the toll collector, however, a law student who wants to make sure she has the facts right can—and indeed she *should*—simply go back and read them again; she gains nothing by repeating them into her bluebook.

Tip #18. Avoid Conclusory Answers

Imagine you and your best friend have just finished reading a great novel like Dostoyevsky's *Crime and Punishment*. You're excited to talk about it and you call your friend on the phone. "Did you like the book?" you ask. "Yes," he says. "Do you think there was any merit to Raskolnikov's original thinking about justifications for murder?" you inquire. "No," he replies. "What do you think ultimately led to Raskolnikov's downfall?" you press on. "Guilt," he mutters. Not much of a conversation, is it?

Your professors can't write like Dostoyevsky. But we do our best to pose problems we find interesting and that we hope will challenge you to think. So, if after a long fact pattern we put a question to you like, "Does Jill's suit have merit?" it is highly unlikely that "yes" (or "no" for that matter) will prove a satisfactory answer. We are at least as interested in why you have drawn a particular conclusion as in the conclusion itself.

Nor is this a mere aesthetic preference. Your professional life will depend on persuading people to act and judges to rule as you wish. It's unlikely that clipped conclusions will push them in the desired direction. You might be able to get by with one-word answers when you are telling a client that "yes" she may go forward with her plans. But if your answer is "no," you had better have a detailed explanation for why and a further consideration of other possible alternatives and why those will or won't work. Explaining why is the watchword of a successful practice, and that goes double for exam performance.

Be wary of conclusory terms.

It is seldom a good idea to begin a point in your essay with phrases like "it is obvious that" or "clearly." If you are correct, and the point you are making is obvious, then the chances are good that this isn't the issue the professor is hoping to see you discuss. So if it is "obvious that Joe will sue Sally for breach of contract," then it's likely the important issues are what defenses

Sally has and whether Joe will ultimately prevail. Alternatively, and still worse, the point you are making may not be obvious at all. Think how unhappy your professor will be to read you saying "it's obvious the rule against perpetuities doesn't apply" when there's a strong argument that it does.

Don't say what, say why.

Law school exams often present ambiguous circumstances. A contract or deed can be interpreted in different ways. A statute can be read to have different meanings. A defendant can be seen as having acted negligently or not. It's important to choose which interpretation of events is more compelling. But it's not enough. In many cases, for example, where there are only two plausible readings, you could pick the right one 50% of the time just by guessing. So it's unlikely the professor will be impressed with a mere conclusion. If an anti-discrimination statute might be read as requiring the defendant to have intended to discriminate and you see no evidence of intent, then it's a good first step to say the defendant isn't liable because the intent element is missing. But if you don't go on to explain why you see intent as an element of the statute—based on the plain meaning of the language, the legislative history, the caselaw interpreting similar statutes, or some other factor—then your answer is stopping short. Every conclusion you draw should have a why attached to it.

Always anticipate rejoinders.

Even after you have spelled out all the reasons why you believe a legal issue should be resolved in a particular way, you are still only halfway home. You should next ask yourself what arguments an imaginary opponent might raise that would push the decisionmaker in the opposite direction. After you have written down how you would respond to the strongest arguments that cut against your position, you will then have truly tackled the question the way it was written. Anyone can reach a conclusion if the arguments the other way aren't adequately presented. But to write a persuasive answer you need to rebut the best that the other side might have to offer. (See Tip #12, "Argue Both Sides.")

Tip #19. Avoid Disquisitions on Topics Outside the Course

Although you may sometimes have your doubts, your professors generally aren't out to fool you by asking questions about topics not covered during the course. We put a great deal of effort into properly explaining the issues we cover, and we want to find out how much you have learned about them. So if you are convinced that the real issue on one of your Property exam questions is whether the defendant violated the antitrust laws, try thinking it over again. The antitrust issue you think you see is probably not there, but in any event there is most certainly a property law issue that you are missing.

This doesn't mean you should never make quick mention of a legal issue you believe is relevant even if you never discussed it in class. Most professors are happy to see creative thinking and even more delighted if you raise facts about the real world that you know from personal experience. But if you find yourself going on and on about something from another course, from some other field, or worst of all from a commercial outline, STOP! The grade you save may be your own.

Know your topics well, and use your syllabus as a guide.

Many of you will be quick to agree that it's foolish to spend time writing about issues not covered in the course. It's one thing, however, to avoid antitrust issues on the Property exam, and quite another to remember every issue covered so as to know whether to include it. There's always the fear that, even though you don't remember covering something, it was in fact a focus of considerable course scrutiny.

Our first reaction to this is that if you are taking school seriously you probably remember a lot more than you think. So if you really don't remember covering something, you probably did not. Often the professor will provide a syllabus with headings that make the course issues easier to remember. And if the exam is open-book, there's probably no better document to have on hand. But here again we'd like to stress that there are no substitutes for knowing the material. Topics discussed in class should be your first study priority. Topics in the readings should be next. These two will keep you plenty busy so that you don't need more.

You can't afford to waste time.

It's the rare exam question that doesn't contain several difficult issues built on the main topics of study. A Constitutional Law question that centers around state action may also involve an issue on the merits and even a standing question as well. You may spot the state action issue and become convinced that if the defendant is found to be a state actor, then there's a follow-up issue of whether the defendant has an absolute or qualified immunity from suit. You may have even written your moot court brief on the immunity of certain public officials. The odds are good, however, that you spent little if any time on immunity issues in your Constitutional Law course. If you insist on showing off to the professor how much you know about immunity, you'll probably run out of time to talk about the merits and may even miss the standing issue altogether. DON'T DO IT! If the professor spent time teaching you about standing, that's probably what she wants to hear about. Remember, you are trying to convince her (see Tip #14, "Remember Who Your 'Judge' Is") that you have learned the course. You'll have plenty of time for disquisitions on immunity elsewhere.

Venturing beyond the course risks extra mistakes.

Going beyond the course material not only wastes time, it increases the odds that you'll make mistakes. You aren't likely to get much credit for material the professor isn't seeking. But the professor is certain to be displeased if you bring up other issues and then get them wrong. Moreover, mistakes are more likely for at least two reasons. First, no matter how well you know another body of law, you aren't likely to know it as well as you know the material that you've focused on like a laser beam while getting ready for the exam. Second, most areas of law offer considerable room for interpretation. You are likely to understand your professor's take on the material that you covered in the course. But you will be hard pressed to predict her understanding of other topics. Material you picked up as gospel somewhere else—whether that be in another course or from a commercial outline—may strike your professor as poppycock. Quoting it back to her isn't likely to improve your performance.

Be brief and you will be saved.

Sometimes you just can't resist discussing other topics. Sometimes you'll even be correct. You'll have spotted an issue from another body of law that actually is more relevant to the problem than anything your professor considered. Your professor will give you enormous credit for creativity if only you have the courage to follow your instincts. Though these occasions will be rare, they will happen, and you don't want knee-jerk tips-following to inhibit you. The answer here is simple. If, upon reflection, or at least as much reflection as you have time for during an exam, you remain convinced that an issue outside the course is crucial, flag it. Explain BRIEFLY why and how you think it's relevant and MOVE ON! You'll get all the credit you can expect, you'll risk little time, and, if you have made a mistake, the professor will care much less if you haven't been distracted from the key issues she is trying to test.

Tip #20. Don't Leave Your Common Sense at the Door

This is a good rule for most of life, but exam pressure makes it hard to follow, especially when you are eager to show off your most recent legal learning. Here are some simple things to remember that will help you sound not only like a good student of your latest lessons but also like someone whom your professor can imagine someday handling a client's affairs.

Rules are made to be broken.

You worked hard all semester learning rules so complicated they made your head swim. You know now that landlords are bound by a warranty of habitability and that if an apartment doesn't comply with the housing code the tenant may cease paying rent. You also know that providing hot water is an essential part of almost every housing code. Rote rule application might lead you to conclude that a tenant in an exam question could stay rent-free for months in a luxury apartment merely because there's no hot water in the Jacuzzi. But you know in the real world this would never happen. It shouldn't happen on your exams either.

Don't ignore your experience.

It's easy to get confused about legal terminology. You may recall that the Supreme Court has found a "fundamental right to travel" without remembering precisely what that means. It might also occur to you that any state rule that restricts your freedom, let's say to hunt as you wish, could be described as interfering with your travel rights. "I can hunt in my home state without any special training in gun safety, so why can't I do that here?" But, however savvy it sounds to your legal mind to challenge state hunting restrictions as unconstitutional infringements on travel, you know in your bones, even if you've never picked up a gun, that states already regulate things like hunting.

Try then to be very careful about reaching exam conclusions that contradict the way you know the world to be organized. In short, if your recollection of the commerce clause cases convinces you that it's unconstitutional for a state to operate a public university, you probably should rethink your recollection before telling your professor at the University of State X to give back his or her paycheck.

Don't demand the impossible.

You have carefully mastered the requirements of "due process of law." Your exam question imagines that to receive a tax credit for college tuition a student must maintain a "B" average. A lot is at stake now in every student grade, and a review of the professor's grades could surely find errors, so your instinct is that every student at a public university has a right to a formal hearing to contest any grade below a "B." STOP RIGHT THERE. However logical this might sound, you know it won't happen. So don't tell the professor that the law now demands it without being very clear you mean this in a purely theoretical sense.

Distinguish the is from the ought.

Suppose you have a creative theory you believe invalidates a practice which your experience tells you goes on all the time. You remember, for example, that the Supreme Court has found it to be unconstitutional state action for a court to enforce a racially restrictive covenant. Your exam question is about a neighbor who holds Ku Klux Klan rallies in his backyard and calls the cops to evict any African-Americans who seek to attend. If you want to argue that *in principle* there's no difference between the cops' involvement here and the courts' involvement in the covenants case, more power to you. Your professor will reward you for creativity, especially if you are sensitive to available counterarguments. But if instead you summarily conclude that the neighbor can't ask the cops to help, you will have confused what you think the law should be with what it is in a way that will hurt you every time.

Tip #21. Avoid Writing Jurisprudence Lectures

Law school classes spend a great deal of energy on time-honored questions of law that transcend individual subjects. When should rules be strictly enforced and when should an exception be made? When should the needs of the community trump the rights of the individual and vice versa? Do citizens owe allegiance to immoral laws? Like most students, you may have developed strong views on such questions. Save them for when the professor asks for your opinion. In the meantime, use your understanding of deeper issues to answer the question at hand. Seeing how your problem is only part of a more general dilemma should help you write a better answer to your problem. It shouldn't spur you toward a lengthy philosophical essay about the dilemma itself.

Always keep the question in mind.

You have studied so hard and learned so much that the temptation is almost irresistible to let the professor know about your newfound erudition. Don't give in! The professor wants your reaction to the question at hand, not your thoughts on big-picture questions or related legal issues. So let's say your Constitutional Law exam has a hypothetical statute that bans cloning and you are asked to discuss a constitutional challenge to the statute. You see right away that Supreme Court cases protecting abortion but refusing to protect sodomy or a right to die may form the background law. GOOD! Now go back and tell us how these cases will help you analyze the cloning statute. Don't spend your time writing about whether the abortion cases are rightly decided, about the ways that privacy has been a contested concept since the time of John Stuart Mill, or about the history of "fundamental rights" analysis.

Analogize with a purpose.

Figuring out how your exam problem resembles certain other problems that you have studied is crucial to top performance. But it's not enough to point out that your case is like Smith v. Jones. You have to show how Smith v. Jones will or won't help solve your case. Dinner table discussion provides the perfect model here. Let's say teenage Jenny sits down and explains a recent problem at work involving a co-worker. Everyone can tell the difference between responses from two types of family elders.

Aunt Sarah, the family sage, might reply as follows. "I faced a problem like that once. Here's how I handled it. Based on my experience, here's what you might try to cope with your situation." Note how Aunt Sarah raised a related issue but then immediately brought the topic back to Jenny's problems. That's what you want to do.

Now consider Uncle Fred's response to Jenny. "Gee dear, that reminds me of a story. Back when I was your age . . . ." Fifteen minutes go by, and Fred is still telling his tale. You recognize Uncle Fred as the family blowhard, and that's how you'll sound if your answer starts off, "This case reminds me of Smith v. Jones," and you then spend the rest of your time merely discussing that case.

Stay at the question's level of generality.

Here's a good chance to remind you once again of the single most important rule of exam-taking: "Read the Question Carefully, and Answer the Question Asked." (See Tip #7.) This time we want to urge you to read the question with an eye toward the level of generality that the professor is seeking.

Thus, if the professor asks whether Jill can sue Sam when Sam draws water from a well lying under tracts of land owned by each, don't write a treatise on the difference between traditional rules of capture and the doctrine of correlative rights. Focus instead on whether Jill will prevail and under what circumstances. If, however, the professor asks for a comparison of the pros and cons of handling conflicts over water via traditional rules of capture, then by all means write at length about the wisdom of competing approaches. Don't switch instead to a more general discussion of whether we should have a private property system or to a less general discussion of whether in one particular case the traditional capture rule would be preferable. Ask yourself for each question whether the professor wants analysis of a particular fact pattern, a competing rule-choice in a narrow area, or a general thematic discussion. Respond accordingly.

Tip #22. Don't B.S.

You open up your Torts exam and carefully read through the first long hypothetical. Terror fills your heart as you realize you just don't quite get what the question is driving at. You do understand that issues of negligence are involved, but you are afraid you won't be able to figure out how. The thought occurs to you that it would be a shame for you to do poorly on a negligence question. After all, you spent hours studying negligence, and you could write a sterling essay on the general characteristics of negligence and how it fits into tort law as a whole. You figure the professor won't penalize you too much if you demonstrate sound command of the general principles, even if you only tangentially refer to how they fit back to the question. These kinds of baloney-filled essays may even have worked for you in college. So you are thinking of trying one again.

Don't even try it. We law professors pride ourselves on our ability to spot exam-dodging evasions, and it will be a matter of professional self-respect that we come down hard on you. There's a pretty simple reason why.

If your experience as law students is anything like ours was, you've probably already figured out that law professors aren't hired on the basis of (a) drop-dead good looks; (b) a sense of humor; (c) compassion for students or other living things; (d) an ability to bring boring material to life; (e) an ability to bring complex material to crystal clarity; (f) an ability to cope with the world going on outside of the "ivory tower"; or (g) an ability to grade exams expeditiously. To be sure, many law professors (present company excluded, of course) possess one or more of these traits, and, if you're as fortunate as we were, you'll even have some who possess almost all of them. But we'll let you in on a deep, dark, dirty secret: There is only one talent that is common to virtually every professor currently teaching in an American law school; moreover, once you understand the nature of this common talent, everything else about legal education—from the way we grade through the selection criteria for Law Review— begins to make an odd sort of sense.

Here's the secret: *What we are good at is taking tests.* Most of us have taken tests successfully throughout our lives. We went to law schools that happen to produce law professors; we did well enough on our law school exams to persuade others who did well on *their* law school exams to hire us for positions as judicial clerks, government attorneys, or associates in blue-chip firms; we even did well enough on our law school exams that our law school professors (who had also done well on *their* law school exams) were willing to recommend us for jobs in the legal academy; and we were ultimately hired by other law professors who in turn hold their own jobs because they too did well on their own law exams.

If you think about it for a little while (and we try not to), test-taking skills are a pretty paltry talent in the grand scheme of things. This may be one reason for the old adage that "A" students become law professors, "B" students become judges, and "C" students become rich. But the one thing you can count on is that a group of people selected for their ability to take tests will be able to spot it when you are bluffing in your efforts to take yours. So go back and read that Torts hypothetical again. Take a stab at what you think the question is really about. Our bet is that you have a better idea than you think. But we're sure you won't get anywhere trying to bull your way through.

Chapter 14

Frequently Asked Questions

We generally offer review sessions prior to our exams during which we entertain student questions about the course and the exam. We also sometimes have feedback sessions at which we answer questions about an exam that we have just given. Here are some of the questions we hear most often. If you have questions that you don't find answered here or elsewhere in this book, you can contact us through our Web site *<http://www.getting2maybe.com>*. Although we can't promise to answer every question, we will from time to time choose a representative sample and post our answers in the on-line version of these tips appearing in the "law student" section of the *Lexis-Nexis for Law Schools* Web site *<http://lawschool.lexis.com>*.

FAQ #1. Do You Need to Cite Cases By Name?

Our answer to whether you should cite case names is both yes and no. Accurately citing cases and describing their holdings is unlikely to hurt you, provided that the cases are relevant to the problem at hand. Moreover, citing cases correctly can often be a useful shorthand to communicate to the professor that you are familiar with relevant law. It is possible, however, to perform superbly on a law school exam even if you forget virtually all of the case names. Above all, case citation is not an acceptable substitute for analysis. Here's what we mean:

Forgetting case names is no cause for alarm.

Law school exams are not memorization exercises. Many are open book, but even those that are not seek primarily analysis, not information. So if you get a question about a state constitutional amendment requiring U.S. Senators to be younger than 70 years old, you'll score well if you say the Supreme Court's invalidation of state-imposed term limits appears to extend to all additional qualifications, including a maximum age. If your analysis is sound, the professor is unlikely to care whether you mentioned the name of the case on which your analysis relies.

Citing cases is not nearly enough.

You won't score well on a question about a state's effort to retire Senators at age 70 if you say that the closest case to your facts is *U.S. Term Limits v. Thornton*, 514 U.S. 779 (1995), but that case isn't really relevant because it involved length of service rather than age requirements. You have remembered the case name correctly. You have accurately identified the way in which your exam problem factually differs from the real case. But your glib distinction between the cases is too pat and misunderstands the Supreme Court's deeper argument about the dangers of legislatively imposed qualifications for federal office. You would have done much better to remember the argument and forget the case name.

Case names are fabulous shorthand.

Pretend for a moment you are writing a history essay about the U.S. Senate in the second half of the 20th century and you want to describe the sudden increase in the number of women following the 1992 election. You could attribute the change partly to the fallout from the Clarence Thomas/Anita Hill hearings. Let's say, however, that your mind went blank for a moment and you just couldn't remember either Clarence Thomas's or Anita Hill's name. You could convey roughly the same point to your reader if you wrote something like, "Female voters were stirred up following a contested hearing before the Senate Judiciary Committee in which a former female subordinate of a Supreme Court nominee accused the nominee of sexual harassment." Certainly, if this were an exam, your grader would be unlikely to penalize you for forgetting the names Thomas and Hill.

But consider the disadvantages. First, it takes a lot longer to describe the event than merely to reference it by name. This is particularly true of law cases, so you'll save time on exams if you cite them by name. Second, if you have to describe the event you will inevitably omit details, which the reader may assume you remember if you just use the name, or you may even make an error in description. By contrast, a mere reference to the Thomas/Hill hearings draws the reader into a shared community in which you both rely on your stock recollections of the event, and conveys that you remember the whole event as it happened. For this reason, we believe case names can prove wonderfully helpful, even though very few professors actually look through answers to see whether the names of the relevant cases are there or not.

FAQ #2. Should You Type Your Exams?

The typical and perhaps most helpful professorial response to the typing issue is that you should do what makes you most comfortable. If you've never spent much time at a keyboard, you would be foolish to start with your law school exams; even if you are worried about your handwriting. By contrast, if you type everything you do, then by all means stick to typing—using a computer (where that's permitted) or a typewriter (if that's what's allowed and you can handle the noise). We believe, however, that there's slightly more to the story.

Speed counts.

Time pressure is a major factor on most law school exams. If you generally write faster than you type, you're taking a big risk in switching to a different format because you are worried about penmanship. On the other hand, if it's handwritten cursive that flows quickly but you find yourself printing exams to ensure legibility, then perhaps you might experiment to see which method is really faster. The good news is that this is an easy thing to check. Take a paragraph or two and write it out in your typical exam style. Then type the same material. Time yourself and see. Then do the same thing when you are actually composing on the page and at the keyboard. If both methods seem about the same, then this factor won't be important for you. But if there's a significant difference, then we recommend that you choose the faster method.

Typewritten legibility helps most students.

All the professors we know do their very best to avoid grading based on factors like legibility. We suspect that most of them fail. We're persuaded that typing helps most students for certain obvious reasons. It's easier for the grader to go back and check to see if certain points are covered. It's easier for the grader to take in the whole answer in a shorter period of time and thus to obtain a better sense of the writer's thought process. Above all, since the grader can easily read the entire answer, there's no risk of losing credit for points you included that the grader might miss because of illegible handwriting.

We haven't done a careful statistical survey to check our intuitions. But in one of our first year classes, 20 out of 560 students were chosen for the law review based on grades. Eleven of the 20 or more than half of those chosen typed their exams, while fewer than 20% of the class as a whole were typists. These numbers are unofficial and could, of course, be pure coincidence. But we doubt it.

Typing can backfire.

The most readable exam in the world won't help you if it turns out you don't understand the material. Worse still, we suspect that typing can actually cut against you. The simplest way of saying this is that good answers seem still better when they are easy to read while bad answers seem worse. Another way of making the point is that typing tends to magnify both the good and bad points of an answer. For example, the grader is more likely to see a contradiction between points early and late in the same essay if the grader can get through it quickly. We know that those of you who read this book won't encounter as many exam problems as your less fortunate classmates. Our point here, however, is that whether you type or write is much less important than *what* you type or write.

FAQ #3. Does the IRAC Method Help?

If we had to answer this question with a flat "yes" or "no," we'd pick "no" without a moment's hesitation. As we said in Chapter 9, in our combined quarter-century of law teaching—and in the thousands of bluebooks we've read over all those years—neither of us can ever recall seeing a first-rate exam answer organized around the so-called IRAC method ("issue-rule-application-conclusion").

In Chapter 9, we also spoke at length about the problems that result from the use of IRAC in the context of a traditional issue-spotter exam question, and we'll try not to repeat that here. What we'll focus on instead are two additional problems that may result from the use of that method.

Not All Questions Are the Same.

Many students conclude that if you try hard enough, you can squeeze *any* question—no matter what size or shape—into the neat little four-corner hole provided by IRAC. You could write an entire book about the salient features of law-exam taking that such a rigid approach ignores; we have, and you're reading it. But the bottom line is that different kinds of questions call for different kinds of answers.

As the first letter of the acronym suggests, IRAC is designed for use with the traditional issue-spotter question—the extended factual scenario full to the brim with legal issues of varying degrees of obviousness. In that setting, you can do pretty well simply by spotting a fair percentage of the more-or-less hidden issues; by identifying the legal rules that govern the resolution of those issues; and by briefly explaining how those rules would apply to the stated facts. Even here, IRAC has severe limits—a point we discussed at some length back in Chapter 9. But properly used in the issue-spotter setting, IRAC may help you get started down the right road.

The problem is that many law exam questions do not follow the issue-spotter format, and IRAC is about as useful in answering them as a bicycle is to a fish. Some exam questions spot the issue and even the rule for you and invite you to focus exclusively on ambiguities in the facts (for example, a question that asks whether an uncle's promise to pay his nephew $5000 if the latter gives up smoking is an offer seeking a bargain or merely a gratuitous promise); other questions call for differing interpretations of a given legal rule (for example, whether a whistleblower statute requires an employee to report wrongdoing to her employer before informing legal authorities); still other questions ask you to explore the pros and cons of one rule vs. another from the perspective of public policy (for example, "Should the State of X adopt a new approach to riparian rights, abolishing prior appropriation in favor of the doctrine of reasonable use?"); and still other questions will give you a conclusion and ask you to fashion arguments based on current law and the stated facts to get there (for example, "What are the best arguments available to a party seeking to challenge the constitutionality of a state law prohibiting affirmative action?").

In the context of exam questions such as these, IRAC is at best a waste of time (*e.g.*, when the question already *states* the "issue" and/or the "rule") and at worst a lens that can seriously distort your reading of the question (*e.g.*, when you ignore competing interpretations of a legal rule—interpretations that were considered at length in class—because you are too busy trying to "apply" the rule to the facts).

IRAC is too slow.

We have stressed all along that law exams put you under tremendous time pressure. Consider then how poorly suited IRAC is to cope with your problem. Although we've devoted our whole book to teaching you how to deal with exam questions where there is no one "right" answer, you can't ever forget that law exams still ask *questions*. You want to answer them as best you can, even if there is more than one way to do so.

Consider how slow IRAC is as a means for answering a question. You pull into a gas station and ask how to get to City Hall. Suppose the person behind the counter says, "I see your issue is that you want to get to City Hall. The rule is that you want to take the most direct route. To apply that rule, take a left at the light, go three blocks and turn right, and you'll come to it in about a mile. So what I want you to do is take a left at the light, go three blocks and turn right." You've got your answer, but you'll probably have to restrain yourself from yelling at the person to get to the point. That's how an IRAC answer may seem to your grader.

Ah, you say, but the City Hall example is unfair, because there was a clear answer and so the question didn't resemble a law exam. Okay, then, imagine that there are two ways to get to City Hall, the scenic route and the quick route. A speedy response might go like this: "Take a left at the light, go three blocks and turn right, and you'll come to it in about a mile. Or, if you want a more scenic trip, don't turn left until your second light, and go the same three blocks and turn right. This takes a bit longer, but you'll go by some nice Christmas lights." Let's say, however, that your town guide is suffering from IRAC disease. So he says to you, "There are two issues here. The first issue is where you want to go, but that one's easy since you are headed to City Hall. The second issue is whether you want the quick route or the scenic route. Now I suppose there are reasons why you might want either. [He then launches into a life philosophy discussion contrasting how the early bird gets the worm with why it's good to stop to smell the roses.] So, if you want the quick route turn left at the first light, go three blocks and turn right and proceed for a mile. If you want the scenic route, turn at your second light, go three blocks and turn right. [He then restates everything he just said to form a conclusion.]" You'll get your answer both ways, but the quickest route in the second scenario would have been to ask someone else for directions.

As we see it, the IRAC method is a product of professorial despair. Having read so many answers where students make analytical errors, professors are striving for a technique that will slow you down to ensure that you think problems through carefully. But we think it's not fair to slow you down when you face so much time pressure in the exam setting. That's why *Getting to Maybe* actually teaches legal analysis so that there will be fewer errors and you won't have to resort to what we feel is the IRAC crutch.

FAQ #4. What If You Realize You've Made a Mistake in Your Answer?

You are halfway through a question on your Criminal Procedure exam when you realize you have been evaluating the constitutionality of a search that a husband made of his wife's suitcase. Suddenly you remember that the Constitution doesn't restrict private actors. What should you do when you have traveled so far down the wrong path?

Don't panic.

Your first instinct may be anger with yourself for having written so much on an issue you now feel was poorly conceived. So you'll have a strong desire to rip up or cross out everything you have done and start over. In a few unusual cases, this may be the right response. Generally, however, you should resist the temptation to overreact. Many mistakes occur because the professor drafted the fact pattern with ambiguities that lure you into error. The question may have involved a husband searching his wife's suitcase purposefully looking for evidence that she committed a crime. The wife may have earlier refused to give the husband the key to the suitcase so he had to deliberately break in. And the husband may have immediately taken the evidence to police headquarters. All this may have been to tempt you into viewing the situation as a police search.

You can bail yourself out without crossing out all you have done. Indeed, in the course of your mistaken answer, you may have made some nice points about search and seizure law that although not directly applicable might still help your grade. You won't get a lot of points for a general statement that the police require a warrant to break into a locked suitcase. But you'll get more credit for an answer you have patched up to take out the worst errors than for no answer at all.

Go back, then, and write in material minimizing your mistake. You might insert a statement such as, "If this had been a police search it would have violated the Fourth Amendment, but since the husband searched his own wife's suitcase no constitutional violation is present." If your original mistake took you off on a tangent, this will minimize your error. But if you are lucky, the question may have been designed to lead you astray for the very purpose of provoking discussion on why a husband should not be constitutionally barred from searching his wife's suitcase. In that case, you'll suffer little and perhaps even gain from a preliminary section indicating why the search would have been illegal had it been conducted by the police.

Go back and signal your mistake before it happens.

Don't simply correct your mistake at the spot in your bluebook where it dawns on you that you have gone astray. Imagine your grader reading along through several pages of largely irrelevant information. Now she comes to a spot where you say, "Sorry, I didn't mean any of what I said for the last 6 pages." In theory, your professor should be able to adjust her view of the last several pages to account for your new found realization. But this is psychologically difficult.

The professor will far prefer it if you go back to the spot in the bluebook where you initially went wrong and signal your error. Write in something like, "In the analysis that follows I treat a search by a husband as if it were a police search for purposes of the Fourth Amendment. I understand that this confuses a basic point about the application of the Constitution to private vs. public actors." This may be the best you can do. If you are lucky, the question may contain facts that enable you to make a silk purse out of a sow's ear. You might say that the husband's quick trip to the police station suggests that he and the police had cooperated in advance on planning the search and that the husband was thus acting as a police agent. This will raise further difficult issues about what a private actor can do when cooperating with the authorities. But at least it will make what was a tangent now seem relevant to the facts. The important point is that an advance signal of your error is your best protection against being graded down severely.

Move quickly and confidently down a new path.

Whatever else it will cost you, a lengthy digression or a mistaken evaluation will take time away from the analysis the professor expects. So if you catch yourself having made a mistake, go back and signal it and THEN MOVE ON! Ask yourself what issues you might have missed because you were busy focusing on something that now seems mistaken. Also, try as hard as you can to resist being flustered by your mistake. Everyone makes errors when confronting complex fact patterns for the first time. When you start down your new path, continue to use the same aggressive, confident tone you had before. You want to learn from your mistakes but not be intimidated by them.

FAQ #5. What If You Think the *Professor* Has Made a Mistake?

You are reading through a long problem on your Property exam that appears to raise issues about the nature of the state action doctrine and its application to judicial enforcement of restrictive covenants. At the end of the question the professor asks, "How does the Rule in *Shelley's Case* apply to these facts?"

You are convinced that the professor has erred. The Rule in *Shelley's Case* is a mostly dead letter doctrine about interpreting grant language in property deeds. You are convinced your professor meant to ask, "How does the rule in *Shelley v. Kraemer* apply to these facts?" *Shelley v. Kraemer* is the leading United States Supreme Court case on the topic of restrictive covenants.

What should you do in such cases of apparent professorial mistake?

Ask about apparent errors.

The first thing to do in an exam situation where you think there's an error is (where permitted) to ask about it. If the professor is present at the exam, ask her. If you are right and the error is a significant one, the professor may have an opportunity to correct it for you and the whole class before it's too late. If you are wrong, the professor may simply tell you there is no error. This will remove any uncertainty you may have had. You may get the silent treatment from either the proctor or the professor. In that case, you are no worse off than you were before. There's no harm in asking, and no need to be bashful.

Flag apparent errors where you cannot resolve uncertainty.

If you can't get to the professor, or the professor won't answer your question, and you still believe there's an error, then explain in your answer how you read the question and how you believe it is supposed to read. This puts the professor on your wavelength as she begins to evaluate your answer. The worst thing you can do, of course, is to assume the professor has made an error, never mention this, and then answer the question that you think the professor meant to ask. If you are mistaken and the question is correct as written, you will score very poorly indeed.

If you have time, answer the question both ways.

If your uncertainty remains unresolved, you must deal with it in your answer. If the final line of the question reads "discuss Carl's causes of action" and you believe the professor meant to ask about Carla's causes of action, then tell the professor about both. First indicate you know what the question says and answer that one first. Then explain how you think the question was supposed to read and answer that one too.

Rethink your assumptions.

Before spending a great deal of time responding to anything other than what appears on the exam, make sure you haven't missed something. Most professors spend a great deal of time proofreading exams, often consulting colleagues for a double-check. Minor, easy-to-miss typographical errors that nonetheless change the meaning of the question sometimes slip through. It's unlikely, however, that you will find major errors. If it seems to you that a professor has really goofed, like asking about the wrong case, stop and think again. If the question is a part of a series of short essays, maybe the apparent mistake is intentional. When the professor asks how does Case A apply, maybe all she wants to hear is "it doesn't."

If, however, you have an hour to analyze the significance of what you are convinced is an irrelevant case—or more generally if you are positive that the question as written isn't what you are supposed to answer—then flag the error and try to cope with it.

FAQ #6. What If You Don't Know What a Word Means?

Your professors will try hard not to use unfamiliar terms without defining them. But occasionally we will forget that something that seems entirely familiar to us may turn out not to be familiar to you. Our favorite example is a Criminal Law exam involving a warrantless search of a Winnebago—a large vehicle on wheels that you can live in for extended periods but also drive around on camping trips. The Supreme Court has granted the police greater latitude to search automobiles than to search private homes. The exam drafter felt that a Winnebago posed the perfect intermediate case which would force his students to consider the reasons for the automobile vs. home distinction. Unfortunately, many of his students didn't know what a Winnebago was, and this ruined the question.

If lots of your classmates don't know a word, then you may be bailed out by general ignorance. It's equally possible, however, that you may be alone or among a few students who don't know a word. Nine times out of ten, your professor won't want a vocabulary difficulty to interfere with performance. (The tenth case will be when the word is one that you specifically should have learned for the course.) Once the exam is over, however, it's very unlikely you'll be able to persuade the professor to make any concession at all. So here's what you should do.

Bring a dictionary to all open-book exams.

The whole point of open-book exams is to allow you to simulate more closely the real world in which attorneys can look things up. Although you are most likely to want to look up cases and statutes, you never know when you might want to check on a definition. This goes double for all of you for whom English is not your first language. If you have taken steps to cope with your language difficulty and still come up blank, a brief statement that the word in question does not appear in your dictionary is likely to persuade your professor that his choice of words—rather than your vocabulary—is the problem. But if you show up without a dictionary, you'll find yourself out of luck.

If the professor is present, ask for a definition.

Many professors check in on their students during exams precisely to ensure there are no unanticipated problems. If you ask, the professor may be more than happy to tell you the meaning of a word. She may decide that the word is harder than she expected and announce the definition to the whole class. Either way, you'll find out what you needed. If the professor won't tell you, at least you'll have tried your best. But if you keep mum, the professor is extremely unlikely to give you a break when you call her the next day and explain your problem.

If the professor is absent, ask the proctor for help.

At some schools, professors don't attend exams, and monitoring is done by proctors. Proctors are much less likely to tell you the meaning of a word, because this might interfere with the professor's goals. A proctor might, however, be willing to call the professor during the exam and check for permission. This is certainly worth a shot, and is a whole lot better than sitting there in ignorance.

If all else fails, highlight in your exam that you don't know a word.

If the professor is not there and the proctor refuses to answer your query or help you out—or, as at some schools, there is no proctor—you should at least flag for the professor that you were confused about the meaning of a word. This may not help you much, but the point of law exams is not generally to test vocabulary. If you explain your confusion in your answer, at least you have a chance that the professor will give you a break.

FAQ #7. Does the Professor Want "Black-Letter" Answers?

We often hear students complaining that Professor X spent all his class time on big-picture questions of social policy and then focused his exam on mundane questions of law. Such complaints miss a basic point. Every law school professor, no matter how abstract or theoretical, will insist that you learn basic legal rules. If you don't, no amount of policy argument, fancy theorizing, or other exam-taking wizardry will save you from a poor performance.

This doesn't mean, however, that your professors are seeking merely "black-letter" law. As we have said elsewhere (see Tip #16, "Don't Regurgitate Legal Rules and Principles"), knowing the black letter is necessary to exam excellence, but it is not sufficient. Your job is to convince the professor that you know how to *use* the rules, not merely that you have memorized them. So your challenge is to demonstrate that you have mastered the black letter and that you can apply it to the problems in the exam. Here are the yin and yang of how to do both.

Use black-letter law to spot issues.

You don't need to have attended law school to recognize certain basic legal issues. A pedestrian struck by a car traveling 90 miles an hour through city streets is likely to have a cause of action against the driver. But the more law you know, the more you will be able to spot subtle problems. Suppose instead that the driver is on an interstate highway traveling at 60 mph when a child runs into the road chasing a Frisbee. The driver swerves, avoiding the child, but a passenger in the car is so frightened he has a heart attack and dies. Can the passenger's family sue the driver? This sounds like a typical Torts exam question.

Every bit of black-letter law you know will help you spot legal issues. If you know there's a legal doctrine called negligence *per se* that renders people liable for damage they cause while violating safety statutes, then you'll want to know what the speed limit was on the highway where the accident occurred and whether it took place in a jurisdiction where negligence *per se* applies. If you know that the negligence *per se* doctrine is sometimes found inapplicable because the injured party is not someone whom the safety statute was intended to protect, then you will see an issue of whether speed limits are really meant to protect passengers from heart attacks. (Passengers seem a likely protected group, but perhaps heart attacks fall outside the scope of intended protection.) If you understand that a tort suit requires proof of causation, then you might see an issue of whether the driver was the proximate cause of the harm. Finally, if you are familiar with so-called "guest statutes" that at various times and places have immunized drivers against suits by certain passengers, then you'll want to know whether any "guest statute" is relevant here. The point is you can't spot any legal issues if you don't know black-letter law. So in one sense your professor wants, even demands, a black-letter answer.

Go beyond black-letter responses.

The whole point of law school exams is to place you in situations in which black-letter law doesn't translate into easy solutions. Suppose you encounter a hypothetical deed in which a rich landowner deeds his large estate, Chic Acres, "to my cousin William, but if William should ever attempt to transfer Chic Acres to a member of Ross Perot's Reform Party, then Chic Acres is to go to my niece Chelsea in fee simple." The first thing that occurs to you is the rule that "restraints on alienation" aren't allowed and that William can thus sell to whomever he wants. But suppose you also remember that courts occasionally make an exception for restraints that prevent transfer to a disfavored branch of the family. If the restrictions on William are looked at in this light, perhaps they might be upheld. Now you are ahead of the game because you have identified black-letter rules on both sides.

BUT YOU ARE NOT FINISHED! You must proceed to analyze the question of whether a court would be more likely to view a ban on sales to Reform party members as a general (and thus invalid) restraint or instead as a limited (and thus permissible) restraint because the ban covers only sales to a disfavored group. You might discuss the size of the disfavored group (the Reform Party has many more members than your brother-in-law's family) or the undesirability of entangling politics and real estate. It's less important which factors you stress than that you recognize that the court has a choice to make. If all you do is prove to the professor that you know the black-letter rules, you won't do well because you won't describe how the choice might be made. In this important sense, black letter is not enough.

FAQ #8. Should You Use Commercial Study Aids?

Let's face it: If we told you that the answer to this question is "no," you wouldn't believe us, for hornbooks, outlines, canned briefs, and the like are as much a part of American law school life as the Socratic method, yearly tuition increases, and the TGIF. Indeed, if we thought there were no place in legal education for commercial study aids, we wouldn't have written this book! But the key word here is "place." There are some things that a high-quality commercial product can do for you, but other things you'll have to do for yourself—other things, in other words, that even the best commercial outline simply cannot replace.

The good news: A high-quality commercial study aid can help you spot the trees in the forest.

The typical law school course tends to treat "black-letter" rules as merely a starting point for analysis. When you study the perfect tender rule in Contracts, for example, your professor may seem to spend about 30 seconds on U.C.C. § 2-601 (buyer may reject goods "if the goods or the tender of delivery fail in any respect to conform to the contract") and devote the next two classes to increasingly complex variations and exceptions (*e.g.*, what if the buyer has invariably accepted similarly nonconforming deliveries in the past? what if the buyer signs for the delivery after the seller notifies him of the nonconformity?). Meanwhile, the individual without any experience in business transactions (*i.e.*, the typical law student) may still be trying to figure out the rule itself. Although the professor is unlikely to test "the rule itself"—and is in fact far more likely to examine the variations and exceptions explored in class—a high quality commercial study aid may nevertheless help the student get the comfort and grounding she needs before she can join the professor "at the next level."

So, you ask, how can I determine which of the many commercial study aids on the market is a high-quality product? The classics—Prosser on Torts; McCormick on Evidence; Farnsworth on Contracts; Chirelstein on Tax; Glannon on Civil Procedure; Tribe on Constitutional Law—are classics for a reason, and you can seldom go wrong with judicious reliance on any of them. Beyond that, the best source for a recommendation is your professor, who may well have a favorite and who may in any event be willing to help you steer clear of the shoddier products on the market.

The bad news: The most useful outlines are made, not purchased.

One terribly important thing a commercial outline cannot do is provide you with the experience of organizing your *own* outline, and, in the end, there is no better way to grasp either the fine details or the "big picture" of a course. Indeed, the very process of outlining—of working your way back through the mass of material before you and of organizing it in a way that helps you make sense of it all—may be the most valuable part of your legal studies. (See Tip #3, "Prepare Your Own Outline of the Course.")

More bad news: The most useful outlines are tailored to your professor's course.

While a commercial study aid may offer a useful overview, nothing will provide a more accurate guide to the particular topics and issues that your professor thinks are most important than what she actually emphasizes in class. Moreover, quite apart from the variety of course content, different professors focus their teaching efforts on different lawyerly skills. As a result, an outline that draws heavily on what *your* professor actually did in class is likely to be your most valuable resource as you prepare for your exams. (Once again, see Tip #3, "Prepare Your Own Outline for the Course.")

Still more bad news: Commercial study aids may emphasize the wrong skills.

Earlier in the book, we quoted a law school classmate who aptly described the experience of reading a case for the first time as akin to "stirring cement with your eyelashes." It is no surprise, then, that many students turn to commercial study aids to help them shortcut this difficult task.

Canned briefs, for example, purport to find legal rules for you, by offering you a pre-digested case analysis for each of the cases covered in the casebook. That they frequently do this shoddily is a defect that we won't belabor here, but the principal problem is that *you* should be undertaking the case analysis yourself; what kind of lawyer would you be if you couldn't give legal advice based upon the current caselaw until that caselaw made its way into a hornbook? There is no better way to learn this vital skill than to brief each case, on your own, *very* carefully. It is a difficult skill to master, and your early attempts may be frustrating, but you simply cannot master legal reasoning unless you learn how to do it yourself.

Moreover, whether you learn a supposed rule by analyzing a case on your own, by reading a canned brief, or by finding it in a hornbook or commercial outline, simply knowing that rule just won't get you very far. The crucial skill—for success on law exams as well as in law practice—is rule-application, and that too is a skill you can only develop with great practice; no commercial product can do it for you.

Perhaps the worst news yet: Commercial study aids may waste valuable time.

It's tough enough to find the time to read the cases for all of your courses; to brief and think about them; to attend all your classes well-prepared and to take good classnotes; and—as exams near—to begin to outline your courses. If occasional or even relatively frequent reference to a high-quality commercial outline helps you clarify your understanding of this or that particular point as you go along, then by all means avail yourself of that assistance. But if you treat your commercial study aid as simply *another* massive text to read, digest, and attempt to integrate with the required materials—or, worse, if you attempt to do this with more than one of the commercial products available for the course in question—you'll find that the added value you get in exchange for all that time and effort will be practically nil. And if your experience of law school is anything like ours was, you don't have that kind of time to waste.

Chapter 15

Putting Maybe to Work: Sample Questions and Answers

Enough talk already. You've gone through a great deal of material telling you what will work and what won't, but you want to see our advice in action. We are happy to oblige. In this final chapter then we will take you through some sample questions from different subjects and point out how our analysis would help you write better answers. These aren't the first examples you have seen, since our book proceeds largely by example. But there is something useful about simulating the longer questions you can expect on a real exam.

We cannot say enough times, however, that our goal in this chapter is not to provide instruction about any of the particular legal topics we select. Our examples are constructed with legal principles common to most basic courses so that they should sound familiar, and, like everything else in the book, they will make more sense to those of you who have studied your class material. We understand, however, that one component of top exam performance is the ability to solve the particular puzzle that each exam question presents. As you read over our puzzles and solutions you may say to yourself, "I just never would have thought of that, and no amount of advice they can provide will change that."

We ask you to put that reaction on hold. First, some of our hypotheticals may be based on issues you haven't covered, and so the solutions will appear much harder than they will to other readers. Second, our experience in solving legal problems is that you just never can predict what solutions might come to you under what conditions. Finally, and most important, this chapter isn't designed to see whether you can solve the particular sample exam questions we present. So the question isn't whether you would have imagined the solution we suggest but whether you can see why the solution appealed to us and how it might help you solve other problems in the future. As we see it, you can improve your exam skills by reading over old exams (especially your professors' old exams) the same way you could improve chess skills by reading over problems. You'll learn a lot, even if you couldn't think of the particular checkmate that the problem-writer had in mind.

Indeed, we can extend the chess analogy as a way of thinking back over what we have covered. The conventional wisdom we have sought to challenge is that successful exam-taking is mostly about whether the answer pops into your head and is therefore a skill that cannot be taught. Of course, even the die-hards agree that answers are more likely to come easily to those who study the material. We agree. But our real beef is with the idea that you can't improve your ability to have the right things come to you at the right time. In Chapter 9, we explained how studying the material with an eye toward, and an understanding of, exam questions can make the actual exam a less intimidating and thus more successful experience. Most of the rest of the book, however, is intended to convey an even more fundamental point.

Consider the easiest chess problems given to beginners just getting past the basics. Beginners often hold fast to first impressions, such as the notion that the Queen is the most valuable piece and cannot be lost. When a chess problem then requires a Queen sacrifice to produce mate, these students may be stuck — not because they lack the ability to imagine the solution, but because their own ideas about the importance of the Queen are getting in their way. So, too, we have sought to show throughout the book how, as beginning law students, you understandably have ideas that may be getting in your way — ideas about what exams should be like that come from undergraduate school, ideas about the need for a certain format, ideas about what your professors are looking for, and mostly ideas about the need for certainty where making peace with ambiguity will do. We are confident that, as you begin to clear away these false ideas, your natural ability will kick in to do the rest. Law school after all is much more about common sense than rocket science.

Finally, we ask you to suppress two additional reactions to our sample questions. You may find that our answers are unrealistically thorough given the time pressure students face. This is clearly true. We have written the questions and answers and have the luxury of writing responses at our own pace—and in the comfort of our faculty offices. We want you to learn from our responses, not to treat them as models. In that regard, you will find citations to legal materials more formal here than they would be in an actual exam answer. We do that so those of you curious about the merits can check our work, not because professors actually expect formal cites on exams.

Alternatively, you may read over our exams and imagine a solution entirely different from the one we propose. Don't get bogged down, however, on the details of any particular question. If you disagree with us, just put that question aside and go on to the next. Later on, if you have time and want to let us know your approach, you can find us by accessing our Web site at *<http://www.getting2maybe.com>* or the *Lexis-Nexis for Law Schools* Web site *<http://lawschool.lexis.com>*. We'll try to write you back, and don't be surprised if we say "maybe" you're right.

A. Torts

One of the easiest ways for your professor to build an exam question is to select a rule you have studied in class or to provide one for you on the exam and to write a fact pattern where categories established by the rule don't quite fit the situation. Here's an example.

Brandishing a large hunting knife, Melissa entered Gary's elegant Coconut Grove mansion and threatened to stab him. Elliott, a free-lance director, was in Gary's living room at the time shooting a commercial for Bedford Falls University, and he captured the moment on videotape. A week later, Suzanna, Gary's fiancée, played a copy of Elliott's tape on Gary's VCR, mistakenly thinking that it was the couple's favorite episode of *thirtysomething*. Upon viewing the tape, Suzanna suffered severe emotional distress, but no bodily injury. Can Suzanna prevail in a lawsuit against Melissa in a jurisdiction that treats § 46 of the Restatement (Second) of Torts as highly persuasive? Why or why not?

Now, if you look at this problem and think, "I've never heard of actions for emotional distress," then you aren't likely to make much headway. Odds are good, however, that either the professor will have spent a great deal of class time on § 46 of the Restatement (Second) of Torts or that you will be provided with a text of the provision on the exam. It states:

(1) One who by extreme or outrageous conduct intentionally or recklessly causes severe emotional distress to another is subject to liability for such emotional distress, and if bodily harm to the other results from it, for such bodily harm.

(2) Where such conduct is directed at a third person, the actor is subject to liability if he intentionally or recklessly causes severe emotional distress

(a) to a member of such person's immediate family who is present at the time, whether or not such distress results in bodily harm, or

(b) to any other person who is present at the time, if such distress results in bodily harm.

A respectable answer might look something like this:

Suzanna will most likely to be able to prove some of the elements of a cause of action based on reckless infliction of emotional distress, but problems in her case—particularly the fact that she was not present at the time Melissa brandished the knife—will, in my judgment, doom her claim.

Suzanna won't have much trouble showing that Melissa's conduct is extreme and outrageous because it is shocking beyond the bounds of society. Making threats while brandishing a knife isn't yet parlor chatter. But Suzanna must also demonstrate

Melissa's recklessness, and, although knife-brandishing is clearly reckless, Suzanna must extend Melissa's state of mind to cover not just Gary and those present but also those who might see the videotape. It's unlikely Melissa missed the fact that Elliott turned the camera on her during the incident, and certainly Melissa could imagine that Gary's loved ones would be emotionally harmed watching it—so Suzanna's case may be strong here.

But Suzanna has two other problems. First, it's unclear whether fiancées fit within the Restatement's definition of family members. Second, Suzanna technically wasn't present in the room when Melissa brandished the knife. Overcoming these obstacles will require her to persuade a judge to extend the straightforward definition of the rule.

Suzanna has a relatively strong case that a fiancée should fit within the definition of family member so that she can escape the Restatement's requirement of bodily injury for non-family. Melissa will argue that a rule is a rule, and that once an exception is made, extensions might be made to include close friends, etc. But Suzanna is in a good position to suggest that fiancées are like family members in all relevant respects—close emotional bonds, serious commitment, etc.—and that including fiancées is unlikely to start us down a slippery slope because fiancées constitute a small, easily identifiable class. Suzanna will be helped here if her engagement to Gary is provable through tangible evidence like the passing of an engagement ring, the establishment of a wedding date, or even their having told lots of friends. The clearer it is that they were truly engaged, the easier it will be to deflect Melissa's point that people might invent a potential wedding as a way of bringing lawsuits within the Restatement rule. All the reasons of fairness and deterring reckless conduct that support the Restatement rule can therefore also be seen as supporting Suzanna's suit.

Suzanna will have a harder time with the Restatement's presence requirement. Certainly she can assert that watching an event on tape has a striking emotional impact very much like seeing it live. But there are two flaws here. First, because a week has passed since the knife incident, Suzanna is likely to be confident that Gary isn't really in danger. True, the tape may not have a date or any recognizable way to establish time, but even so Suzanna is watching it in Gary's house so presumably she knows nothing untoward has happened there. Second, given the proliferation of videotaping, interpreting the "presence" requirement to include seeing an event on tape is likely to lead to a dramatic expansion of liability for infliction of emotional distress. My guess is that despite the obvious pain to Suzanna, and Melissa's obvious culpability, a court would be reluctant to rule for Suzanna due to the potential for multiple lawsuits arising from all family members who view emotionally distressing news footage.

Finally, if she is rebuffed under the Restatement, Suzanna might argue that she meets the stiffer requirements of the old common law. But it is unlikely that Suzanna can show Melissa had a desire to harm her or that Melissa knew her outrageous conduct was "substantially certain" to cause harm to Suzanna since Melissa had no way to know that Suzanna would ever view the tape. Suzanna is thus unlikely to prevail.

Comments: This question is relatively straightforward and calls upon several of the basic skills we have explained. Note that the response starts with a summary answer to the question that draws the reader into the longer discussion. Plus it "answers the question," because a conclusion is reached about whether Suzanna will prevail, but at the same time it "argues both sides" because arguments supporting Suzanna are put in their best light ("close emotional bonds"/"obvious pain she felt"). Note further that the main device of the question is to put the reader in doubt about whether a fiancée is a family member and whether watching a videotape counts as "presence." The answer avoids two common mistakes. It would be easy to lose points by simply concluding without argument that a fiancée was not a family member or that the presence requirement is not met. And it would be equally understandable to be thrown by a question that talks about a fiancée when you know the rule covers family members and you have never studied a rule for fiancées. What the answer does is to treat the unsettled issues as an opportunity for discussion and then attempts to resolve them by drawing on facts in the question (Suzanna is unlikely to see Gary as still in danger) and policy arguments about the future (videotapes may generate too many lawsuits).

* * * * *

Another common exam technique is to pose a hypothetical that would be resolved one way under one rule and another way under a competing rule. Unlike the previous question, where rule-choice arises only briefly at the end, here you are expected to focus on which rule should apply and why. Good answers will include discussion about how the rules relate to each other (e.g., statutes trump common law) and policy arguments about which rule is superior. Here's a question like that.

> A tiger escapes from its locked cage in Chicago's Lincoln Park Zoo and attacks Lynda Tripe as she exits her apartment building, which is located about a block from the zoo. Ms. Tripe brings an action against the zoo seeking recovery for her injuries. The zoo argues it need not pay, since it has complied in every respect with the detailed Illinois statutes regulating the construction and maintenance of cages "for the keeping and public display of animals." Who will prevail and why?

One possible answer might look like this:

I'm going to assume that the Lincoln Park Zoo is a private entity subject to lawsuit like any other, since our course didn't go deeply into questions of sovereign immunity or suing governments. The hard question then is whether the zoo's compliance with the statutes should preclude Tripe's suit or merely help the zoo establish that it was not negligent.

The zoo's position is the more straightforward. It complied with the statutes, which the zoo will say represent the legislature's considered judgment about regulating the caging and "keeping" of animals. The "details" in the statute suggest the legislature meant to cover the waterfront, and courts shouldn't step in and impose additional liability. Moreover, if complying with safety statutes is insufficient to immunize zoos against lawsuits, the cost of keeping animals will rise beyond what the legislature intended and may make the economics of zoos entirely infeasible.

Ms. Tripe has several possible counterarguments, and a closer reading of the Illinois statutes might be necessary to make an educated judgment about who will likely prevail. Her easiest argument is that nothing in the statutes explicitly indicates that the legislature intended to foreclose common law actions. Thus a private law action could be a desirable supplement to the legislative rules. To the extent that the statute modifies the common law rules, it could be read merely to establish the standard for negligence. But Ms. Tripe could argue that the keeping of tigers is an abnormally dangerous activity governed by the common law rule of strict liability (as opposed let's say to what the rule might be if a sheep got loose and bit someone). To support this position from a broader policy perspective, Ms. Tripe might also stress that her injuries are just another cost of running a zoo and that the zoo should bear those costs or pass them on to the public in terms of higher admission prices. The zoo has a relatively strong rejoinder, however, in that the existence of relatively detailed regulations makes it doubtful that the legislature meant to leave a system of strict liability in place that would leave zoos vulnerable to suits even if they complied with the regulations.

So what Ms. Tripe needs to do is convince a court that there's a way to square the Illinois regulations with a generous system of strict liability tort recovery. One way to do that would be to look closely at the regulations to try and show they were aimed at something other than public safety, such as humane treatment for the animals. A second alternative might be to suggest that the legislature was regulating the "public display" of animals so as to prevent the otherwise easily foreseeable injuries to spectators, but that zoos have a separate common law duty to prevent the actual escape of dangerous animals. Since Ms. Tripe is a neighborhood resident, not a zoo-goer, she should be entitled to rely on the common law.

Both of Ms. Tripe's arguments here depend on learning more about the text and background of the Illinois statutes. And each is sufficiently credible that a court, interested in placing the loss on the deeper pocket or the more responsible party, could easily conclude that the zoo was liable. Absent something unusually helpful in the statute to support a narrow construction or a court eager to spread losses, however, I would expect the zoo to prevail on grounds that it complied with Illinois statutes.

Comments: As we explained in Chapter 9, you will often find yourself arguing over which rule governs a particular situation, and you need to understand both the arguments for and against each rule and the difference it makes to the outcome of choosing one rule over the other. Here you are forced to argue the choice between the common law of strict liability (which favors Ms. Tripe) and applying the statutory safety standard to the question of private liability (which favors the zoo). What makes this answer better than many is that it not only grasps the importance of the rule choice but also generates multiple arguments for each choice, including arguments based on economic policy. Note also that the proposed answer again "answers the question" (the zoo will prevail) yet gives enormous weight to Ms. Tripe's arguments to the point where you can barely distinguish between the clear conclusion and the equally clear presentation of the alternative position. Note further that the answer explicitly tackles issues that appear confusing, like the possibility that the zoo is a public entity, by letting the professor know that you spotted the issue but didn't believe it was meant to be part of the question. The assumption here, of course, is based on what was covered in the actual course. Finally, it should be clear here, as elsewhere, that top performance depends upon careful study of the "rules" —e.g., those governing strict liability for abnormally dangerous activities —and of the relationship between statutes and the common law.

B. Property

A common variation on the rule vs. counter-rule problem is the situation that doesn't quite fit either Rule A or Rule B. In that setting, policy arguments will obviously figure prominently when you try to choose between them. It's particularly interesting when it turns out that the policy arguments that ordinarily support Rule A turn out to support the application of Rule B in an unusual set of facts. That's the case in the example that follows:

Bobby Donnell owned a large, beautiful ranch called "Practice Estates." When he turned 80, Bobby decided to convey Practice Estates to his two children, Jimmy and Eleanor. The deed reads as follows: "I hereby convey Practice Estates to Jimmy and Eleanor Donnell as joint tenants, with right of survivorship, it being my express wish that the ranch will one day be owned outright by my longest-lived child. During the first ten years of the joint tenancy, either joint tenant may sever the joint tenancy through voluntary transfer of his or her interest, but I further declare that, after ten years of uninterrupted joint tenancy, neither Jimmy nor Eleanor should attempt to convey his or her interest, if either of them learns he or she is terminally ill. If, upon being diagnosed with a terminal illness, either Jimmy or Eleanor does attempt to transfer his or her interest in Practice Estates, then his or her interest shall be extinguished and 100% ownership of Practice Estates shall immediately become vested in the co-owning child (*i.e.*, the child not seeking to transfer his or her interest).

After 30 years of uninterrupted joint tenancy, during which time Jimmy and Eleanor got along beautifully and shared many pleasures at Practice Estates, Jimmy's doctor informs Jimmy that he has incurable lung cancer. Jimmy wants to be sure his son Eugene can continue to enjoy the good times at Practice Estates. So, without consulting a lawyer, Jimmy conveys his "undivided one-half interest in Practice Estates to my son Eugene." Eleanor learns of this conveyance and hires an attorney who immediately files suit seeking a court order that title to Practice Estates now rests exclusively with Eleanor.

Make the strongest case you can for Eugene that he is now owner of one half of Practice Estates as a tenant-in-common with Eleanor, and make the strongest case you can for Eleanor that she is owner of all of Practice Estates. How would you resolve the dispute and why?

Possible Answer: Eugene's argument calls for a straightforward application of the rules governing joint tenancy and the rule compelling courts not to enforce Bobby's deed as written because it is an unlawful restraint on alienation. Joint tenants such as Jimmy are customarily entitled to transfer their half interests thereby creating a tenancy in common between the recipient (Eugene) and the former joint tenant (Eleanor). Jimmy's only obstacle to this is Bobby's deed provision prohibiting transfer, but this is most likely void because fee simple owners (and a joint tenant is a fee owner for this purpose) are generally not permitted to have their interests encumbered by provisions causing forfeiture upon transfer. The rule prohibiting restraints on alienation is typically justified on the ground that former owners (like Bobby) shouldn't be allowed to prevent current owners (like Jimmy) from making decisions about the best use of the property under today's conditions. The general idea is that a single current owner is likely to make the most educated judgments about the highest and best use of land. Rules that fragment ownership between present and former owners may interfere with the efficient use of resources.

Eleanor can win only through enforcement of the provision in Bobby's deed. She can start with the idea that the plain language of the deed should be respected, and that courts should enforce Bobby's clear intent. The rule Jimmy relies on prohibiting restraints on alienation is an exception to the more general rule in property law to respect the grantor's intent. Even so, to prevail Eleanor must successfully argue that Bobby's is not an unlawful restraint. To do that she can analogize this situation to those in which courts have permitted restraints on alienation as long as those restraints are *partial*. The typical partial restraint involves a prohibition on a sale to a particular person or family. Courts, for example, have allowed grantors to leave land to their children in fee simple and yet have upheld forfeiture provisions that would prohibit the children from transferring land to (say) their spouse's family. Eleanor can't make the simple argument that Bobby's restraint on Jimmy is partial merely because it does not cover Jimmy's entire period of ownership. Courts have found that a restraint on alienation for a period of time, like ten years, will be considered total even though the restricted owner could sell once the ten years was over. [Here, the answer might cite a case from the course.]

To convince the court that Bobby's restraint was valid because partial, Eleanor will have to stress the equities of the situation. First, unlike the typical case in which the restricted owner is bound for a period and then released, Jimmy here had an initial ten year window in which to sever the joint tenancy. If Jimmy wanted to hold a transferrable interest, he could have conveyed the land to someone in a straw (*i.e.*, not real) transaction who would then reconvey to him. Thus, Jimmy himself is responsible for the existence of the current restriction that now bars him from transferring to Eugene. Second, although Bobby's restraint doesn't fit into any recognizable category, it is obviously extraordinarily limited in scope. Only when a terminal illness is diagnosed does the restraint take effect. So, if ever a restraint was partial within the literal meaning of the word, this one is. Finally, Eleanor has an interesting policy point as well. Under the facts of this case, if Bobby's restraint is enforced, total ownership will be consolidated in her, whereas if the court voids the restraint, ownership will remain divided between Eleanor and Eugene. Thus, the goal of consolidating ownership (normally supportive of the rule prohibiting restraints) will, on these unusual facts, be best served by respecting Bobby's intent.

Despite these unusual facts, I would find for Eugene and against Eleanor. Bobby had other ways (such as creating a trust) of keeping his property in the hands of his children (not to mention that Jimmy's transfer is to his own son). If courts start creating unusual exceptions to the rule barring restraints on alienation, their enforceability will become a matter of continued litigation. This restraint on alienation is sufficiently like those courts have invalidated, and I wouldn't hesitate to do so here.

Comment: Clearly the key to this question is knowing the general rule that bars total restraints on alienation and the exception that permits partial restraints. But many students familiar with both of these rules will still write poor answers to this question. One clue to figuring out what the professor is seeking is to think back to Chapter 9's section on "themes and issues." Virtually all Property teachers spend some time on the general tension between respecting a grantor's wishes (Bobby here) so as to encourage contemporary transfers (his transfer to his kids) and promoting the marketability of property by unencumbering titles (such as Jimmy's here). This question, then, is a vehicle for discussing that theme, even though it's not explicitly a "theme" question. But you are likely to recognize this only if you react to the rather unusual fact pattern by asking, "Why did the professor write it this way?" rather than merely despairing that you have never quite seen a case like this. Other things to note about the answer include the relentless insistence on demonstrating not only the different rules but the consequences of applying one rule rather than another (see Chapter 9's discussion of "what difference does it make"); the ability to deploy policy arguments (like consolidating ownership and the dangers of the slippery slope if an exception is made to the rule against restraints) once the competing rule-choices are identified; and, of course, that the answer carefully addresses each of the questions in the problem, offering arguments for each side and then drawing a conclusion.

* * * * *

It is common for many areas of law to be organized around multi-factor tests in which courts are charged with looking at each factor before reaching an ultimate conclusion. (Compare our discussion of "Running the Gantlet" in Chapter 6.) These areas of law pose challenges for exam writers who attempt to invent fact patterns that call for careful analysis of each of the many factors. That's the case in the following example. Moreover, professors are very aware that exams they write in year one will be read by many of their students in years two, three, and four. Sometimes, then, a professor will attempt to provoke thought by tying together, through unusual facts, two parts of the law that don't immediately seem connected. (See our discussion of "competing domains" in Chapter 7.) That's the case in the next example as well.

It's 1999, and President Clinton has grown tired of watching the Justice Department play antitrust footsie with Microsoft. He delivers the following speech on national television:

"The public interest clearly won't be served if consumers have no choice but to embrace the industry's sole surviving computer operating system, Windows 2000. The track record suggests that even the most vigorous antitrust enforcement won't succeed in bolstering private competitors to Microsoft. Accordingly, I am today authorizing a no-holds-barred government effort to develop a public operating system to serve as an alternative to Windows 2000. My intention is that when this system is complete, the federal government will pursue every means necessary to ensure its successful introduction to the marketplace."

In 2005, President Gore announces the completion of the government's new operating system, which has come to be known as Big BOSS (Big Brother's Operating System, Silly). Unfortunately, Big BOSS can't hold a candle to Sunroof 2004 (the latest operating system from Microsoft). Big BOSS works half as well and costs twice as much. So, in the first year, sales of Big BOSS proceed at a snail's pace, helped along only by computer zealots who feel the need to have the latest thing. Then government gets into the act.

1. The first government to respond is the town of Singerville. Singerville is facing a drastic shortage of electric power, and must take every possible measure to conserve. So Singerville arranges to alter the electric current running into every Singerville home and business. To use the new form of current, each electric appliance or lamp must have an adapter that fits between the plug and the wall outlet. The special adapters can be purchased only from the town public works department, and for each adapter the user must complete an application form indicating the intended use. Singerville then adopts an ordinance requiring that no adapter shall be sold for use with any computer manufactured in 2005 or later that does not have Big BOSS already loaded onto it. At a press conference, Singerville's Mayor explained the ordinance: "We have only a limited amount of power in this town, and we want to ensure it's spent on computers that are part of the effort to break the Microsoft monopoly rather than those which are part of the problem."

2. Congress also decides also to support President Gore's computer policies. It passes the Big BOSS Support Act of 2005, which reads in pertinent part:

"No personal computer made after the year 2006 shall be sold in the United States, unless at least half of the memory available for running operating systems is devoted to the running of Big BOSS. The National Scientific Administration will ensure that different versions of Big BOSS are available to accommodate even the most powerful computers. Moreover, each computer must be sold to the consumer with Big BOSS already loaded on and with no way of removing it."

Sam Works lives in Singerville and is one of the last true Macintosh lovers. He wants to purchase an adapter for his new Macintosh (2005 vintage) which does not contain the less efficient Big BOSS. William Yates is a Singerville computer manufacturer who makes machines running Sunroof 2004. He claims the cost of installing the government's cumbersome operating system will impair his business.

Both Mr. Works and Mr. Yates hire you as their attorney. Works wants to challenge the Singerville ordinance, while Yates wishes to contest the congressional statute. Evaluate the challenges available to each of your clients under the Takings Clause of the Fifth Amendment, and comment very briefly on any insights the problem suggests concerning the wisdom of current Takings doctrine. Do not discuss potential First Amendment challenges or any other constitutional problems.

Because this is a long, complicated question, organization will be key. One possible answer might look like this:

The key difference between the Singerville ordinance and the congressional statute is that the statute actually requires Yates to include Big BOSS whereas the ordinance offers Works a trade — include Big BOSS and get the adapter. This difference calls for a separate discussion of each claim.

Sam Works — There is a superficial relationship between this case and *Loretto v. Teleprompter* [458 U.S. 419 (1982)]. Both cases involve the installation of a small device designed to power electronic equipment. A crucial distinction, however, prevents straightforward application of the pro-claimant *Loretto* rule to Sam's case. The apartment owner in *Loretto* was required by law to install the offending cable box. Here, Singerville hasn't required Sam to put in an adapter.

Sam might respond by arguing that electronic current is a contemporary necessity and so the town's conservation requirements *in effect* force the adapter upon him. It is unlikely, however, that the courts will want to expand the *per se* rule governing permanent physical invasions to this situation. Singerville's ordinance is basically an environmental regulation, and the courts have consistently refused to treat as *per se* takings situations in which the invasion has been invited (here Sam wants the adapter). (See the case about mobile homes, in which the park owner had to keep renting to the home owner [*Yee v. City of Escondido*, 503 U.S. 519 (1992)], and the Florida Power and Light case, in which the electric company was forced to continue carrying cable wires at a government mandated low rate [*FCC v. Florida Power Corp.*, 480 U.S. 245 (1987)]). So Sam is unlikely to prevail under the *Loretto* rule.

Sam, however, has a much stronger argument under the cases of *Dolan v. City of Tigard* [114 S. Ct. 2309 (1994)] and *Nollan v. California Coastal Commission* [488 U.S. 825 (1987)]. These cases establish that, when a landowner is required to provide physical access to his or her land (or to cede some land to the government) in exchange for a permit, the local government must show "an essential nexus" between the harms the government seeks to prevent and the condition imposed on the owner. Sam should start with the straightforward argument that there is no connection at all between Singerville's need to conserve power and its desire to spread the Big BOSS operating system. Moreover, even if a court finds some nexus, Sam can rely on *Dolan*'s requirement that there be a "rough proportionality" between the harm prevented and the condition imposed. Here Sam can argue that if he uses only one computer there is no evidence it will burn any more power without Big BOSS; indeed, both the Macintosh and the Sunroof operating systems burn less than Big BOSS. Sam has a powerful argument that Singerville is acting unconstitutionally by imposing this condition.

Singerville could try to defend the condition with a broad argument about the general importance of conserving power and using it only for important things. If power is scarce, Singerville will argue, why shouldn't the town be able to limit its use to the most desirable computer systems? This argument has some policy appeal, but today's courts are unlikely to accept it. After all, the Coastal Commission in *Nollan* tried to persuade the Court that beaches were a scarce resource and should be managed accordingly. But the Court insisted that the Commission show a tight fit between its refusal to allow an owner to build and its requirement that this same owner grant passers-by access to the beach. Here, Singerville will have a tough time showing a tight connection between its need to save power and its desire to spread Big BOSS. It would be a different matter if Big BOSS were a more energy efficient system.

Singerville could also attempt to distinguish *Nollan* and *Dolan* on the ground that those cases involved physical access to land while this case is merely a regulation about power usage. Although *Nollan* and *Dolan* have not yet been expanded to cover cases like ours, this seems a poor case to push Singerville's proposed distinction because the connection between Singerville's power goals and its computer policy appears so weak. Singerville will stress the idea that if courts start inspecting things like power conservation regulations to determine whether they are roughly proportional to their goals then we'll be headed back toward *Lochner*-era judicial decisions. Sam may try to rebut Singerville by once again noting that this particular regulation does include government's physically appropriating space (the adapter space — *Loretto* in a new guise). This argument is a bit far-fetched, however, since Sam's complaint isn't about the space the adapter occupies. So in the end he's best off stressing the complete lack of connection between power conservation and computer systems. In today's climate of judicial receptivity to these kinds of takings claims, Sam will probably prevail.

William Yates — Mr. Yates has arguments under many components of the Supreme Court's multi-factor inquiry in takings cases. First, Yates will argue that the congressional statute's requirement constitutes a permanent physical invasion of the space on his computer's hard drive. Although none of the physical invasion cases discuss memory space (a point the government may stress in rebuttal), there is no reason why computer memory deserves any less protection than land. Indeed, in the modern economy it may become more important than land. Here the government is forcing Mr. Yates to accept an intrusive and unwanted operating system. This may be a *per se* taking.

If the court rejects the physical invasion analogy, Mr. Yates can stress the loss of economic value (half his memory cluttered with an unnecessary operating system) and the damage to his reasonable investment-backed expectations (government seldom acts in such Draconian fashion). He can also characterize government's actions as using his computers to procure the public benefit of fighting monopoly.

The diminution in value argument is a bit murky since the Court has never been clear on quite how much a claimant must lose to mount a successful takings challenge (clearly Yates hasn't lost everything like the claimant in *Lucas* [v. *South Carolina Coastal Council*, 505 U.S. 1003 (1992)]). Moreover, the facts don't say how damaging the government's rule is. (What percentage of value would be lost by doubling the memory capacity, loading Big BOSS on an unused half and running Sunroof on the other half?) It's fair to say, however, that Yates's loss will be substantial, and the government must justify such a harsh requirement. Yates will stress the weak government justification and the unexpected nature of the requirement, and Yates will once again revive the argument that the physically invasive nature of the regulation warrants invalidation.

The government will counter Yates by noting that he should have expected regulations like this, especially given President Clinton's 1999 speech, which gave him years to prepare. Moreover, the statute can be defended as a mere economic regulation that leaves Yates free to continue making money from computer sales. Finally, the government can portray its rules as preventing Yates from participating in the harmful system of monopoly that would otherwise prevail.

Courts have historically been sympathetic to economic regulations, and thus Yates has a tough road. I bet, however, that he would be successful either through persuading the court to treat this as a *per se* physical invasion or by emphasizing the substantial harm to his business. What turns the case for me is what I perceive to be a likely judicial hostility to such severe regulation that is both unusual and threatening to an important industry.

Implications for Takings Law—Although I predicted that both Works and Yates would win, it is odd that Works seems to have the stronger case. Why should it be that a regulation that offers a trade is more likely to be held invalid than one that forces action upon an individual? Perhaps this suggests the Supreme Court plans to use the Takings Clause more as a way of policing the regularity of government actions (do conditions imposed fit with government's stated reasons?) than as a way of constraining government's substantive decisions.

Comments: The phrasing at the end of this question is very sketchy, but you can't let poorly worded questions leave you in a quandary about exactly what "evaluate" claims means. Note how the suggested answer adopts the familiar style of not only pressing the arguments for the claimants but also suggesting how the government might respond. See also how the answer copes with many of the techniques within the exam that we have described in earlier chapters. When a question seeks evaluation of a multi-factor test (here the one for takings), you want to hunt for facts that permit discussion of each factor. In this case, the economic information about Big BOSS facilitates discussion of the diminution in value; Clinton's speech is relevant to expectations analysis; and of course the occupation of computer memory is designed to raise the issue of physical invasions. Note also how the answer hinges on identifying both "forks in the law" and "forks in the facts." In Sam's case, for example, it's not clear whether Nollan and Dolan are meant to apply to cases that don't involve physical takings, so the answer identifies this as a rule still needing to be determined. In Yates's case, the question whether the occupation of memory is a "physical invasion" is a classic question of characterization. Finally, once again note how the answer sticks precisely to the question, including a last comment designed to address the big-picture issues.

C. Constitutional Law

The next question vividly illustrates why merely memorizing laws and cases won't be enough on law school exams. Virtually every constitutional law student learns the framework in which government classifications that discriminate on the basis of race receive strict judicial scrutiny; those based on economic factors receive rational-basis review; and those based on gender ar-

guably fall in between. But the following question tests not merely the familiar framework, but also the more fundamental issue of what constitutes "discrimination." The question also attempts to place a set of facts between two cases, another example of a "competing domains" problem. Finally, the question involves both structural issues involving the separation of powers and individual rights issues involving equal protection. Unless you follow Chapter 9's advice to continue past the first issue you see, it's easy to focus exclusively on one topic and miss the other one altogether.

After Al Gore is elected President in the year 2000, William Rehnquist resigns as Chief Justice of the United States. President Gore nominates Mario Cuomo to replace him. Sixty U.S. Senators sign the following letter to the President:

"Dear Mr. President: We believe Mario Cuomo is eminently qualified to serve as Chief Justice. We will not, however, vote for his confirmation. It is our sincere belief that the time has come to have a woman as Chief Justice of the U.S. Supreme Court. We will not vote for a man to fill that post. We urge you to withdraw the nomination."

President Gore refuses to treat the Senators' letter as the final word. He makes an impassioned plea to the public and the Senate that Cuomo is the person for the job. Finally, Gore and the new Senate majority leader, Paul Wellstone, work out a deal. The Senate agrees to reconsider the Cuomo nomination in exchange for Gore's promise to sign "The Rotating Gender Chief Justiceship Qualification Act of 2001." The Act reads as follows:

"The President shall not appoint nor shall the Senate confirm any person to serve as Chief Justice of the United States who is the same gender as the person previously holding that high office." After Cuomo is confirmed, the Congress passes this measure by large margins and the President signs it into law.

Discuss all plausible constitutional challenges to this statute. Will it survive constitutional scrutiny? Why or why not?

There are no easy issues here, so a good answer will launch right into the thick of it. Here's what one might look like:

It's not immediately clear who would have standing to challenge a statute like this, since presumably someone must show an "injury in fact." Eventually, however, a President may wish to nominate someone of the gender disallowed by the statute, and that person might have standing to sue. I'll assume for purposes of the question that someone has standing.

One obvious problem with the statute is that it's a legislative as opposed to constitutional change in the framework of our government. The Constitution clearly gives the President the power to appoint the Chief Justice, and it's not at all clear that his options may be limited by statute. There is a strong analogy between this case and *U.S. Term Limits v. Thornton* [514 U.S. 779 (1995)], in which the Supreme Court invalidated Arkansas's effort to put an additional qualification (term limits) upon those seeking to appear on the ballot to be elected to the House and Senate. On this theory, the additional qualification that the new Chief Justice be of the opposite gender must be added by constitutional amendment.

Defenders of the statute might start by noting that limiting the President's appointment power may not be the same as imposing a "qualification." Certainly statutes can create federal officers and require the President to choose individuals of different political parties. True, the office of the Chief Justice is based on the Constitution, not just statutes. But suppose a statute required the President to select a lawyer. Would that be an unconstitutional infringement on presidential prerogative? So then the statute's defenders might point to the standard set out in *Morrison v. Olson* [487 U.S. 654 (1988)] for judging the constitutionality of statutes that limit the President's power to remove certain executive officials. In *Morrison*, the Supreme Court said that the President's removal power could be limited as long as there was no impediment to the President's ability to exercise his or her core executive functions. Here the argument would be that limiting the President's choices by gender would hardly be overly restrictive, since there are plenty of men and women qualified to serve as Chief Justice. Indeed, it might be said that the President won't suffer any real limitation at all.

The analogy to *Morrison*, however, is probably not as strong as to the term-limits case. First, *Morrison* is about removal, a topic not clearly mentioned in the Constitution. The Rotating Gender Act puts limits on appointments, a matter clearly spelled out in Article II. Second, *Morrison* dealt with independent counsels, whom the Court clearly determined were inferior officers under the constitutional definition. Obviously, there is no more important office subject to Presidential appointment than the Chief Justice, so the Court might be more concerned with a statutory limit on Presidential authority. Third, the Senate's "advise and consent" power is clearly the constitutional means for the Senate to have its say over Presidential appointment of judges. This statute alters that constitutional mechanism. For all these reasons, I doubt the courts would undertake a qualitative assessment of whether the President's prerogatives were unduly limited and rely instead on a formalistic approach prohibiting statutory modification of the power to appoint constitutional officers like the Chief Justice.

A second, unrelated challenge to the Rotating Gender Act would be based on the equal protection component of the Fifth Amendment. (Equal protection in the Fourteenth Amendment applies directly to states, but the Supreme Court has held the same principles applicable to the Federal government through the due process clause of the Fifth Amendment)[*Adarand Constructors, Inc. v. Pena*, 515 U.S. 200 (1995)]. The Supreme Court has gotten increasingly tough on government classifications based on gender. Although such classifications don't yet receive the same strict scrutiny as racial classifications, the Court requires government to demonstrate "an exceedingly persuasive justification" (the VMI case) [*United States v. Virginia*, 518 U.S. 515 (1996)]. I doubt the statute can survive this test.

Presumably, the government will defend the statute on the ground that it will help remedy past discrimination—there has never been a woman Chief Justice—and on the ground of promoting diversity on the Court. It's not clear that alternating the gender of the Chief Justice achieves meaningful diversity on a nine-member panel. But in any event, cases in which the Court accepts diversity as a rationale for race- (and thus presumably gender-) based classifications tend to be those involving education, *Bakke* [*Regents of Univ. of Cal. v. Bakke*, 438 U.S. 265 (1978)] or the media, *Metro Broadcasting* [*Inc. v. Federal Communications Commission*, 497 U.S. 547 (1990)]. Extending the diversity rationale to permit gender quotas in constitutionally significant governmental bodies like the Supreme Court seems inconsistent with the Court's direction of rejecting even much more limited affirmative action programs. See *Adarand*. And, as for remedying past discrimination, the statute's most obvious flaw is that half the time it will require naming a man. Beyond that, even past discrimination hasn't justified rigid quotas, *Bakke*; the total number of people who have filled the post is so small as to make proving discrimination difficult; and the statutory requirement is permanent rather than merely remedial. All this leaves the statute on very uneasy footing.

The government might also argue that the statute shouldn't be evaluated under the typical standards for gender-based classifications because previous cases involved situations where the classification favored one gender over another. Here, the statute merely calls for "rotation." There is no "discrimination" and thus the government could argue for a "rational basis test." Even cases like *Craig v. Boren* [429 U.S. 190 (1976)] involved discrimination against men whereas here, over the long term, this statute can be characterized as gender-neutral. In theory this is a strong argument. But based on what I know about Constitutional Law, there is no obvious way to decide whether the right time-frame is at the moment of choosing one particular Chief Justice or over the long haul. In practice, however, I doubt the courts will accept it. It would pave the way for all sorts of gender rotations and, worse still, racial rotations. (Could a statute say every sixth Chief Justice must be African-American?) And the courts seem committed to the idea that job selection should be based on criteria other than race and gender. For this reason too, then, I believe the courts would find the Rotating Gender Act unconstitutional.

Comments: This answer gives you an opportunity to review several test techniques. First, the question's phrasing asks you to "describe plausible challenges" and thus it's unclear whether you are to consider procedural issues like standing. So the answer flags the issue, hits the most important point, and then moves on—*covering bases if you were supposed to discuss it but giving short shrift to standing on the theory that the question isn't getting at that. Second, the answer finds a way to cope with the "competing domains" problem and shows how to take uncertainty and turn it to your advantage. Thus, the answer exploits the way in which the exam facts fall between one often-studied rule ("the term limits case") and another ("the* Morrison v. Olson *rule"). And once this ambiguity is spotted, the answer doesn't stop, instead teasing out reasons that the court might be likely to resolve it one way rather than the other.*

Perhaps the answer's most important aspect is that it keeps going even after a good discussion of the structural issue. It's tempting to assume that if you have found one good issue you have answered the question. But this is often deadly. Certainly, you won't do as well as you hope unless you also discuss equal protection. Once again, this answer is good because it reflects knowledge of the rule structure governing equal protection. Yet it doesn't stop there either. The whole point of the question is to make it difficult to apply the rule structure to unusual facts. This answer recognizes that rotation is unusual and then goes on to consider how a court might react to the novelty. Once again it turns uncertainty into a friend.

* * * * *

Like the previous question, this one also involves a professor's effort to take two different parts of the constitutional law course (here commerce clause and equal protection) and test them both in the same question. There are also familiar wrinkles involving competing legislative purposes and the application of complex legal standards (like strict scrutiny).

Abdul Jones, an Arab-American, owns a chain of car dealerships throughout the upper midwestern United States. For the last 20 years, he has earned a fortune selling cars manufactured in Detroit and overseas. Last year, however, he invented a new, six-wheeled automobile ("the Pistol") that he began manufacturing at his home base in Greater Minneapolis.

Soon after its introduction to the market, the Pistol became a huge success among Arab-American and other customers, particularly in Minnesota and Michigan. In a short time Abdul was able to bankrupt other dealers in certain Michigan neighborhoods. Many buyers of the Pistol were families who valued the slightly wider passenger compartment that the three wheels across (front and back) afforded. Although the car was no wider than many large luxury cars, it did afford more room than similar family sedans.

A second category of buyers, however, began to arouse regulatory concern. Young Arab-American males started to buy the car and drive it very fast. Print ad campaigns aimed at this audience touted the ability of the driver to control the car during highway driving. Moreover, rumors were flying that the extra wheel base gave the car extra stability during rapid acceleration such as that found in drag racing. In fact, all scientific studies showed that although the Pistol was a safe vehicle, top sports cars, like the Corvette or the Miata, could outperform it in terms of acceleration and road stability. But the youth market refused to credit these studies, reported repeatedly in national press, in favor of the "common sense" view that the extra wheels would reduce the chance of tipping over.

Then, one day, tragedy struck. Two eighteen-year-old Arab-American males were drag racing two Pistols on the outskirts of Detroit. The cars brushed against each other, sending each out of control. One car went off a cliff, killing the driver. The other car crashed into the group of spectators assembled to watch the race, and five people, including the driver, were killed.

The next day, the Speaker of the Michigan House of Representatives introduced legislation banning the sale of six-wheeled passenger vehicles in the state. On the floor of the House, he railed against the "evil influences of this demonic vehicle, shipped into our state for the purpose of profiting from the passions of our misguided youth." He further commented that "even if we can't actually ban driving the Pistol, the least we can do is stop sales of this vehicle from taking bread out of the mouths of Michigan manufacturers." Two weeks later, his proposed bill became law.

Because it was now a crime to sell the Pistol in Michigan, Abdul had to close down many of his dealerships, which had come to rely heavily on Pistol sales. He filed suit against the

State of Michigan, challenging the new statute under the United States Constitution.

What arguments might Abdul make? What is his best argument? How is a federal court likely to respond to his various claims?

Possible Answer: Abdul clearly has standing to challenge the Michigan statute. It prevents him from selling the Pistol and making a profit, and invalidation of the statute would be an effective remedy.

His challenges are likely to be along two lines. First, he may contend that the statute violates the commerce clause because Michigan is discriminating against an out-of-state manufacturer. Second, he may argue that the statute offends the equal protection clause of the Fourteenth Amendment.

Equal protection is probably the weaker of the two claims. One way to view the statute is purely as an economic regulation. It bars a particular type of vehicle on the ground of safety. Here Michigan needs to prove only that there is a rational relationship between the statute and the safety goal. Abdul's argument against this is not frivolous. He will contend that the vehicle is perfectly safe and that all evidence supports him. It's irrational, he will argue, to ban a safe vehicle on grounds of safety. Michigan's response, however, may be definitive. A vehicle may be perfectly safe when used properly, yet dangerous if used incorrectly. Michigan's experience is that people are using the Pistol dangerously. If the legislature decides that controlling improper use is too difficult, it may conclude an outright ban is the best way to protect the safety of its citizens. Given the fatal accident prompting the legislation, a court is highly unlikely to upset Michigan's determination on the ground that it's irrational.

Abdul may also argue that the courts should apply strict scrutiny under equal protection because the state statute discriminates against Arab-Americans. Certainly, Arabs would meet the definition of a "suspect class," but Abdul's problem is that the statute is so clearly neutral on its face. The prohibition is of a certain type of vehicle, and it is not a classification based on national origin. Abdul may counter that the statute is discriminatory in effect, because the Pistol is the only popular six-wheeled vehicle, and Arabs are a principal user and the sole manufacturer. But under *Washington v. Davis* [426 U.S. 229 (1976)], mere discriminatory impact is not sufficient to show an equal protection violation. Instead, Abdul must show that Michigan intended to target Arab-Americans. His best and only evidence here comes from the Speaker's remarks about "demonic influences." This could be a code word for anti-Arab sentiment. And Michigan's rationale for the ban is rather flimsy. One suggestive comment by a bill's sponsor, however, is hardly enough to persuade a court of a discriminatory motive on the part of the entire legislature. Indeed, the courts are much more likely to believe either that the statute was a reaction to the danger (permissible) or an effort to protect Michigan's auto manufacturers (perhaps impermissible under the commerce clause but not ill-intentioned with respect to an equal protection claim based on national origin).

Abdul's commerce clause argument is similar in structure to the equal protection claim but is more likely to succeed. Once again there is a facially neutral statute. The law bans six-wheeled vehicles, not those made in Minneapolis.

Here, however, the illicit protectionist motive flows not only from the Speaker's comment about "Michigan manufacturers," but also from the context. Everyone knows that Detroit is the auto capital of the U.S., and any threat to dominance from a different state will be taken very seriously. Although the Michigan statute will hurt some Michigan dealers, far larger constituencies (*i.e.*, the Big Three and the UAW) are likely to favor a statute that hurts an out-of-state manufacturer. Thus, this is just the kind of case where the courts are needed to step in in the name of the free-flow of interstate commerce.

Finally, the weak safety rationale may also help doom the statute. Although there is nothing inherently illegitimate about banning a vehicle based on frequent abuse, the courts may be unwilling to swallow this rationale in light of the obvious potential for protectionist abuse. This statute just looks like a way for Michigan auto manufacturers to punish a successful competitor. Although Abdul will face a stiff argument that Michigan is merely reacting to a tragic accident, I would bet on him to prevail on this part of his claim.

Comments: This answer succeeds in part because it divides the arguments available to Abdul into discrete sub-parts. By contrast, the answer's selection of the commerce clause argument as the stronger case is relatively unimportant. You could do equally well arguing that one comment by a legislator isn't enough to render a facially neutral law protectionist, and perhaps you might conclude it's more important for courts to ferret out closet racism than closet protectionism. What is key is to spot both arguments and the weaknesses in each. Note also how the answer copes with some of the question's wrinkles. It's odd to think that a statute banning a demonstrably safe car can be justified on safety grounds. Once you notice this, you need to decide whether the legislature's judgment or the scientific reality needs to be respected in this context. Your answer would be equally rewarded if it concluded that the car's actual safety prevents the legislature from hiding behind the safety rationale. You would, however, then need to supply an argument for why the legislature may not rely on "danger in practice" as sufficient evidence of a valid safety rationale.

D. Contracts

As we have repeatedly explained, the most common exam technique is to write a question with some facts on each side of a familiar boundary and insist the student discuss which side the court should ultimately select. Better answers link such "forks in the facts" to one or more "forks in the law." Here's a classic example.

At lunch on Monday, Seller and Buyer, both merchants, negotiated an oral contract for the sale of goods at a price of well over $500. On Tuesday morning, Seller sent Buyer a (signed) letter confirming the agreement and outlining the details (including the price, quantity, delivery, and payment terms) as she understood them. Buyer received the letter on Wednesday and immediately dispatched the following (signed) response, which Seller received on Friday: "Thank you for your letter. I spoke with my lawyer after our meeting on Monday, and he pointed out serious problems with our deal that I just hadn't contemplated. I hope you'll understand, but I'm afraid I won't be able to go through with it." Attempts at settlement having failed, Seller sues Buyer for breach of contract, and Buyer raises the Statute of Frauds as a defense. How should the court rule on Buyer's defense? Explain your answer.

This question is unusual because it spots the issue by telling you to discuss the Statute of Frauds. We include it to highlight that even when you know the issue, there's still plenty to discuss. Moreover, you can get to the point quickly. Here's an answer that does so.

Although Buyer has a quite plausible case under the Statute of Frauds, it's one the courts should ultimately reject. Buyer's case begins with the simple observation that since this is a sale of goods for more than $500 and the sale is "between merchants," U.C.C. §§ 2-201(1) and (2) apply. Seller must therefore show something in writing to enforce the deal, and there is no written document signed by Buyer establishing the contract. Seller, however, will assert that Seller's letter confirming terms is sufficient to satisfy the Statute of Frauds unless Buyer has sent a timely "notice of objection." So Buyer's case concludes with the argument that Buyer's Wednesday letter was such an objection.

I doubt a court will accept Buyer's position because of the wording of Buyer's letter; it is not really an objection to the "contents" of Seller's letter, as the plain meaning of § 2-201(2) would require. Buyer does not quarrel with Seller's description of the terms agreed to over lunch. Rather, Buyer is now saying that the deal appears unattractive. Indeed, Buyer's admission that there are unanticipated consequences of "our deal" probably constitutes an admission that a deal was struck and a signed writing that will itself satisfy the Statute of Frauds.

Even a court that took a purpose-based approach is very likely to rule against Buyer to facilitate trust among business parties engaged in oral transactions. Buyer isn't arguing that no deal was struck or that there is a disagreement about what deal was struck. Those points would strengthen Buyer's Statute of Frauds defense because the Statute is designed to prevent parties from inventing deals or mistakenly relying on terms that were never actually agreed to. Of course, Buyer may argue that the principal reason for the Statute of Frauds is "cautionary": to give contracting parties more time to think about entering deals. The writing requirement serves to slow things down. This goal, however, is less important in deals between merchants who are presumed better able to take care of themselves. Accordingly, Buyer's defense should fail.

Comments: Notice how this answer is very short but everything builds toward the conclusion. Once again the whole question begins with the ambiguous wording in Buyer's letter that creates a "fork in the facts." Is this an objection or not? The answer is then clear on how resolving this "fork" will determine the outcome. Finally, the answer introduces arguments based on the plain-meaning vs. purpose-based and "competing purposes" interpretations of the Statute of Frauds as a way of pointing the reader toward techniques for resolving the ambiguity. By the end, both sides have been fully considered, yet the answer returns to the facts—always a good move!—to defend a choice between them.

* * * * *

Okay, we know that most of the questions so far are a bit shorter and less complicated than the gargantuan issue-spotters preferred by some professors. Lest you think we have forgotten these, our final question weaves in more than enough for even the most challenging exam. Pay particular attention to the strategy the sample answer uses to stay organized. It's the best strategy of all: ANSWERING THE QUESTION.

When Sweeny Todd, Inc. (STI)—a large grocery wholesaler located in Omaha, Nebraska—wanted to upgrade the duck-processing operation at its poultry plant, company officials contacted Keyser Soza Co. (KSC), a local firm specializing in the design, construction, and installation of machinery for slaughterhouse use. In January 1996, representatives of KSC visited the plant and then met with STI officials on several occasions to discuss the latter's needs. Working together, they developed a detailed "joint proposal" for a new duck-processing system. Among other things, the parties agreed—and the joint proposal specifically stated—that STI would be forced to cease duck-processing operations at the plant for a period of "no more than 45 days" to permit KSC engineers to install the new hardware.

On March 15, shortly after the last planning session, STI sent KSC a facsimile requesting KSC's "lowest price" for the project outlined in the joint proposal. On March 22, KSC responded with a brief fax of its own: "We would be willing to consider undertaking the project in question for a total price to you of $512,000, payable upon completion of the project. If you agree to these terms, please forward a purchase order at your earliest convenience, so that we can commence work immediately."

On March 25, by overnight delivery, STI sent KSC its standard-form purchase order—inserting the words "as per our joint proposal" in the "description" column and "$512,000 (terms per 3/22/96 FAX)" in the price column. In reply, KSC sent its standard-form "acknowledgment of order," which accurately recapitulated the terms of the purchase order, but added the following statement in large, bold type across the bottom of the front side of the document: "This acceptance of Buyer's purchase order is expressly conditional on Buyer's assent to the terms that appear on the back of this form. Any variance from those terms must be secured in writing from Seller's officials. Otherwise, Buyer's acceptance of and/or payment for any items covered by this Acknowledgment constitutes assent to and an unconditional acceptance of the terms of this Acknowledgment." On the back of the form, in smaller but perfectly legible typeface, was a provision that purported to bar Buyer from recovering "any consequential damages arising out of any defect in the design, hardware, assembly, or installation of any machinery or other goods covered by this Acknowledgment." (STI and KSC had not discussed the issue of consequential damages during their protracted negotiations, and STI's purchase order was silent on the subject.)

KSC procured the materials necessary for the project and, during April and May, assembled most of the hardware at its own plant. On July 1, KSC began the installation work at the STI plant, and STI ceased duck-processing operations. In late July, however, STI entered into a contract for the sale of the plant to multi-millionaire H. Ross Turow. Under the terms of that contract, the deal was to close on August 15, when Turow was to pay $2,500,000 in cash for the plant, including the new duck-processing system. (STI officials were thrilled

with that price, which was about $600,000 above the approx-
imate market value of the plant, even with the new system in
place. Turow, it seemed, was willing to pay a premium because he liked the way the place smelled. "Reminds me of
Washington, D.C.; that's the beauty part," STI officials heard
him say.) The contract further provided that Turow had the
right to back out of the deal entirely if the plant was not
fully operational by the closing date. Upon execution of the
contract with Turow, STI immediately forwarded a copy of
the document to KSC officials, with a cover note outlining
the basic terms of the deal and emphasizing the resultant
need for a timely completion of the installation work by
KSC.

In fact, however, KSC did not complete the installation until
August 22. As a result, Turow called off the sale on August
15, and STI lost approximately $12,000 in profits during the
additional week that the duck operation was down. In the
meantime, Dahmer-Lechter, Inc. (DLI)—owner of the
rapidly growing "Just Like Chicken" chain of fast-food outlets—has offered to purchase the plant from STI for
$1,800,000. As it happens, DLI has no interest in the duck-
processing operation and plans to convert that area of the
plant to other purposes.

It is now August 24, and—pending resolution of the possible
DLI deal—STI has not yet resumed its duck-processing operation. Instead, STI officials have turned to you, their General
Counsel, for legal advice. They would like to sell the plant to
DLI, they explain, and want to know whether there is "some
legal way to avoid paying those scoundrels at KSC the money
for that damn duck-processing system, since DLI wouldn't
need it." Indeed, the officials would also like to know whether
they have any legal right to recover the lost profits from the
Turow deal—or at least the lost profits from the prolonged
shutdown—from KSC. What will you tell them?

Possible Answer: 1. I doubt that a court would allow STI
to escape altogether from paying for KSC's considerable
work. First, although doubt over whether this is a sale of
goods or a service may generate substantial debate over

whether the U.C.C. governs the transaction, either way a contract between the parties existed. If the U.C.C. is held applicable (more on this later), then at the very least the parties have a contract by conduct under § 2-207(3). But even if the common law mirror-image rule applies, at the latest a contract was formed when STI accepted KSC's counter-offer by performance (*i.e.*, by cooperating in the installation of the new system).

STI's stronger argument for refusing to pay will be that KSC breached the contract by failing to complete the work on time. Given the manifest injustice of allowing KSC to complete a half-million-dollar job and receive nothing, and given the impact such injustice would have on future commercial dealings, I would expect courts to strain very hard to find STI liable to pay the contract price—minus any legitimate damages. And here, under either the U.C.C. or the common law, the court won't have to strain too hard. True, the U.C.C. follows the "perfect tender rule" and if the duck-processing equipment is treated as a "good" then that rule will apply here. But even under the U.C.C., STI continued to accept delivery of the equipment after the due date, even though it knew delivery was late. If STI wanted to rely on the goods being late to reject delivery, it should have done so right away. It was unreasonable and lacking in good faith for STI to accept late delivery and then argue that it doesn't want to pay, especially since that argument is clearly a product of STI's subsequent discovery that its new buyer, DLI, doesn't want the equipment. Accordingly, the perfect tender rule is unlikely to be conclusive in STI's favor.

And, STI is likely to fare worse still if it contends that the entire contract isn't governed by the U.C.C. because it involved construction services rather than the sale of goods. Under the common law, KSC has clearly completed "substantial performance" so that STI's efforts to back out will be unsuccessful. Moreover, STI probably doesn't want to argue here that the U.C.C. doesn't apply, since it won't help on this issue and may hurt on the question of consequential damages (see below). STI will have to pay for the equipment minus any damages recoverable under a theory of breach.

2. Our next issue is whether STI can recover for the loss of profits suffered as a result of the collapse of the Turow deal. For this issue, we need not resolve either the applicability or the meaning of KSC's clause regarding consequential damages on the back of the acknowledgment. Even if STI can recover consequential damages under the contract, it can't recover for the collapse of the Turow deal. True, STI did inform KSC about the Turow deal and the need for timely completion. But this notice came long after the making of the contract (itself a clincher) and at a time when it would probably have been infeasible for KSC to take Turow's offer into account. Under the common law rule of *Hadley v. Baxendale,* consequential damages must be reasonably foreseeable to the parties at the time of contract formation, and the U.C.C. § 2-715 takes a similar approach. Where potential damages constitute "special needs," they must be disclosed at the time of contracting. Here the need to comply with Turow's unusual insistence on a date certain was highly unpredictable. Turow's offer came after the negotiation of the KSC/STI contract; his willingness to overpay (which generated the "lost profits") was highly unpredictable; and even if damages from a lost sale could be expected from late performance, damages of this magnitude could not. Accordingly, STI can't recover for this loss.

3. By far the most complicated issue is whether STI can recover for its purported $12,000 in lost profits for the week between August 15 and August 22. As General Counsel to STI, I would urge its officers to try to fit the contract within the U.C.C. by arguing that it involves basically a sale of goods. I would stress the fact that the hardware assembly occurred mostly at KSC and that installation was just as if you bought an air conditioner or a refrigerator. Plus, I'd emphasize that the deal is between sophisticated merchants, the kind the U.C.C. is best-equipped to handle. The advantage of U.C.C. treatment would be that KSC's acknowledgment operated as an acceptance under § 2-207(1), but its disclaimer is out under sub-(2) as a material alteration to which STI never agreed.

KSC will, of course, counter by saying the common law should apply because the contract involves a "service." It will stress the importance of "installation," and perhaps attempt to argue that the deal involved both goods and services and that the dispute is now about the timeliness of the service "installation." (Of course, I'll call this "delivery.")

If I do win on this point and the U.C.C. prevails, I'm almost home to the $12,000 because "lost profits" are the classic kind of consequential damages recoverable for breach. KSC might respond with the "new business" rule—contesting our right to recover lost profits since this was a new duck-processing system—but that claim would be weak on the facts (we are an established poultry-processing firm) and weaker still on the law (it's not at all clear that the common law new business rule applies under the U.C.C.). KSC could also argue that my lost profits are really a fiction. They could argue that, although I might have made $12,000 during the week between 8/15 and 8/22, this assumes I would have re-opened the plant. The timing of DLI's entry into the picture is unclear, but I'll bet KSC will claim that we were already in negotiations with them, that they don't want the operation, and that we wouldn't have gone to the trouble of restarting only to shut down again so soon. I think a court might buy this, but the question seems to treat these lost profits as a fact—not an allegation—so I'll assume that STI recovers the $12,000 under the U.C.C.

STI may also prevail even if the common law applies. Now KSC will claim the consequential damages disclaimer is part of the contract because its acknowledgment should be treated as a counter-offer and STI's beginning performance should be seen as acceptance of that term. Certainly the disclaimer was sufficiently prominent to avoid any claim of surprise. But I think STI has several compelling responses. First, the battle of the forms can be read so as to interpret KSC's March 22 fax as itself an offer and STI's March 25 fax as an acceptance. The March 22 fax is the classic ambiguous document where the language "we would consider" suggests negotiations but the phrase "if you agree, forward an order so we can start work" suggests an offer. I'd expect a court to grab onto this to rule for STI because the claim for lost profits seems fair. If this reading of the forms doesn't work, STI can argue that the terms of the disclaimer itself don't apply since the consequential damages don't stem from a "defect" in the equipment or installation but instead from late delivery. Here STI can cite the classic argument that the language should be construed against the drafter. Once again, I think STI will win for the same policy reasons. And, once the disclaimer is held inapplicable, it will be no trick at all for the court to find "lost profits" to be the kind of consequential damages recoverable at common law and to reject KSC's arguments to the contrary.

My client has to pay KSC the contract price, but it is entitled to the $12,000 set-off for lost profits. It is not, however, entitled to any money for loss of the Turow deal.

Comments: This is the kind of question that could easily tie anyone in knots. One of us wrote the question and the other the answer, and it wasn't easy. The advice in Getting to Maybe, *however, proved very useful. First and foremost, the answer uses a three-numbered organizational scheme built directly from the three questions given in the problem. Second, "forks in the facts," like sale vs. service, are analyzed only when they prove relevant to an actual outcome. So in the first part that issue is quickly passed over to get to the point. Third, for each "fork" that's identified (and there are many), the relevance to the outcome is emphasized and the reasons a court might choose one over the other discussed. Finally, and perhaps most important, the answer maintains its organizational structure by dealing with each issue quickly enough so as not to lose sight of how it fits into the overall scheme. It takes patience and practice to do all of this. But we've given you all the help we know how. Go for it, folks. You're on your own!*

Sources

As we noted in the acknowledgments, we have been particularly influenced by the work of Karl Llewellyn and Duncan Kennedy. We cite their works formally here, along with those of the many authors whose ideas we found invaluable to our project. We strongly encourage readers to review these works for a broader understanding of American law that is not limited to a focus on law school exams. Finally, we include citations to some of our own earlier efforts to contribute to legal education, just so you'll see that this isn't quite a "first novel."

Terence Anderson and William Twining, *Analysis of Evidence: How to Do Things with Facts Based on Wigmore's Science of Judicial Proof* (Boston: Little Brown & Co. 1991).

J.M. Balkin, "The Promise of Legal Semiotics," 69 Texas Law Review 1831 (1991).

J.M. Balkin, "The Rhetoric of Responsibility," 76 Virginia Law Review 197 (1990).

J.M. Balkin, "The Crystalline Structure of Legal Thought," 39 Rutgers Law Review 1 (1986).

Jamie Boyle, "The Anatomy of a Torts Class," 34 American University Law Review 1003 (1985).

Steven Burton, *An Introduction to Law and Legal Reasoning* (Boston: Little Brown & Co. 1985).

Richard Michael Fischl, "The Question That Killed Critical Legal Studies," 17 Law & Social Inquiry 779 (1992).

Richard Michael Fischl, "Privileged Positions," 17 Law & Social Inquiry 831 (1992).

Richard Michael Fischl, "Some Realism About Critical Legal Studies," 41 University of Miami Law Review 505 (1987).

Gerald E. Frug, "The Ideology of Bureaucracy in American Law," 97 Harvard Law Review 1276 (1984).

Jennifer Jaff, "Frame-Shifting: An Empowering Methodology for Teaching and Learning Legal Reasoning," 36 Journal of Legal Education 249 (1986).

Mark Kelman, A Guide to Critical Legal Studies (Cambridge, MA: Harvard University Press 1987).

Mark Kelman, "Interpretive Construction in the Substantive Criminal Law," 33 Stanford Law Review 591 (1981).

Duncan Kennedy, A Critique of Adjudication (fin de siècle) (Cambridge, MA: Harvard University Press 1997).

Duncan Kennedy, "A Semiotics of Legal Argument," 42 Syracuse Law Review 75 (1991).

Duncan Kennedy, "Freedom and Constraint in Adjudication: A Critical Phenomenology," 36 Journal of Legal Education 518 (1986).

Duncan Kennedy, "Form and Substance in Private Law Adjudication," 89 Harvard Law Review 1689 (1976).

Edward H. Levi, An Introduction to Legal Reasoning (Chicago: University of Chicago Press 1949).

Laura E. Little, "Characterization and Legal Discourse," 46 Journal of Legal Education 372 (1996).

Karl Llewellyn, The Bramble Bush: On Our Law and Its Study (Dobbs Ferry: Oceana Publications 1960).

Karl Llewellyn, The Common Law Tradition, Deciding Appeals (Boston: Little Brown & Co. 1960).

Soia Mentschikoff and Irwin P. Stotzky, The Theory and Craft of American Law—Elements (New York: Matthew Bender 1981).

Frances Olsen, "Statutory Rape: A Feminist Critique of Rights Analysis," 63 Texas Law Review 387 (1984).

Jeremy Paul, "The Politics of Legal Semiotics," 69 Texas Law Review 1779 (1991).

Jeremy Paul, "A Bedtime Story," 74 Virginia Law Review 915 (1988).

Pierre Schlag, "Rules and Standards," 33 UCLA Law Review 379 (1985).

Pierre Schlag and David Skover, *Tactics of Legal Reasoning* (Durham: Carolina Academic Press 1986).

Joseph William Singer, "The Player and the Cards: Nihilism and Legal Theory," 94 Yale Law Journal 1 (1984).

Deborah Stone, *Policy Paradox: The Art of Political Decisionmaking* (New York: W.W. Norton 1997).

William Twining and David Miers, *How to Do Things With Rules*, 3rd Ed. (London: Weidenfeld and Nicholson 1991).

Roberto Mangabeira Unger, *The Critical Legal Studies Movement* (Cambridge, MA: Harvard University Press 1986).

Patricia J. Williams, *The Alchemy of Race and Rights: Diary of a Law Professor* (Cambridge, MA: Harvard University Press 1991).

Steven L. Winter, *A Clearing in the Forest: How the Study of the Mind Changes Our Understanding of Life and Law* (University of Chicago Press; forthcoming 1999).

Steven L. Winter, "An Upside/Down View of the Counter-Majoritarian Difficulty," 69 Texas Law Review 1881 (1991).

Steven L. Winter, "On Building Houses," 69 Texas Law Review 1595 (1991).

Steven L. Winter, "Transcendental Nonsense, Metaphoric Reasoning, and the Cognitive Stakes for Law," 137 University of Pennsylvania Law Review 1105 (1989).

About the Authors

Richard Michael Fischl is Professor of Law at the University of Miami in Coral Gables, Florida, where he teaches Contracts and various courses in labor and employment law. A 1975 graduate of the University of Illinois, he received his law degree from Harvard in 1978. Prior to his teaching career, Professor Fischl was an appellate attorney with the National Labor Relations Board in Washington, D.C., and was the principal author of the Board's briefs and petitions in a number of cases before the Supreme Court. At Miami, he has also taught Torts and Evidence, and he has conducted courses in comparative labor law at University College London and Eberhard-Karls-Universität Tübingen in Tübingen, Germany. His articles have appeared in *Columbia Law Review*, *Law & Social Inquiry*, and *Legal Times*. He has been lecturing first-year law students on exam-taking techniques for over a decade, and he estimates that he has graded nearly 5000 sets of bluebooks since 1983.

Jeremy Paul is a Professor of Law at the University of Connecticut in Hartford, where he teaches Constitutional Law, Property, and Jurisprudence. A 1978 graduate of Princeton University, he received his law degree from Harvard in 1981. In addition to his long-term career in teaching, Professor Paul has served as a law clerk to Judge Irving R. Kaufman of the U.S. Court of Appeals for the Second Circuit, as Professor-in-Residence at the Appellate Staff of the Civil Division of the U.S. Department of Justice, and as Assistant to the President of TravelersGroup. He has taught at the University of Miami (as both Assistant and Associate Professor) and at Boston College Law School (as a Visiting Professor). Professor Paul's writings have appeared in the *Texas Law Review*, the *Michigan Law*

Review, the *University of Southern California Law Review*, and the *Washington Monthly*, and include an introduction to legal reasoning entitled "A Bedtime Story," 74 Virginia Law Review 915 (1988), that has been used at many law schools. Perhaps most important, Professor Paul has graded roughly 2,000 exams.

Both authors encourage readers to find out more about them and about *Getting to Maybe* by visiting their website at http://www.getting2maybe.com.